DONALD W. SMITH

2006

# HADRIAN'S WALL IN THE DAYS OF THE ROMANS

# HADRIAN'S WALL IN THE DAYS OF THE ROMANS

*Drawn by*
RONALD EMBLETON, R.O.I.

*Text by*
FRANK GRAHAM

Maps vignettes and inscriptions by Gill Embleton, Eric Dale and David Thompson

*Published by*
FRANK GRAHAM
6 Queen's Terrace, Newcastle upon Tyne NE2 2PL

First Published 1984

I.S.B.N. 0 85983 177 9



Printed by Howe Brothers (Gateshead) Limited

# CONTENTS

Preface ....7
Introduction ....10
The Wall ....15
The Roman Army ....23
South Shields ....32
Hadrian's Monument ....43
Wallsend Fort ....45
Newcastle upon Tyne ....47
Benwell Fort ....52
Rudchester Fort ....57
Rudchester to Haltonchesters ....72
Reconstruction of a Turret ....74
Haltonchesters Fort ....78
Haltonchesters to Chesters ....90
William Hutton at Planetrees ....96
Chesters Fort ....98
Chesters Bridge ....111
Chesters to Carrawburgh ....114
Carrawburgh Fort ....117
Housesteads Fort ....130
Housesteads to Greatchesters ....152
Haltwhistle Burn Fort ....169
Greatchesters Fort ....172
Greatchesters to Carvoran ....181
Carvoran ....187
The Stanegate ....195
Corbridge ....204
Vindolanda Fort and Civilian Settlement ....210
Willowford Bridge to Birdoswald ....233
Birdoswald Fort ....235
The Maiden Way and Gillalees Beacon ....242
Bewcastle Fort ....243
Birdoswald to Castlesteads ....245
Written Rock of Gelt ....251
Castlesteads Fort ....251
Netherby Fort ....264

Birrens Fort ....... 272
Risingham Fort ....... 276
High Rochester Fort ....... 288
Chew Green ....... 301
Cappuck Fort ....... 301
Newstead Fort ....... 305
The Devil's Causeway ....... 309
Stanwix Fort ....... 312
Carlisle ....... 313
Index ....... 319

Roman Pottery. Carlisle.

# PREFACE

For the past ten years Ronald Embleton and I have been trying to show what Hadrian's Wall was like in the days of the Romans. After considerable research over 400 paintings, line drawings and plans have been created showing almost every aspect of Roman life on the northern frontier. Hadrian's Wall is the grandest monument of Roman rule in Britain and the greatest attraction for visitors to Northumberland. Vast archaeological treasures have been found and many more remain to be discovered on the northern frontier. Only a fraction of the Roman Wall has been scientifically excavated. This book tries to reconstruct the colourful life of this huge military area.

Many of Ronald Embleton's drawings have already been published by us in a series of booklets on the same theme as the larger volume now appearing. They have attracted world-wide notice and are acknowledged to be among the best reconstructions of Roman life from both an artistic and historic viewpoint.

The immense amount of research and work embodied in the present book is difficult to appreciate, and to produce it in colour the financial cost has been heavy. Many people have assisted us with advice and information, some of whom are mentioned in the text. But the most important inspiration and help came from the late Russell Robinson. If he had lived long enough to assist with the entire work the quality and historical accuracy would have been even higher.

This book is not our final contribution to illustrate the living history of the Wall. We hope in future editions to add to and improve many of the illustrations.

Many travellers and antiquaries have written about the Wall but the most interesting was William Hutton who at the age of 78 travelled the Wall from end to end in 1801. We have occasionally quoted from his amusing and readable book and have inserted three colour plates showing incidents on his journey. Since Hutton, thousands have made the same journey and have enjoyed the same excitement and pleasure.

The Wall is not only one of the wonders of the World. It is also built in one of the most beautiful parts of Britain. Visitors can not only enjoy an historic experience but travel through a scenic paradise.

*Opposite: One of the men who built the Wall*

Ronald Embleton

## INTRODUCTION

### Historical Survey

In 55 and 54 B.C. Julius Caesar raided Britain and defeated the tribesmen of Kent, but events in Gaul prevented him from continuing with the conquest of the island. A century later in A.D. 43 four Roman legions crossed the Channel to conquer Britain. At the Medway a decisive battle took place and the southern king Cunobelinus eventually surrendered at Colchester, his tribal capital. The Emperor Claudius came over from Rome to accept the homage of the eleven kings of southern Britain. For many years the Romans slowly advanced to the west and north where they encountered considerable resistance. It was Julius Agricola, governor of Britain, who finally subdued the north of England. He advanced into Scotland, meeting very little opposition and won a great victory at *Mons Graupius* (A.D. 84) in the Grampian mountains. As he advanced Agricola built roads and forts to consolidate his conquests. One of these roads was the *Stanegate* which linked the two supply bases of Carlisle and Corbridge. He built a string of forts to guard the highland passes in central Scotland but he was recalled before his work was completed. The years after he departed are obscure. Scotland, south of the Highlands, was held for a few years but then a gradual withdrawal set in. By A.D. 90 the frontier was based an Oakwood and Newstead in southern Scotland and the Stanegate line was strengthened. Troops were withdrawn from Britain to withstand barbarian attacks elsewhere. The crack 9th Legion, stationed at York, disappears from the pages of history. It was either destroyed or disbanded after disgracing itself on the battlefield. The forts north of the Tyne, and Solway (including Corbridge) were abandoned and twenty years after Agricola's drive into Scotland the northern parts of Britain were lost (c. A.D. 105). The Emperor Trajan decided to make the Stanegate the northern frontier. He rebuilt and increased the number of forts especially in the central sector and it has been suggested constructed a frontier line *(limes)* a little to the north with regular forts and signal stations.

On Trajan's death the new Emperor Hadrian visited Britain. He decided to establish the frontier across the most easily defended part of the island within easy reach of the legionary fortresses of York and Chester and for this purpose to erect a continuous Wall which would be 76 Roman miles long. Hadrian did not stay long and the work was carried out by Aulus Platorius Nepos, who was legate of Britain from A.D. 122 until A.D. 126.

Hadrian's successor in A.D. 138 was Antoninus Pius who decided, for reasons now unknown, once again to attempt the conquest of Scotland. He entrusted the campaign to Lollius Urbicus who was sufficiently successful that a new wall (The Antonine) was built across the narrow Forth-Clyde gap (40 Roman miles), with a string of outpost forts to the north. Hadrian's Wall was to all intents and purposes abandoned. Fort gates were removed and sections of the Vallum filled in to afford easy crossings for military and civilian traffic. But peace was very fragile and in A.D. 155 the Antonine Wall was abandoned for a brief period (the retreating soldiers burnt almost all the forts). The Roman Army soon returned rebuilding most of the forts. Their work was hardly completed when about A.D. 161 the Antonine Wall was finally abandoned for military and political reasons. (For an up-to-date study of the Romans in Scotland see *Roman Scotland, A Guide to the Visible Remains* by David G. Breeze, 1979). Hadrian's Wall with its outposts forts was now the Roman frontier.

In 180, when Commodus was emperor, trouble broke out. A Roman general was killed and his soldiers massacred. The native tribes crossed the Wall and committed large scale devastation. The forts of Rudchester, Haltonchesters, Corbridge and Birdoswald were destroyed along with many milecastles and turrets. Ulpius Marcellus was sent out by Commodus and he quickly restored order. Newstead and possibly Risingham were abandoned after the restoration of the damaged forts.

On the last day of 192 Commodus was assassinated and civil war raged for the next four years. One of the claimants was Clodius Albinus, governor of Britain, who was defeated at Lyons in February 197. When he crossed to Gaul Albinus undoubtedly took some of the Wall garrison with him but stories that the northern tribes seized this opportunity to detroy the Wall are now discounted. The only literary evidence (Cassius Dio) states that the Malatae caused trouble and Severus's new governor Virius Lupus had to buy them off with a large sum of money in exchange for prisoners they held.

Meanwhile many of the forts were being rebuilt by a new governor Alfenus Senecio who rebuilt Risingham and Rochester north of the Wall and did work at Chesters, Housesteads, Corbridge and Birdoswald. However, the situation deteriorated and events turned against the Romans.

Herodian tells us the governor wrote to Severus "that the barbarians had risen and were overrunning the country, carrying off booty and causing great destruction, and that for effective defence either more troops or the presence of the emperor was necessary". Severus came to Britain in 208 with his sons Caracalla and Geta. Extensive preparations were made for the invasion of Scotland. At South Shields 20 new granaries were built, and the fort at Cramond on the Firth of Forth was restored so that the main supplies could be sent by sea. In two campaigns (starting in 209) Severus overcame the Caledonians and almost reached the utmost end of Scotland. But he died at York in February 211. He had taught the Caledonians such a lesson that peace reigned here for almost a century. His two sons Caracalla and Geta returned to Rome after making peace with the northern tribes. Southern Scotland became very friendly, almost a Roman protectorate. The Ravenna Cosmography lists eight places *(loca)* in North Britain where meetings or assemblies could be held. They include the *locus Moporu, locus Manavi, locus Dannoni,* the *Segloes* and the *Tava.*

Peace brought changes on the Wall. Many turrets were built up, milecastles had their gates narrowed, the Vallum was abandoned and civilian settlements increased in size. The outpost forts were re-occupied and the number of cavalry on the Wall increased. While the Roman Empire suffered many crises in the third century it was a period of peace on the Wall. The forts were developed and repaired, the conditions in the army were improved and the civilian settlements on the Wall flourished and expanded. By the end of the century the Wall garrison was reduced in size and many of the forts were only partially used and buildings were becoming ruinous.

In 287 Carausius who commanded the fleet in the Channel revolted and took control of Britain. He was overthrown in 293 by another usurper Allectus. In 296 Constantius Chlorus reconquered Britain and decided to restore the frontier defences. Extensive restoration was carried out at Housesteads and Birdoswald,

*Building the Wall*

*Opposite. Various 1st Century Roman Cavalryman*

Vindolanda was almost rebuilt and repairs were done at South Shields and Carrawburgh. Strangely Halton and Rudchester were allowed to decay. Perhaps it was thought that the outpost forts more or less replaced them. Constantius came to Britain in 306 and died at York after a campaign in the north of Scotland.

The fourth century was a period of peace in the north apart from trouble in Scotland in 343 and 360. In 367 a great disaster took place when barbarians combined in overwhelming force. Of the two Roman commanders of Britain the Count of the Saxon Shore was killed in battle. In the north a new Pictish war broke out. But here a new factor was entering into the problem of the north. For a long while before the Pictish War many of the auxiliaries on the Wall had been recruited locally. This was one of the factors which gave stability to the century following Severus, since it meant that the local population now had an interest in the preservation of peace. But as the Roman Empire declined economically and increasing burdens were placed on the local population, due to the continuous dynastic struggles, the loyalty of the local troops became doubtful. So in 367 when Britain was almost overrun by the barbarians they made common cause with the Picts and Scots and treacherously betrayed the Wall. Collingwood well describes this new state of affairs when he states — "The local militia of Britain were at this time hardly to be trusted as watch-dogs of a peaceful and wealthy diocese. All but barbarians themselves, and a peasant militia rather than a well-disciplined army, it is hard to resist the impression that their sympathies were more on the side of the barbarian without and the peasant within, the potential invader and the potential rebel, than the rich landowner whose property they were ordered to protect".

Count Theodosius immediately brought new troops to Britain who quickly drove out the invaders but the *Pax Romana* north of the wall was now over. The Wall, but not the outpost forts, was restored by 369.

The history of the Wall was now reaching its end. In 383 Magnus Maximus, Governor of Britain, took the main part of the Wall garrison over to Gaul to assist him in the struggle for the Imperial throne, there to be defeated by Theodosius. Archaeological evidence takes us down to 383; after that the history of the Roman garrison, if in fact any was left there at all, is shrouded in mystery.

**THE WALL**

The Roman Wall was a composite military barrier with four main parts.

1. A stone wall with a V-shaped ditch in front.

2. A regular series of forts, milecastles and turrets to house the garrison needed.

3. A ditch and attendant earthworks to the south called the Vallum.

4. A road network for the movement of soldiers and supplies.

The outpost forts to the north and the series of forts and towers along the Cumbrian coast completed the work.

The Wall extends 80 Roman miles (73½ English) from Wallsend-on-Tyne to Bowness-on-Solway. The Vallum, except where the topography dictated otherwise, ran an average 70 yards to the south. It is now agreed that the Vallum and

Wall were built at the same time and were the work of Hadrian. The Wall was built by the Roman legionaries who were the only soldiers available with the necessary skills, although it was garrisoned by the auxiliaries.

The Wall, as originally planned, was to be 10 Roman feet wide and probably 15 feet high with a parapet. The facing was of carefully cut stones set in mortar, obtained from nearby quarries, and the filling was formed with rubble and lime cement or occasionally puddled clay. The foundation for the ten foot Wall was laid for 23 Roman miles from Newcastle westward and in sections further west. However it was decided very soon after work had started to decrease the width to eight or in some cases six Roman feet, so that the Wall varies in width. In some cases milecastles and turrets were built for the broad wall before a change in width was decided upon. West of the river Irthing stone of the right quality and limestone were not readily available, so a turf wall, with milecastles and turrets of wood, was substituted. Sections were however replaced in stone after only a few years elapsed. The ditch to the north was constructed throughout its length except where cliffs or the terrain made it unnecessary. Occasionally the ditch was left unfinished, usually where rock outcrops made the work difficult.

**Forts, milecastles, turrets**

In the original Hadrianic plan the patrol garrison would have operated from milecastles and turrets only with the forts to the rear to reinforce and relieve them. However at a very early stage a decision, to place the forts on the Wall itself, was taken. The forts were all of the same shape (like playing cards) but varied in size from three to five and a half acres. A third of the fort usually projected beyond the Wall. The gates and fort ditches were generally of a uniform pattern with four main gates, one on each side and two minor gates, one on each of the

Reconstruction of a Milecastle ~

*FLAVINUS: Standard bearer of Ala Petriana.*

This magnificent drawing is based on a gravestone now to be seen in Hexham Abbey. The inscription tells us that Flavinus was the standard bearer of the troop of Candidus of the *ala petriana.*

*Opposite. ROMAN OFFICERS.*

*LEGATUS.* Usually a Senator appointed by the Emperor. 2nd in command of the Legion.

*TRIBUNUS LATICLAVIUS.* Chief Tribune. Identified by the broad purple stripe on his tunic.

*LEGION COMMANDER.* and the Primus Pilus. Chief Centurion.

longer sides. The *milecastles,* as their name implies, were a Roman mile (1620 yards) apart. They were constructed early with broad wingwalls to link with the Wall itself, which in many was built to the narrow gauge. Massive gateways opened to the south and to the north through the Wall. The gates are of three distinct types. Barracks and facilities for cooking and storage, of a uniform pattern, were provided. The garrisons varied in number but a maximum would be sixty-four.

Two *turrets* at an average distance of 540 yards are found between each milecastle. They seem to have been built to a uniform pattern about twenty feet square and recessed into the Wall. On the ground floor were cooking facilities with a movable ladder giving access through a trap door to the upper storey. Here sleeping accommodation would be provided for a garrison, probably of four, two

Reconstruction of a Turret ~

of whom would always be on patrol. There used to be a tradition that the Romans used pipes through which they signalled between turrets, one of those numerous legends about the Wall not supported by archaeological evidence. Michael Drayton in his *Poly-Olbion* (1613) tells us:—

*Towns stood upon my length, where garrisons were laid.*
*Their limits to defend and; for my greater aid,*
*With turrets I was built where sentinels were plac'd*
*To watch upon the Pict; so me my makers grac'd*
*With hollow pipes of brasse, along me still they went,*
*By which they in one fort, still to another sent,*
*By speaking in the same, to tell them what to doe,*
*And soe from the sea could I be whispered through.*

**The Vallum**

To the south of the Wall was a large earthwork called the Vallum. Unlike the ditch to the north it was flat bottomed and twenty feet wide and ten feet deep. The upcast was usually piled in two continuous mounds at a distance of thirty feet. The total width of these earthworks, two mounds, two berms and ditch was 120 feet. At the forts the Vallum was crossed by a stone causeway (see Benwell). The Vallum was intended as a rear boundary not a military fortification. The Vallum went out of use about A.D. 140 and at regular intervals of 45 yards the two mounds were breached and their soil used to form a causeway across the ditch. Whether the Vallum was ever used again is uncertain.

Lateral communications along the Wall was possible along the parapet walk or possibly by a patrol path. Heavy supplies could be brought along the Stanegate from which lateral roads led to the Wall forts. But after some years a *Military Way* was built. Its date is uncertain but it was probably built subsequent to the destruction of the Vallum (A.D. 140). It ran from milecastle to milecastle with paths to the turrets. It is now completely overgrown but can be traced in places. It was a typical Roman road, twenty feet wide with kerbs.

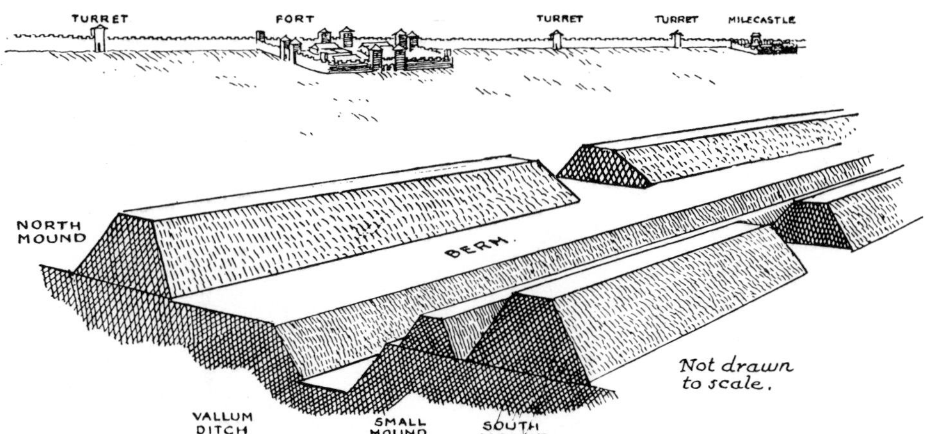


**Bridges**

At places the Wall had to cross rivers. Good examples can be seen at Chesters and Willowford. The Tyne also had to be crossed by roads at two points — Newcastle and Corbridge. Small streams were carried through the Wall by culverts. The engraving of the one which existed at Denton Burn is of great interest (page 66). In many other places (examples can be seen east of Birdoswald) the Wall had small openings at ground level to allow water through where there was a danger of pools forming.

**THE ROMAN ARMY**

The Roman Army was divided into the legions and the auxiliaries. It was the legions who built the Wall and the auxiliaries who garrisoned it. The legions were each about 5,500 strong and were composed of Roman citizens. They were mainly well trained, heavily armed infantry with a small contingent of cavalry. They were crack troops with a wide variety of skills. They were fighters, engineers and builders. Their length of service was sixteen to twenty years.

A legion was divided into ten *cohortes* each containing six *centuriae* except for *Cohors I* which had ten *Centuriae.* The commander was called a *legatus legionis* and held praetorian rank. The second in command was the *praefectus castrorum* who was a professional soldier. The headquarters staff was formed of six military tribunes, the first of whom was a senator, the other five belonging to the equestrian class. The tribunes served in the army as the first step in a public career. The

LEG

*A Centurion and a Standard Bearer*

*Opposite: Roman Legionaries of the 2nd century with their packs.*

backbone of the officer class was the commander of the century called a *centurio*. Under the centurion was an *optio* or second in command, and a *signifer* or standard-bearer. The centuries were divided into ten eight-man sections called *contubernia* and each contubernium shared a common tent and feeding arrangements. (The term century is rather confusing. Originally the unit was 100 strong but by the time of Hadrian had been reduced to 80 men, although the traditional title was maintained).

There were three legions stationed in Britain (a tenth of the whole legionary force) and from Hadrian's time had permanent headquarters at Caerleon-on-Usk (Second *Augusta*), Chester (Twentieth *Valeria Victrix*), and York (Sixth *Victrix*). York was the legionary fortress nearest the Wall and was intended as support for the Wall garrison.

The equipment used by the legionaries was remarkably uniform and was probably mass produced at centres in Gaul, Italy and the eastern Empire. A bronze helmet was worn which had a projecting piece at the back to protect the neck, and a similar ridge at the front to protect the face with ear protectors. As weapons each legionary carried a sword *(gladius)* and two javelins *(pilum)*. The sword was two edged and about two feet long. Each legionary had a large rectangular rounded shield *(scutum)* made of wood with a metal boss. The rectangular bronze centrepiece found at the mouth of the Tyne, illustrated on page 42, came from such a shield. The soldier's name — IVL MAGNI IVNI DVBITATI — (belonging to Junius Dubitatus of the century of Julius Magnus), and his legion — LEG VII AVG — can be seen among the decoration. The legionary also had well-designed body armour as can be seen in our illustration.

The auxiliaries differed from the legionaries in many ways. They were recruited from the non-Roman tribes of the Empire and were organised in smaller groups. The unit was a cohort of either 480 men (6 centuries) or 800 men (10 centuries). The smaller cohort was called *quingenary* (nominally 500) and the larger *milliary* (nominally 1000). A cohort might be part mounted *(equitata)*. There were also cavalry units *(alae)* which were divided into 16 or 24 *turmae* commanded by decurions. The turmae had 32 men so a quingenary *ala* had 512 men and a milliary *ala* 768 men. The milliary cohort was commanded by a tribune and the quingenary cohorts and all cavalry by a prefect. Auxiliaries served for 25 years.

A third section of the Roman army appears on the Wall in the third and fourth centuries. They were irregular or native infantry units. They used their own equipment and they were led by their own chiefs. They were essentially mercenaries. An infantry unit of such men was called a *numerus* and their cavalry counterpart was known as a *cuneus*. Another unit is sometimes found, a *vexillatio*. This is a special detachment used for a special purpose and formed from a legion or an auxiliary unit.

The equipment and uniform of the auxiliaries presents us with infinite variety. Russell Robinson's book *What the Soldier's Wore on Hadrian's Wall* deals with the subject in great detail. Numerous discoveries have now made it possible to describe many of the auxiliaries who included armoured cavalry *(cataphractarii)* lancers or spearmen, sharp-shooters (slingers and bowmen) and a wide variety of troops who were often equipped on the basis of the region from which they originally came.

Little is known of the Roman Navy in the North. Whether they had a base at South Shields is not known. The Navy was considered inferior to the Army and was under its control. An inscription at Benwell records building work done by the British Navy *(Classis Britannica)*.

When an auxiliary was released at the end of his service he was presented with a bronze diploma giving details of his service and confirming the grant of Roman citizenship. Fragments of a diploma found at Chesters are shown here. Part of another diploma was found at Vindolanda.

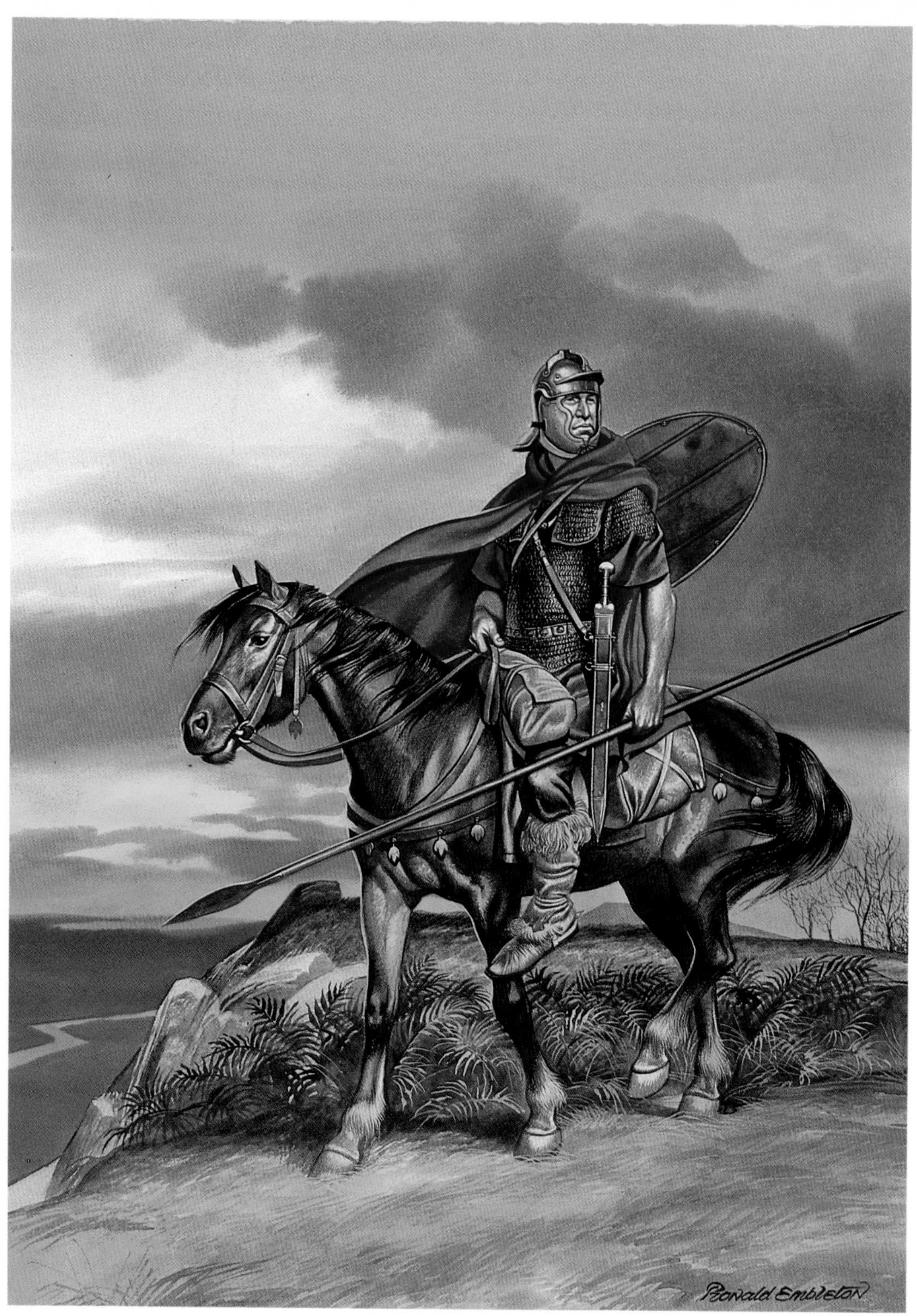


*Roman Cavalryman*

## GARRISONS AND NAMES OF THE WALL FORTS

The Roman names of the forts are derived from several sources. The best (although rare) are inscriptions. The documentary evidence is provided by the *Antonine Itinerary,* the *Notitia Dignitatum* and the *Ravenna Cosmography.* The *Rudge Cup* and the *Amiens Skillet* provide a few names.

The *Antonine Itinerary* is a collection of 225 post roads in the Empire. It was compiled in the reign of the Emperor Caracalla (211 to 217 A.D.), one of whose names was Antoninus. It provides names of places and distances. The Wall Forts are only mentioned near the roads which crossed it at Carlisle and Corbridge. Fifteen routes in Britain are described.

The *Notitia Dignitatum* is an official document recording among other information a list of army units under the generals of the Empire. Its date is c. 410 A.D., near the end of Roman rule in Britain but is based on earlier sources. It provides a partial list of the Roman Wall garrison.

The following is the list of officers and stations as given in the *Notitia.*

ITEM PER LINEAM VALLI

Tribunus Cohortis Quartae Lingonum Segeduno.
Tribunus Cohortis Primae Cornoviorum Ponte Aeli.
Praefectus Alae Primae Asturum Conderco.
Tribunus Cohortis Primae Frixagorum Vindobala.
Praefectus Alae Savinianae Hunno.
Praefectus Alae Secundae Asturum Cilurno.
Tribunus Cohortis Primae Batavorum Procolitia.
Tribunus Cohortis Primae Tungrorum Borcovicio.
Tribunus Cohortis Quartae Gallorum Vindolana.
Tribunus Cohortis Primae Asturum Aesica.
Tribunus Cohortis Secundae Dalmatarum Magnis.
Tribunus Cohortis Primae Aeliae Dacorum Amboglanna.
Praefectus Alae Petrianae Petrianis.
Praefectus Numeri Maurorum Aurelianorum Aballaba.
Tribunus Cohortis Secundae Lingonum Congavata.
Tribunus Cohortis Primae Hispanorum Axeloduno.
Tribunus Cohortis Secundae Thracum Gabrosenti.
Tribunus Cohortis Primae Aeliae Classicae Tunnocelo.
Tribunus Cohortis Primae Morinorum Glannibanta.
Tribunus Cohortis Tertiae Nerviorum Alione.
Cuneus Armaturarum Bremetennaco.
Praefectus Alae Primae Herculeae Olenaco.
Tribunus Cohortis Sextae Nerviorum Virosido.

## RAVENNA COSMOGRAPHY

A road map of the Roman Empire compiled by a seventh-century cleric at Ravenna and based on earlier road maps. It is a mere list of more than 5,000 names but for Britain is the fullest source available. It lists the Wall forts from east to west in tabulated form. It is extremely confusing. We here give all the Wall names mentioned in the *Ravenna List* together with modern names.

*Serduno* — Wallsend.
*Condecor* — Benwell.
*Vindovala* — Rudchester.
*Onno* — Halton Chesters.
*Celunno* — Chesters.
*Brocoliti* — Carrawburgh.
*Velurtion* — Housesteads.
*Esica* — Great Chesters.
*Banna* — Birdoswald.
*Uxelludamo* — Stanevix.
*Avalava* — Burgh-by-Sands.
*Maia* — Bowness.
*Fanocodi* — Bewcastle.
*Vindolande* — Vindolanda.
*Magnis* — Carvoran.
*Gabaglanda* — Castlesteads.
*Bribra* — Beckfoot
*Alauna* — Maryport.
*Gabrocentio* — Burrow Walls.
*Juliocenon* — Moresby.
*Bremenium* — High Rochester.

**RUDGE CUP**

This is a small enamelled bronze bowl found at Rudge in Wiltshire in 1725. It is decorated with a frieze representing the Wall and an inscription reading:—

A MAIS ABALLA VXEL(L)OD(VN)VM
CAMBOGLAN(NI)S BANNA

The date of the cup is uncertain but probably the first half of the 2nd century. The decoration shows the Wall with crenellations, the only evidence surviving of the Wall's superstructure.

**AMIENS SKILLET (PATERA)**

A closely similar vessel, but with a long handle, was found in 1949 at Amiens in France. The inscription reads:—

MAIS ABALLAVA VXEL(L)ODVNVM
CAMBOG(LANI)S BANNA ESICA

It has been suggested that these vessels were part of a table service which would give the names of all the forts. They were probably sold as souvenirs.

# MILITARY UNITS ON HADRIAN'S WALL AND THE NORTHERN FRONTIER

**ALAE**

Fifteen cavalry regiments have been recorded in Britain. Six were certainly on the Wall and three more in the hinterland.

**ALA II ASTURUM**

Under Uepius Marcellus it is recorded at Chesters. It was the third century garrison there and is also mentioned in the *Notitia.*

**ALA I HISPANORUM ASTURUM**

Originally raised in Asturia (north west Spain) before 43 A.D. and probably part of the invasion army. Stationed at Benwell from A.D. 205 to 367. Mentioned in the *Notitia.* The tombstone of a freedman of a trooper of this *ala* from South Shields does not prove it was stationed there, but it does present problems.

**ALA HISPANORUM VETTONUM C.R.**

Originally raised from the Vettonians of central Spain. Two fine inscriptions record their stay at Binchester in the late second century or early third century. They assisted in restoring the bath-house at Bowes in 197 A.D.

**ALA I PANNONIORUM SABINIANA**

Originally raised in Pannonia (modern Hungary). An inscription records it at Haltonchesters in the third century and it is mentioned in the *Notitia* at the same fort. A lead seal found at South Shields raises the question whether it was stationed there in the second century but now agreed the seal is no proof.

**ALA I TUNGRORUM**

Raised from the Tungri of Gallia Belgica (Belgium) it is recorded in an inscription at Burgh-by-Sands in the second century (L.S. 514). During the first occupation of the Antonine Wall an inscription was found at Mumrills (RIB 2140).

**ALA AUGUSTA**

Three Alae Augustae have been recorded in Britain namely Ala Augusta Gallorum Proculaeana stationed at Old Carlisle in the second and third centuries, the Ala Augusta Gallorum Petriana attested at Stanwix and the Ala Augusta Vocontiorum raised in Gaul but recorded at Newstead during the first Antonine occupation of Scotland.

Recently however, a remarkable altar to Discipline has been found at Chesters. It was almost certainly erected by the first garrison and is unique in providing the name of the only original garrison known in any Wall fort. It was an Ala Augusta showing there was clearly a fourth *ala* of that name in Britain.

**ALA AUGUSTA GALLORUM PROCULEIANA**

From 185 to 242 it was at Old Carlisle.

**ALA AUGUSTA GALLORUM PETRIANA MILLIARIA CR BIS TORQUATA**

Originally raised in Gaul and named after one of its prefects T. Pomponius Petra. In the first century it was stationed at Corbridge as shown on a tombstone (RIB 1172). It was then a quingenary unit. One of the torques was given by Domitian, the other by Trajan in the Second Dacian War. It is assumed to have been the garrison of Stanwix, from the time of Hadrian, since the fort was named Petriana after it, but the first reference to the fort is in the *Notitia.* A stone recording the unit has been found at Carlisle (RIB 956) suggesting its presence there at some pre-Hadrianic date. This was the only milliary *ala* of the army of Britain.

**ALA AUGUSTA VOCONTIORUM C.R.**

Raised from the Vocontii of Gallia Narbonensis. During the first occupation of the Antonine Wall they are recorded on an altar at Newstead (Trimontium).

**ALA AUGUSTA OB VIRTUTEM APPELLATA**

This cavalry regiment was styled Augusta for valour. It was the garrison of Chesters in the reign of Hadrian. From 185 until 242 it is recorded at Old Carlisle, a stone recording this unit has been found at Carlisle but it may not have been stationed there (RIB 946).

**COHORTES MILLIARIAE**

Only seven cohortes milliariae have been recorded in Britain and all were stationed on the Wall for most of the time.

**COHORS I AELIA DACORUM MILLIARIA**

Raised in Dacia (Romania) early in the second century. It is recorded c. 130 A.D. building the Vallum of Hadrian's Wall (RIB 1365). For reconstruction see page 66. Under Hadrian it may have been the garrison of Bewcastle (RIB 991). In the third and fourth centuries it was the garrison of Birdoswald where it is also recorded in the *Notitia.*

**COHORS I NERVANA GERMANORUM MILLIARIA EQUITATA**

Raised in Dacia (Romania) early in the second century. It is recorded c. 130 A.D. building the Vallum of Hadrian's Wall (RIB 1365). For reconstruction see page 66. Under Hadrian it may have been the garrison of Bewcastle (RIB 991). In the third and fourth centuries it was the garrison of Birdoswald where it is also recorded in the *Notitia.*

**COHORS I AELIA HISPANORUM MILLIARIA EQUITATA**

Raised by Hadrian in Spain about 119 A.D. as a quingenary unit. It built the fort at Maryport and was the first garrison. Mid-way through Hadrian's reign it was doubled to a *milliaria.* It left Maryport early in the reign of Antoninus Pius and took part in the conquest of Scotland where it won the honorific title *Aelia.* In the third century it was stationed at Netherby where in 222 A.D. it built a cavalry drill-hall as attested in a magnificent slab. The *Notitia* records a Cohors Hispanorum as the garrison of Axellodunum which some equate with Netherby. However the *Antonine Itinerary* gives Netherby the Roman name of *Castra Exploratorum.*

**COHORS I TUNGRORUM MILLIARIA**

Originally raised from the Tungri of Gallia Belgica (Belgium). In its first years a *cohors quingenaria* it was one of the Tungrian cohorts which fought at Mons Graupius in Scotland. It is recorded on a diploma of 103 A.D. as a *cohors milliaria.* A recently discovered diploma fragment from Vindolanda dated 146 A.D. suggests it was then in garrison there. Late in Hadrian's reign part of the unit was engaged in building at Carrawburgh. After Houseteads was rebuilt by Severus it was stationed there and is so recorded in the *Notitia.*

**COHORS II TUNGRORUM MILLIARIA EQUITATA**

Originally raised from the Tungri of Gallia Belgica (Belgium). Originally it was a *cohors quingenaria.* It was recorded in 158 A.D. on a building inscription for Birrens where it stayed for most of the century. In 241 A.D. it was stationed at Castlesteads but was omitted from the *Notitia,* probably in error. In the second century it was given the title C.L. whose interpretation is doubtful.

**COHORS I VANGIONUM MILLIARIA EQUITATA**

Originally raised from the Vangiones of Germania Superior (Upper Rhineland) it came to Britain with Cerialis. An inscription from Chesters refers to the daughter of a tribune of this unit and is dated late second century. An altar to Antenocitus at Benwell dated about 180 A.D. was erected by a prefect of the Vangiones. The thousand cavalry were probably split between the two forts. In the third century (from 205-8) it was the garrison of Risingham. While there it was supported by a *Numerus Exploratorum,* or Unit of Scouts and a detachment of *Raeti Gaesati* or Raetian Spearmen. Since the fort at Risingham could not have held so many troops, large numbers must have been stationed regularly at outlying posts.

**COHORS I FIDA VARDULLORUM MILLIARIA EQUITATA CR**

Originally raised from the Vardulli of northern Spain it was a *cohors quingenaria* when first recorded in Britain in 98 A.D. Under Pius it is recorded at Castlecary on the Antonine Wall. About this date a vexillation of this unit erected an altar to the mother-goddesses outside Milecastle 19. An inscription found at Corbridge in the second half of the second century is unclear and could refer to the *Cohors Tungrorum.* From 175 A.D. it was at Lanchester and from 213 A.D. at High Rochester.

**COHORTES QUINGENARIAE**

**COHORS I AELIA CLASSICA**

Raised during life of Hadrian. The *Notitia* records it at Tunnocellum, a fort still missing but probably at the mouth of the Eden.

**COHORS I AQUITANORUM EQUITATA**

It is recorded at Carrawburgh in the reign of Hadrian.

**COHORS II ASTURUM EQUITATA**

Raised from the Astures of northern Spain. In the third century was the garrison at Greatchesters. The *Notitia* mentions a First Cohort of Asturians, which is probably a slip for Second.

**COHORS I BAETASIORUM C.R.**

*ob virtutem et fidem*

Raised from the Baetasii of Lower Germany. Garrison of Bar Hill in the first period of the Antonine Wall. In the second period it is recorded at Old Kilpatrick. Late in the second century they were stationed at Maryport.

**COHORS I BATAVORUM EQUITATA**

It is recorded on building stones near Carvoran, and was the garrison of Castlesteads in the second century. In the third century it was stationed at Carrawburgh where it is recorded by the *Notitia.*

**COHORS VIII BATAVORUM**

Recorded only on one of the Vindolanda writing tablets. Could have been in garrison there c. 100 A.D.

**COHORS IIII BREUCORUM**

One of eight cohorts raised from the Breuci of Pannonia, and the only one which served in Britain. It was building at Bowes under Julius Verus (130-133). Three inscriptions at Ebchester suggest it was the garrison there in the third century.

**COHORS I CORNOVIORUM**

This was the only British fort garrison on the Wall. The Cornovii came from the Cheshire, Staffordshire and Shropshire districts. The only record of it is in the *Notitia Dignitatum* (early 4th century), where it is stationed at Newcastle.

**COHORS I ULPIA TRIANA CUGENORUM CIVIUM ROMANORUM**

Originally raised in Germania Inferior (Lower Rhine). An inscription of 213 A.D. gives it as the garrison of Newcastle. An inscription at Carrawburgh of the second half of the second century records a soldier of this unit. It came to Britain with Cerialis.

**COHORS I DELMATARUM EQUITATA**

Originally raised in Jugoslavia. It is recorded at Maryport in the reign of Pius. There is a building inscription for the unit from Chesters early in the second century. An inscription from High Rochester of the late second century refers either to this unit or I Dacorum.

**COHORS II DELMATARUM EQUITATA**

An undated inscription (RIB 1795), but probably of the third century records this unit at Carvoran. It is also placed here by the *Notitia.*

**COHORS IIII DELMATARUM**

Recorded as building at Hardknott Fort in the reign of Hadrian.

**COHORS I FRISIAVONUM**

The name of a tribe in what is now the Netherlands. They came to Britain with Cerialis. The *Notitia* calls them *Frixagorum.* They were stationed at Rudchester in the third century and later. An undated altar to Coventina at Carrawburgh from an *optio* of this unit does not mean it was in garrison there.

**COHORS II GALLORUM EQUITATA**

An inscription records it at Old Penrith in the third century.

**COHORS IIII GALLORUM EQUITATA**

In the first century it was at Templeborough (Yorkshire) and stamped tiles found at Castleford (Yorkshire) are of the same period. Two altars from Castlesteads show it was the garrison there either during time of Hadrian or Pius. At Castlehill during first occupation of Antonine Wall. Under Marcus Aurelius it is attested at Risingham. The unit was the third century garrison of Vindolanda (RIB 1705), where it is recorded in the *Notitia.*

**COHORS V GALLORUM**

This is the first attested garrison of South Shields, and the proof is an inscription recording the installation of a water supply dated 222 A.D. (RIB 1060). Before this date it was stationed at Cramond in Scotland. It has been suggested the cohort was split between the two sites but that is unlikely and such an explanation is not heeded.

**COHORS I HAMIORUM SAGITTARIORUM**

This unit of Hamian archers was raised in Syria. In Hadrian's time it was the garrison of Carvoran. It left to become the garrison of Bar Hill during the second period of occupation of the Antonine Wall, returning to Carvoran in the reign of Marcus Aurelius (c. 163-166).

**COHORTES I—V LINGONUM**

These five cohorts were raised in Upper Germany and four were sent to Britain with Cerialis who was governor in 71 A.D. The fifth went to Dacia. All were *equitata.*

**COHORS I LINGONUM EQUITATA**

It was at High Rochester under Lollius Urbicus during first period of occupation of the fort. In the third century it was stationed at Lanchester where several inscriptions record rebuilding work in the reign of Gordian (A.D. 238-44).

**COHORS II LINGONUM EQUITATA**

Recorded on an altar at Moresby in the second century. In the reign of Marcus Aurelius it was stationed at Ilkley. In the third century it is recorded on a lead seal from Brough-under-Stainmore. The *Notitia* places it at Congovata which is generally accepted as being Drumburgh. Since Drumburgh is only two acres in size only part of the Cohors II Lingonum could have been stationed here.

**COHORS IIII LINGONUM EQUITATA**

It was stationed at Wallsend in the third and fourth centuries. It is first on the list of the *Notitia Dignitatum.* The inscriptions found here are not dated but probably 3rd century.

**COHORS I MORINORUM**

This unit was originally recruited from the sea-faring tribe living around Calais and Boulogne. In the *Notitia* it is recorded at Ravenglass *(Glannoventa).* A single inscription gives the name of this unit as COHORS I MORINORUM ET CERSIAEORUM, the second name being that of another tribe living in the same area.

**COHORS II NERVIORUM CIVIUM ROMANORUM**

Six cohorts of Nervians were raised in Gallia Belgica (modern Belgium) and sent to Britain with Cerialis. None were *equitata.* The second cohort is recorded at Wallsend (RIB 1303) and a detachment at Carrawburgh (RIB 1538) in the second century. An altar found near Vindolanda suggests a connection with that fort. In the third century it was stationed at Whitley Castle.

**COHORS VI NERVIORUM**

An inscription, probably of Hadrian's reign, records it at Greatchesters. In the second century was at Rough Castle in Scotland and in the third at Bainbridge fort in Yorkshire.

**COHORS I PANNONIORUM**

A tombstone found in Milecastle 42 near Greatchesters has been ascribed to the first cohort of Pannonians, although the number is missing (RIB 1667). See page 166.

**COHORS II PANNONIORUM**

Raised in Pannonia (Hungary) an inscription records it at Beckfoot (BIBRA) probably in the second century. It is also recorded on a lead seal from Vindolanda but it need not have been stationed there since such seals were placed on goods at their place of origin.

**COHORS VI RAETORUM**

One of eight cohorts raised in Raetia (Switzerland). It is first recorded in Britain at Greatchesters (166-169) in the reign of Marcus Aurelius. The only other record is a lead seal of the third century found at Brough-under-Stainmore.

**COHORS I THRACUM EQUITATA**

It is recorded on a building stone (RIB 1323) found near Newcastle (Hanover Square) but probably records only their work on the Vallum. In the third century it was the garrison of Bowes (RIB 730).

**COHORS I THRACUM CR**

Originally raised in Thrace (Bulgaria). It is recorded on a building inscription at Birdoswald (RIB 1909) (A.D. 205-8). Must not be confused with Cohors I Thracum Equitata.

**COHORS II THRACUM EQUITATA**

This Thracian unit was at Mumrils during the second occupation of the Antonine Wall. Two inscriptions, one of which is probably of third century date, record it at Moresby (GABROSENTUM). The *Notitia* also places it there.

**NUMERI**

Irregular army units.

**CUNEUS FRISIONUM ABALLAVENSIUM**

This regiment of irregular cavalry was raised in Frisia (Holland). It is mentioned in two inscriptions at Papcastle fort c. 244 A.D. Its name however shows it as the garrison of Burgh-by-sands (Aballava).

**CUNEUS FRISIORUM VER**

Originally raised from the Frisii of Holland it is only recorded on an inscription from Housesteads in the reign of Severus Alexander (222 — 235). The letters VER have been suggested as an abbreviation of the Roman name of Housesteads namely Vercovicium.

**CUNEUS FRISIORUM VINOVIENSIUM**

A cavalry unit raised from the Frisii of Holland. It is recorded on a third century altar, now lost, from Binchester, Roman name VINOVIA (RIB 1036).

**NUMERUS BARCARIORUM TIGRISENSIUM**

This unit of Tigris Lightermen is given as the garrison of South Shields in the *Notitia.*

**NUMERUS CONCANGIENSIUM**

Third century garrison of Chester-le-Street. The *Notitia* gives: *Praefectus numeri Vigilum, Concangios.* A tile found at Binchester and inscribed N CON was probably made at Chester-le-Street.

**NUMERUS EXPLORATORUM BREMENIENSIUM**

Stationed at High Rochester in reign of Gordian (238-41). No other reference to it except perhaps Portchester in the south. The name means "scouts".

**NUMERUS EXPLORATORUM HABITANCENSIUM**

Recorded at Risingham from 213 A.D. (RIB 1235).

**NUMERUS HNAUDIFRIDI**

This unit is recorded on an inscription at Housesteads in the third century. It came from Germany and was named after its commander one Notfried. Recorded nowhere else.

**NUMERUS MAURORUM AURELIANORUM**

Raised in North Africa the name suggests it was formed by Marcus Aurelius in the second century. First recorded on an inscription of 253-8 A.D. (RIB 1576) at Burgh, it is still placed there by the *Notitia.*

**VENATORES BANNIENSES**

Only record is at Birdoswald probably in the third century (inscription undated). Venatores does not necessarily mean they were animal hunters.

**VEXILLATIO GAESATORUM RAETORUM**

Only record is at Greatchesters in the third century. This unit is probably distinct from the following (RIB 1724).

**VEXILLATIO RAETORUM GAESATORUM**

Stationed as Risingham in the third century. Also mentioned on an inscription found at Jedburgh which probably came from Cappuck (RIB 2117).

## SOUTH SHIELDS

South Shields (or ARBEIA in Roman times), although south of the Tyne was part of the Roman Wall defences. It was basically a seaport and supply depot with a large civilian settlement.

The fort was probably built about 129 A.D. in stone during the reign of Hadrian when the system of northern defences was being established as the Roman Wall. Pottery has suggested a Flavian origin but if so the fort must have been sited somewhere else on the hill top. When Severus came north in 208 A.D. the fort was turned into a supply base with a very small garrison. Fourteen granaries have already been found. When the Scottish campaigns were over the fort returned to its former use and some of the granaries were changed into barracks. An inscription shown below records the building of a new aqueduct in 222 A.D. by the Fifth Cohort of Gauls.

*The "Aqueduct Stone"*

The fort seems to have been abandoned late in the 3rd century and not used again until well into the 4th. The last coins found in the fort are two of the Emperor Arcadius who reigned from A.D. 395 to A.D. 408.

The original 2nd century garrison seems to have been a cavalry regiment, the *ala Sabiniana,* 500 strong, followed by the First Ala of Asturians (name mentioned on a tombstone). An insctiption mentions the 5th Cohort of Gauls at the beginning of the 3rd century with, later in the 4th century, a unit of Tigris Lightermen (numerus Barcariorum Tigrisiensium) mentioned in the *Notitia* along with the name of the fort ARBEIA. They were probably only here for a short time since South Shields went out of use by *c.* 400 A.D. These bargemen were probably used for ferrying troops and stores up the Tyne.

The fort in its final form measures 620 by 320 feet, covering an area of just over five acres. Its defences are a stone wall backed by a turf rampart with a gateway in each of its sides. In front are two ditches.

A very large collection of Roman material has come from the site. There are two magnificent funereal monuments. The one to Regina, with its inscription in two languages (unique in Britain), is shown on page 136.

*South Shields Harbour*

Roman skillet *(patera)* cast in bronze. Early 3rd century. Probably made in Gaul. Found in the wreck of a ship on the north sands at South Shields. *Paterae* were used for many purposes in Roman cookery, such as boiling stews and decocting wine, and sometimes had strainers. Each Roman soldier carried one.

*Stone Mason's Workshop*

*The funereal monument to Regina*

The first part of the inscription is in Latin and reads in translation — "To the divine shades. To Regina a freed woman and (his) wife, Barates a Palmyrene (erected this) monument. She was) by nation a Catuvellaunian, (and lived) thirty years". It ends with a line in the Palmyrene language, translated — Regina, freedwoman of Barates, alas!". Regina is shown with a distaff and spindle in one hand while the other raises a decorated chest supposed to hold her personal possessions. At the other side is a basket containing weaving materials. Barates was a merchant who supplied military standards and his own epitaph was found at Corbridge where he died aged 68 years.

It has been suggested that this tombstone was the work of a Palmyrene living at South Shields. Being a large seaport and an important civilian settlement Shields would have had a large polyglot population.

The domestic scene recorded on this funereal monument is shown on our coloured plate (page 39).

Tombstones are the most common of all remains surviving from Roman times. There were special workshops of monumental masons where stocks were kept of various designs and at different prices. The relations would select the stone they liked and the name of the deceased and suitable words would be inscribed and then painted in red. Such a scene is shown by R. Embleton (page 35). The masons would also manufacture temple altars, some of which are shown in the drawing.

Roman funerals were elaborate affairs. The dramatic picture shown on page 38 illustrates a funereal procession of a wealthy inhabitant of *Arbeia*. The people depicted are, from left to right — family mourners and friends, slaves carrying the *lectus funebris,* funeral manager *(Dissignator),* hired mourners *(Praeficae)* and flute players *(tibicines).*

*Roman ship passes Tynemouth on its way back to Rome*

However Shields was not the centre of the funeral trade on the Wall. It had a thriving commerce, some local manufacturers, and numerous shops. One of these trades was the manufacture of jet ornaments, many of which have been found along the Wall (see Vindolanda). Our illustration shows a jet worker at his bench. The methods of manufacture and the tools used were almost identical with those employed at Whitby in the last century (page 58).

*A Roman anchor*

DIS
MANIBVS
FLAVIUS
DM
PERVICAE
FILIAE

Ronald Embleton

*A merchant's wife at South Shields*

*Opposite: A Roman funeral*

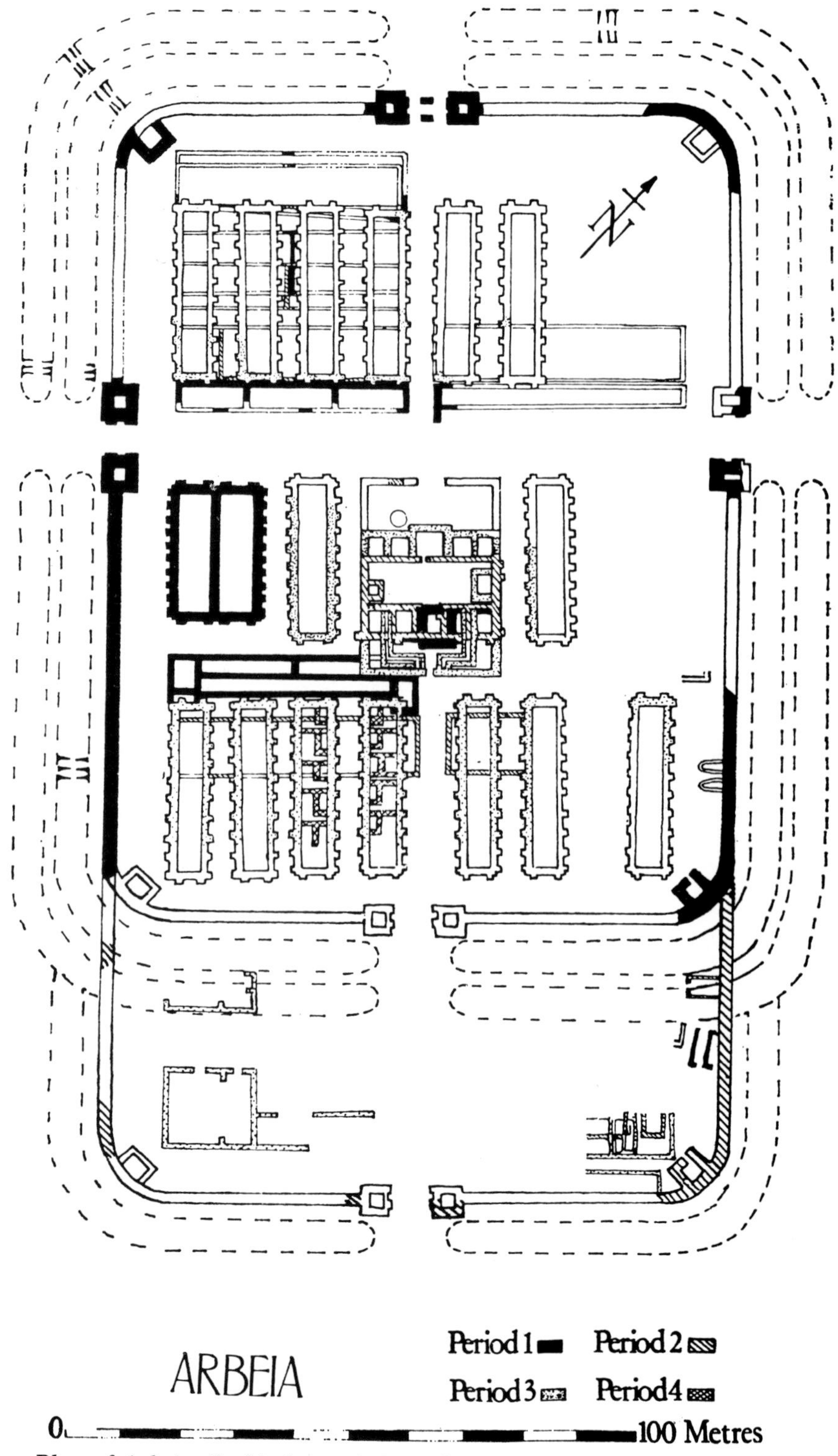

*Plan of Arbeia. By kind permission of Tyne and Wear Museum Service*

Gill Embleton

*Roman Cutter's Shop*

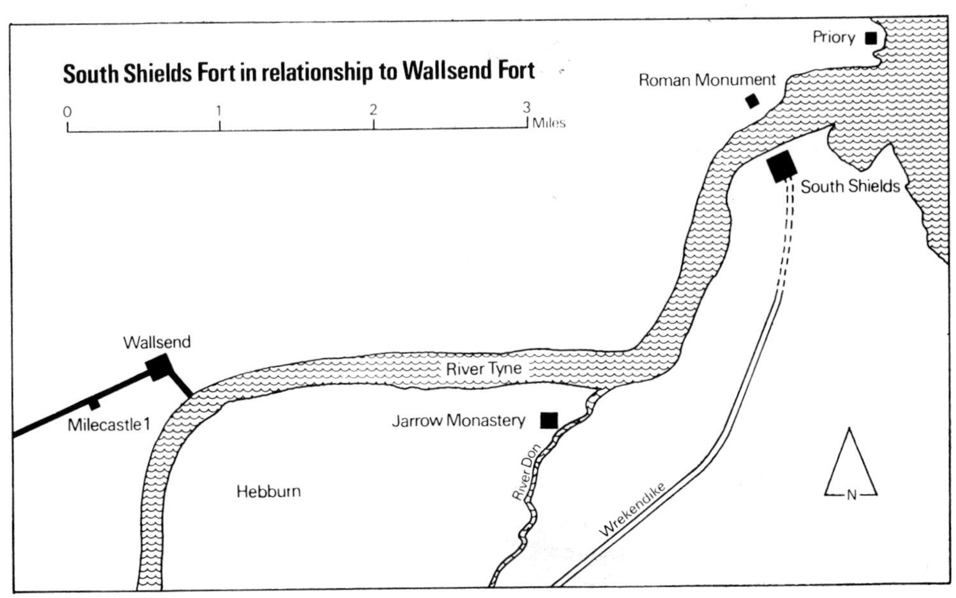
South Shields Fort in relationship to Wallsend Fort
0
1
2
3
Miles
Priory
Roman Monument
South Shields
Wallsend
River Tyne
Milecastle 1
Jarrow Monastery
River Don
Hebburn
Wrekendike
N

*Boss of a Roman shield found in Tyne*

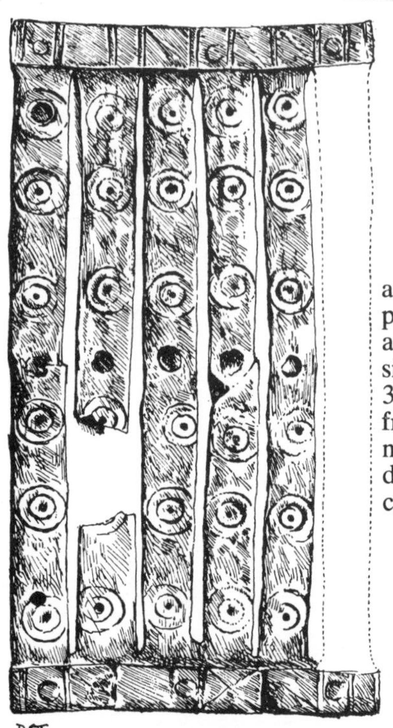

DST.

At South Shields an interesting domestic article has been found in a good state of preservation. It is a bone weaving frame, and consists of a perforated bone plate with silver mountings, rather small, being only 3½ x 1¼ inches in size. It is a heddle frame used for weaving narrow bands of material such as belts, head bands and decorated cloth for embellishing women's clothes.

**HADRIAN'S MONUMENT**

The Roman Wall, with its camps, roads, towns and villages, was the greatest single building achievement of the ancient world. The men who planned and executed this great mural barrier must have been proud of their work. The emperor Hadrian would almost certainly have erected some monument to record his achievement. His patron and predecessor Trajan had built a magnificent war memorial on the eastern front to commemorate his victories there and to mark the boundary of the Roman Empire. His enormous monument at Adamclisi in modern Rumania has now been completely restored in all its magnificence.

The eastern and western ends of the Wall were probably chosen by Hadrian for identical monuments. At a later date Severus may have recorded his rebuilding of the Wall with a memorial near the centre. Was the huge "mausoleum" outside Corbridge, near the main Roman road north, the work of Severus?

In 1866 when the nave of Jarrow church was being rebuilt two inscribed Roman stones, used by the original Saxon builders, were discovered. One of the stones was finally presented to Burlington House, London, and the other to the Blackgate in Newcastle. In 1943 Ian A. Richmond and R. P. Wright published an article in *Archaeologia Aeliana* suggesting the two stones belonged to a monument erected by Hadrian after the Wall was built.

The original inscribed stone was probably six feet square and formed part of a large war memorial or *tropaeum.* Although less than quarter of the original inscription was left the two authors were able to suggest more than half of it. The Blackgate fragment (with the additions) in translation reads:—

*The emperor Caeser Traianus Hadrianus Augustus son of all his divine ancestors, decided it was necessary on the advice of the gods to fix the boundaries of the Empire in the second consulship . . .*

OMNIVM · FIL
*AIANVS*
HADR *ITA*
NECESSITAT
VATI DIVINO
PR SII
Roman lettering on the Blackgate fragment.

The Burlington House fragment tells us:—

*The barbarians were scattered and the province of Britain freed. A boundary was established between the two oceans a distance of 80 miles. The army of the province built the Wall under the command of Aulus Platorius Nepos imperial legate and propaetor.*

DIFFVSIS
PROVINC
BRITANNIA
· AD
VIRVMQVE
· O
EXERCITVS
· PR SVB CV R
Roman lettering on the Burlington House fragment.

If I. A. Richmond and R. P. Wright are correct where would this monument have been? Clearly not at Jarrow. It was too low lying and of no importance. Shields could have been the site but the fort itself stood on the highest land and such a war memorial would not have stood out. Tynemouth is clearly the place and the Collingwood Monument or the Priory probably stand on the spot. The *tropaeum* would have been clearly visible from the large base at South Shields and also to every ship that entered the Tyne.

When the Saxon church at Jarrow and the medieval priory at Tynemouth were built Hadrian's memorial would have been a good source for stone and was probably completely removed.

Ronald Embleton's reconstruction has been based on the monument at Adamclisi.

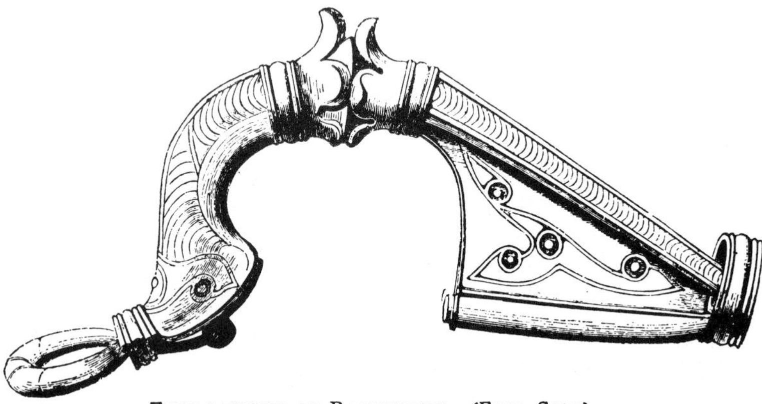

FIBULA FOUND AT BACKWORTH. (FULL SIZE.)

A silver gilt *fibula,* used to hold parts of a garment together. Celtic in style it almost certainly came from somewhere on the lower Tyne. (Part of the so-called Backworth Hoard).

**WALLSEND FORT**

Wallsend, as its name implies, was at the east end of the Wall. The *Notitia Dignitatum* puts it first on the list, under *Item per lineam valli,* as *Tribunus Cohortis quartae Lingonum Segeduno.* The name is Celtic and signifies a *hill* of some kind. The fort occupies a good site, with a wide view in every direction, and being on an angle of the river dominates the stretches to the east and west. We do not know the original garrison but in the second century the Second Cohort of Nervians was stationed here. In the third and fourth centuries the part-mounted Fourth Cohort of the Lingones was here. Both garrisons were 500 strong.

From the south-east angle of the fort the Wall continued to the river and extended into the stream at least as far as low water level. In 1903 part of this Wall (6 feet 6 inches wide) was discovered and re-erected in Wallsend Park and in 1912 remains of the east gate, found when Simpson's Hotel was built, were also transferred to the Park. Many Roman relics, coins and pottery have been found on the site and dateable evidence suggests occupation almost down to 400 A.D.

There appears to have been a civilian settlement in the angle between the Wall and the fort stretching along the river bank. A bath-house, a temple and two or three streets have been recorded and there is evidence of a potter's kiln. Several early writers also noted remains of a possible Roman quay just below the fort.

The interior of the fort, as often happens, altered over the centuries and our reconstruction has tried to show Segedunum in the 3rd century. It is based on information supplied to us by C. M. Daniels.

The Wall between Wallsend and Newcastle was 7 feet 6 inches wide on a foundation of 8 feet. Milecastle 1 (The Grange) is found 800 yards from the fort (normally the distance is a Roman mile — 1,620 yards). Milecastle 2 (Walker) was a short distance east of the summit of Byker Hill, the Wall continuing over the highest part of the hill. Stukeley came here in 1725 and was so impressed with the view of the Wall from Byker Hill to Newcastle that he made a sketch of it which was published in his *Iter Boreale,* 1776, *View of the Tract of the Picts' Wall, Newcastleward, from Byker Mill Hill, 4 Sept.,* 1725. The Wall was then standing in good order. Ronald Embleton shows the same view in Roman times.

Milecastle 3 (Ouseburn) is shown in Stukeley's View. Milecastle 4 (Pilgrim Street) in conjectural.

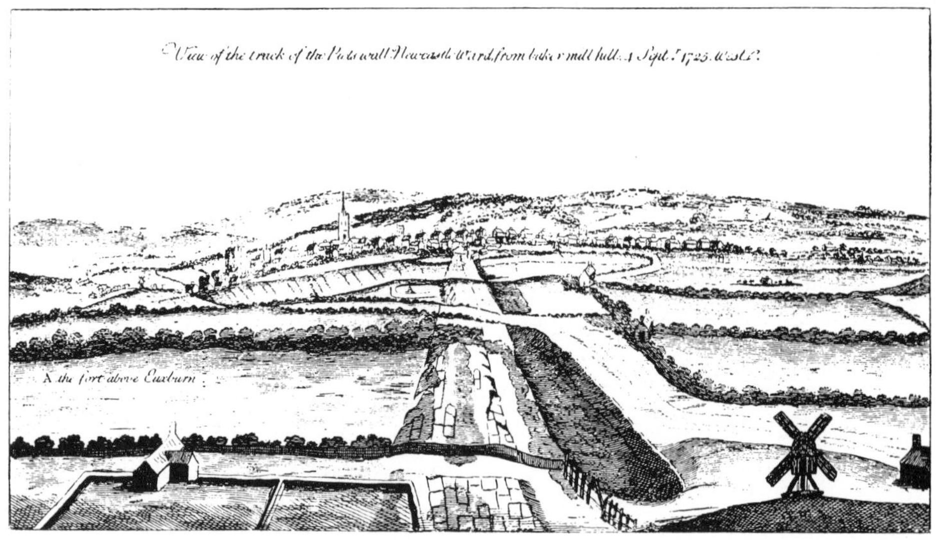


*View from Byker Hill looking west. 'A' marks the Ouseburn milecastle*

*Grinding corn on a mill*

**NEWCASTLE UPON TYNE (PONS AELIUS)**

Newcastle was originally the beginning of the Wall. This is assumed because the stretch between Newcastle and Wallsend is the Narrow Wall and the stretch to the west is Broad Wall. The milecastles to the west are spaced exactly from the bridge. Probably the Romans found there was too much penetration by marauders down the denes between Newcastle and Wallsend so the Wall had to be extended.

We know the exact site of the bridge but the fort is not so certain. During their 400 years of occupation of the North the Romans built three bridges over the Tyne, one on practically the same site as the present Swing Bridge, the second at Corbridge and the third at Chesters. In the case of Newcastle the remains of only two piers have been found. However, two fine altars dedicated respectively to Neptune and Oceanus have been dredged from the river. They came from a shrine on the bridge, built by the Sixth Legion, to protect the structure from floods and tides.

The Newcastle Bridge was built by the Emperor Titus Aelius Hadrianus about 120 A.D., and was called *Pons Aelius,* and the camp guarding it received the same name. Few Roman frontier posts bear Imperial names. The length of the bridge to the banks of the river has been calculated at 735 feet. The piers were used later by the medieval bridge. The third pier from the south was found in 1872 when the Swing Bridge was being built.

The pier had a cutwater both up and down stream. Its width was 16 feet and the parallel sides were 20 feet long. The oak timbers, black with age, were found. They had been shod with iron and driven into the bed of the river. Heavy timber

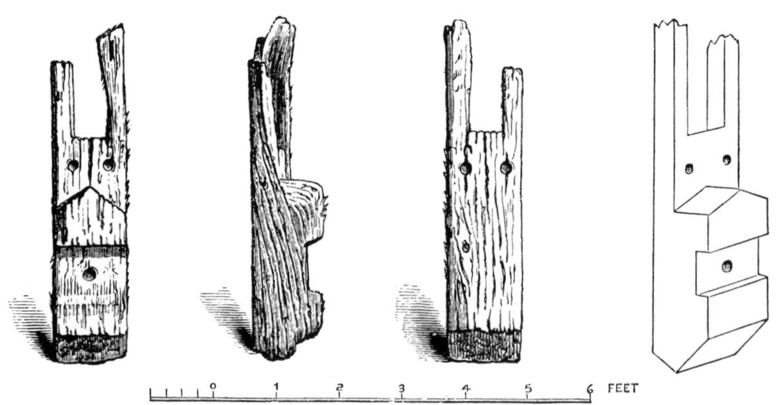


*Roman timbers from the bridge at Newcastle*

*Roman altars which stood on the bridge at Newcastle*

*The altar to Neptune reads: NEPTUNO LE(GIO) VI(CTRIX) P(IA)* F(IDELIS). *To Neptune, the 6th Legion, Victorious, Pious and Faithful.*

*The altar to Oceanus reads:* OCIANO LEG(IO) VI VI(CTRIX) P(IA) F(IDELIS). *To Oceanus, the 6th Legion, Victorious, Pious and Faithful.*

was laid across them to provide a foundation for the stone pier. There appear to have been ten piers and two abutments.

For long the site of the Roman fort has been a subject of controversy, however, recent excavations by Miss Barbara Harbottle show that the Castle Keep is on the site of the fort. Remains of the headquarters and commanding officer's house were found adjoining the Keep.

In the early 4th century the garrison was the First Cohort of Cornovii. This was the only British fort garrison on the Wall. The Cornovii came from the Cheshire, Staffordshire and Shropshire districts. A tablet recording work done by the 1st Cohort of Thracians has been found at Newcastle (south side of Hanover Square) but probably records only their work on the Vallum.

An important stone recently found at Newcastle is of great importance. It is one of a series set up by the army in Britain in 230 A.D. to express their loyalty to the Emperor Caracalla. It is dedicated to the Dowager Empress Julia Domna, the mother of Caracalla, and gives the garrison at that time as *Cohors Ulpia Traiana Cugernorum.* They were a quinqenary peditate cohort raised in the lower Rhineland (Holland) and brought to Britain about A.D. 103.

From Newcastle a road led south to Chester-le-Street with an eastward branch to South Shields. It has also been suggested that a road ran north, joining the Devil's Causeway near its crossing of the Coquet.

The reconstruction by Ronald Embleton shows the chapel on the bridge at Pons Aelius. We have also reproduced H. B. Richardson's drawing made *c.* 1840. It is purely imaginary but very accurate bearing in mind that it was one of the earliest attempts to show Hadrian's Wall as it was originally.

Punishments in the Roman army were very severe. The soldier here being stoned to death outside the walls of Pons Aelius was probably guilty of cowardice.

*Inscribed slab from the Tyne Bridge by Julius Verus c.* 158 A.D.

Size, 2 feet 1 inch by 1 foot 6 inches.

This altar was found built-up in a wall of Mitchell's printing premises, St. Nicholas' Churchyard.
It probably came from Pons Aelius.

*Dea(bus) / Matribus Tramarinus / Patri(i)s Aurelius Iuuenalis / s(acrum).*

'To the Mother Goddesses of his native land from overseas Aurelius Juvenalis made this offering'.

**THE BENWELL TORC**

At Benwell during the excavations of 1937 a fragmentary bronze torc was found, the only Roman military decoration discovered in the north. It came from a building in the *retentura* of the fort. Information about Roman military decorations is somewhat fragmentary. The decorations awarded to soldiers of the rank of centurion and below were torcs, *armillae* (bracelets) and *phalerae* (embossed discs). Higher officers received *hastae purae* (small silver spears), *vexilla* (flags) and *coronae* (crowns).

The torc found at Benwell is usually thought to be of Roman, not Celtic origin, and to be a military decoration. There are problems since military decorations were only awarded to Roman citizens and the garrison of Benwell were auxiliaries and not citizens of the Empire.

The torc is about six inches in diameter and was worn on the chest suspended by a leather strap.

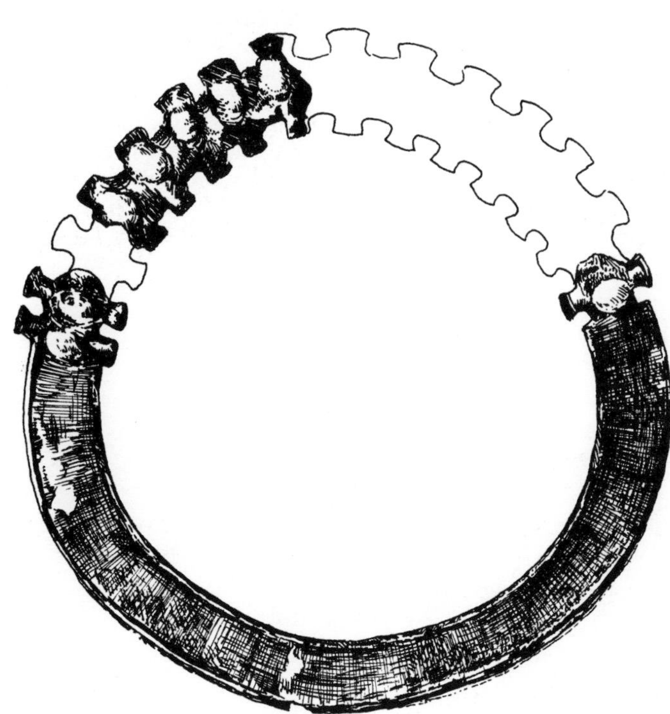

*The Benwell torc*

## BENWELL FORT (CONDERCUM)

The third fort on the Wall was Condercum standing near the top of Benwell Hill, with an extensive view in all directions. The distance from Newcastle is just over two miles and to Rudchester 6¾ miles. The reason why Benwell was built only two miles from Newcastle was probably because Newcastle was a very small fort only intended to defend the bridge and the first opportunity to erect a large fort was taken at Benwell. Today the northern part of the fort is covered by a reservoir and cut by the Newcastle-Carlisle road. About two thirds of the fort lies to the south of the road.

In the second century the first milliary cohort of the Vangiones was stationed here. In the *Notitia* the garrison is described as *Praefectus Alae primae Asturum Conderco.* The Astureans came from northern Spain. The term *ala* means a body of cavalry (in strength just over 500 men). Cavalry were chosen for Benwell because the flat open country here was suitable for their use. The Astureans were the garrison from A.D. 205 to 367. A dedication of about A.D. 240 has been preserved.

The fort measurements seem to have been about 570 feet from north to south and 400 feet east to west with an area of just over five acres. The fort was built in Hadrianic times and extensively rebuilt towards the end of the second century. It continued in occupation until late in the fourth century. It is a typical oblong fort with rounded angles.

The original building of the fort was carried out by the second legion as can be seen in a fine dedication, now in the British Museum. The stone bears the symbols of a Capricorn and a Pegasus confronting a *vexillum* (Standard).

The most important remain to be seen at Benwell today is the Vallum crossing. The *vallum* can be traced right round Benwell fort. Only at Birdoswald can a similar diverted vallum be completely traced. The *vallum* at Benwell is however unique because the vallum crossing has been preserved and can be seen today. It is a causeway of undug earth (the fort either existed or was planned before the vallum was built) with gaps through both mounds. The straight sides of the causeway were reverted in well dressed stone with a drain on each side of the southern section. In the centre of the crossing resting on the east and west revetments are the massive foundations of a gateway. The passage is 12 feet wide and was closed by two doors opening to the north. The massive foundations seen today would have been built up and joined by some form of arch making an imposing entrance. The vallum crossing here was used for a long time as successive periods of road are visible on the north looking like a series of steps.

Size, 1 foot 3 inches by 10 inches

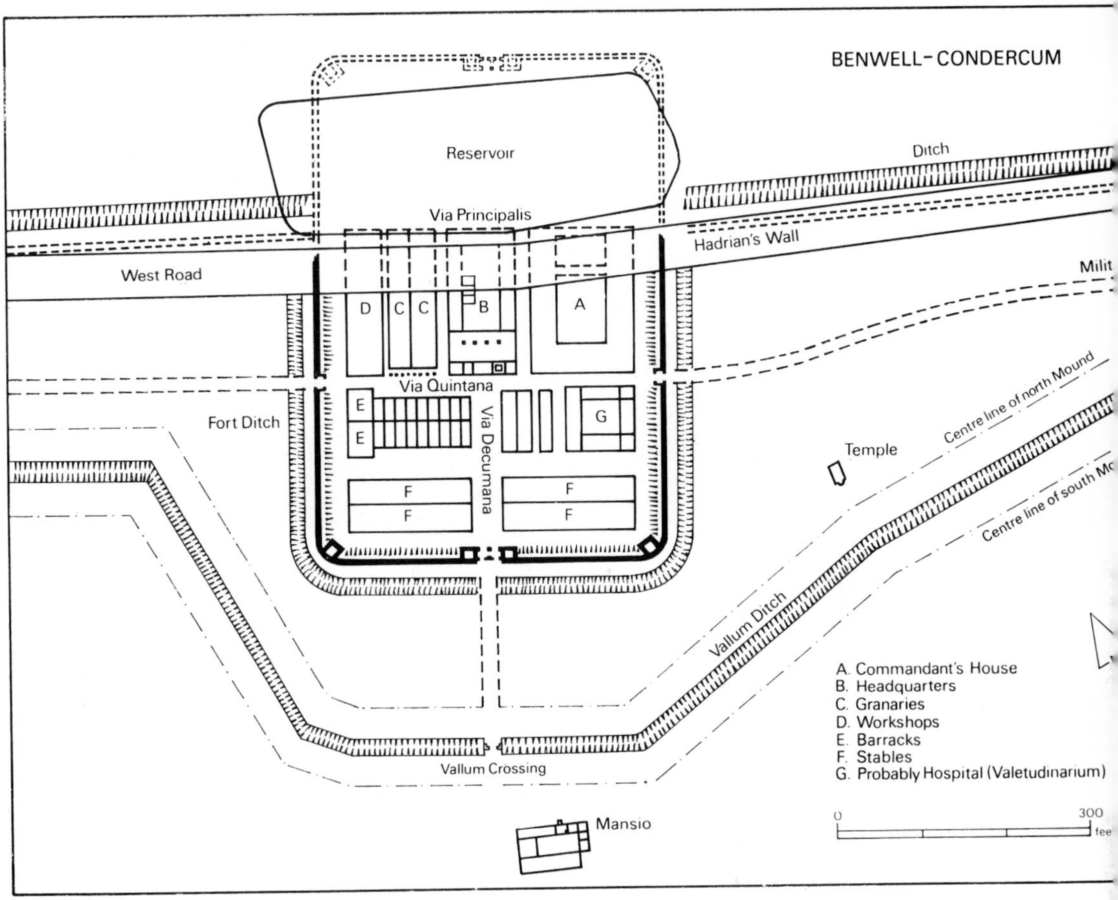

BENWELL-CONDERCUM

Reservoir

Ditch

Via Principalis

Hadrian's Wall

West Road

Via Quintana

Fort Ditch

Via Decumana

Temple

Centre line of north Mound

Centre line of south Mo

Vallum Ditch

Vallum Crossing

Mansio

A. Commandant's House
B. Headquarters
C. Granaries
D. Workshops
E. Barracks
F. Stables
G. Probably Hospital (Valetudinarium)

0 300 feet

*Roman children's games*

GATEWAY OF VALLUM CROSSING AT BENWELL

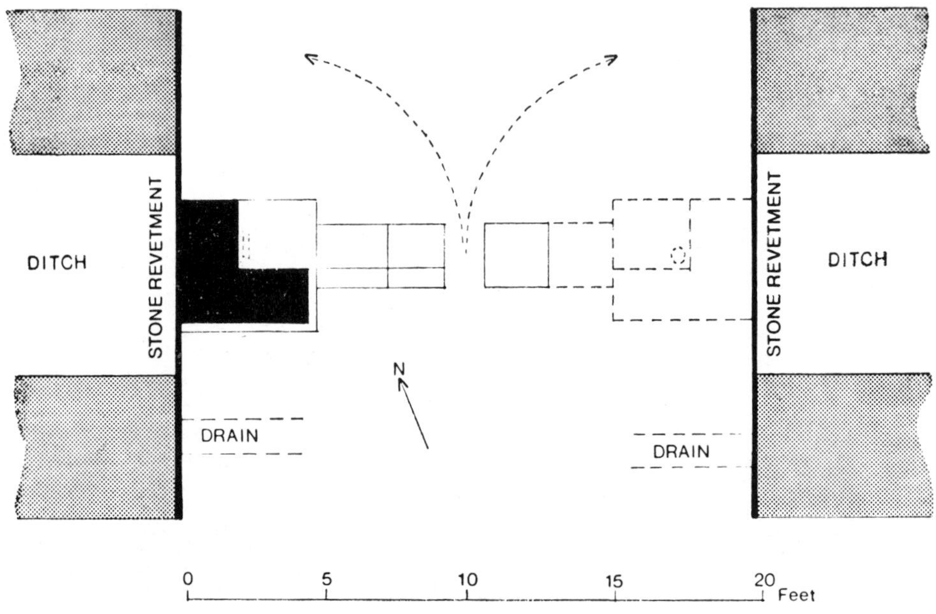

## TEMPLE OF ANTENOCITICUS AT BENWELL

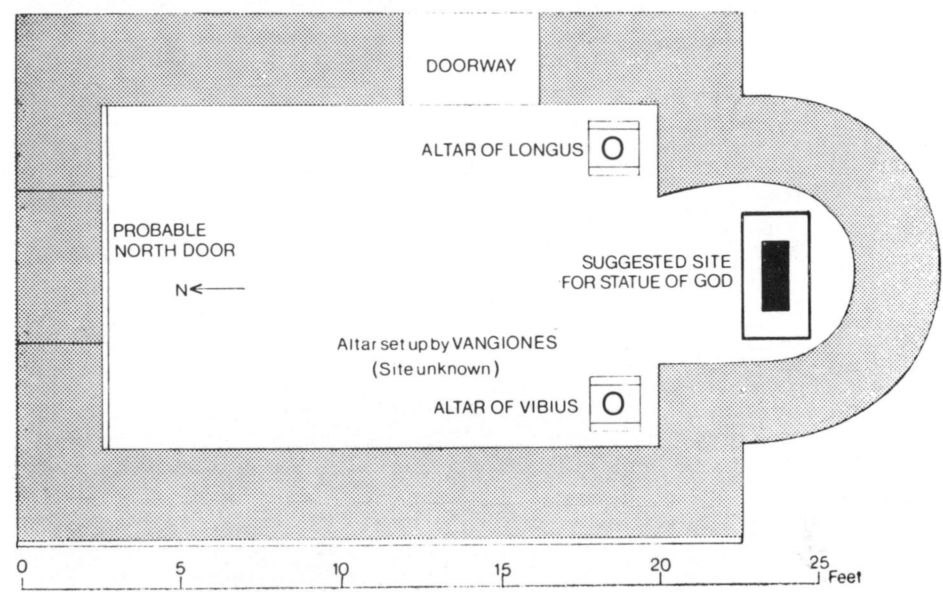

**Temple of Antenociticus**

Many gods were worshipped on the Roman Wall. Besides the official gods such as the soldiers' deities Mars and Hercules there were numerous native gods and foreign ones brought in by the auxiliary troops. Because of the variety there were no large temples but a multitude of smaller ones. The god at Benwell was Antenociticus who had his own temple, the remains of which can still be seen. There appears to have been a large civilian settlement at Benwell. The bath house was 300 yards south west of the fort, the *mansio* 300 yards to the south and the temple of Antenociticus 200 yards to the east. The Military Way was lined with buildings north and south of the vallum.

The temple of Antenociticus was discovered in 1862 in the grounds of Condercum House, south east of the fort within the line of the Vallum. It now lies in Broomridge Avenue open to view. The internal measurements are 18 by 10 feet plus the apse. The entrance is on the east but in its early form was probably on the north as shown in the plan. Two altars were found face down but *in situ.* Another altar in fragments was found but its original site is unknown. A full-size head with fragments of arm and leg was also found, almost certainly the statue of the god. It probably stood in the nave. Evidence from the excavation of the temple suggest it was deliberately destroyed late in the 2nd century and never rebuilt.

The interior view of the temple shows the two main altars (of Longus and Vibius) with the statue of the god in the apse. Only the head of the god has survived "ovoid in shape, with wild hair and Celtic neck torc". The floor was covered with fine sand. Whether Antenociticus was a local god or imported by the Vangiones we do not know. He has only been found at Benwell.

*"To the god Antenociticus, Tineius Longus, who was given senatorial rank and appointed quaester designate while he was cavalry prefect, by decree of our best and greatest emperors under the consul Ulpius Marcellus".*

## HOSPITAL (VALETUDINARIUM)

Few hospitals have been found in the auxiliary forts on the Wall but many had them, especially *ala* forts and *milliary* cohort forts. Probably a hospital provided medical treatment for a group of forts. There was almost certainly a hospital at Wallsend as well as the better known one at Benwell.

Doctors were of centurion rank and some have been recorded on tombstones. A doctor at Binchester, M. Aurelius Abrocomas, was doctor to a group of cavalry of Vettonians, and dedicated an altar to Aesculapius and Salus. Under the doctors were bandagers *(capsarii)* and orderlies *(medici)* who cared for the wounded on the battlefield and in hospitals. The doctors were fairly skilled since they had plenty of practice and a variety of medical instruments have been found on the Wall. Surgeons were held in more esteem than physicians, many of whom were quacks.

There is some evidence that medical herbs were grown on some sites for use by the garrison.

The hospital at Benwell stood behind the Commandant's house on the south side of the *via quintana* and measured 74 by 81 feet. This quiet and secluded position was usually chosen for a hospital because the rest of the fort was very noisy. Although never completely excavated due to the presence of modern buildings, it was revealed as a courtyard building with the wings divided into small rooms.

Anaesthetics were limited and consisted largely of preparations made from poppy, henbane and mandrake. The Roman writer Celsius says that a good surgeon should learn to ignore the cries of his patient.

*A Roman Bakery*

There was a large civilian settlement at Benwell since the site was pleasant and fertile. The Roman road behind the Wall was lined with buildings. There were several temples, an inn for travellers, and a bathhouse whose plan has been preserved.

Benwell however is of great social interest because here coal was first mined and used for industrial purposes. In the fort workshops coal has been found which probably came from open-cast working nearby.

From Benwell the Roman Wall follows the line of the main Carlisle road. The area is now built up but in Roman times was open country. Between the *vicus* of Condercum and the fort of Vindobala (Rudchester) there were no civilian settlements for almost 7 miles. An observant traveller would however have noticed almost midway between two milecastles (now designated 7 and 8), a fine culvert under the Wall which carried the stream now called the Denton Burn. In 1867 Bruce recorded this culvert, which was the only one left on the entire Wall, and probably identical with many others built where streams crossed the mural barrier (see page 65).

*A jet worker at South Shields* *Opposite. Hadrian's Monument*

*A Potter at Work*

Mass produced pottery was brought to the *vici* on the Wall from the south but some pottery was produced locally, especially at Corbridge where there is evidence that it was made on a large scale. A potter's kiln was traced in the *vicus* at Wallsend.

*Roman flask depicting a slave boy*

*Below: Monumental slab from the Granary at Benwell*

Benwell Fort

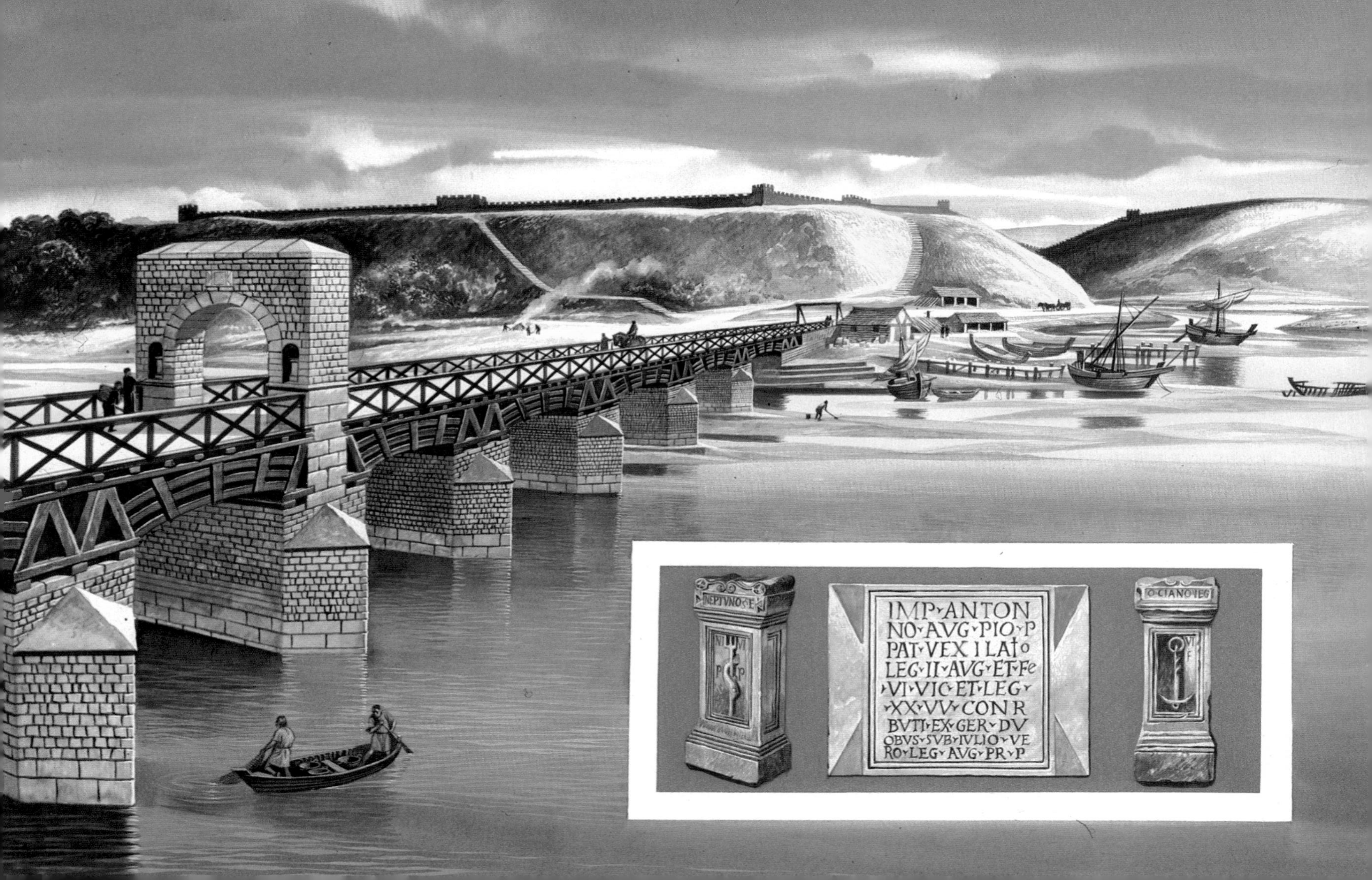
NEPTVNO LE
IMP ANTON
NO AVG PIO P
PAT VEX I LATO
LEG II AVG ET FE
VI VIC ET LEG
XX VV CON R
BVTI EX GER DV
OBVS SVB IVLIO VE
RO LEG AVG PR P
O CIANO LEG

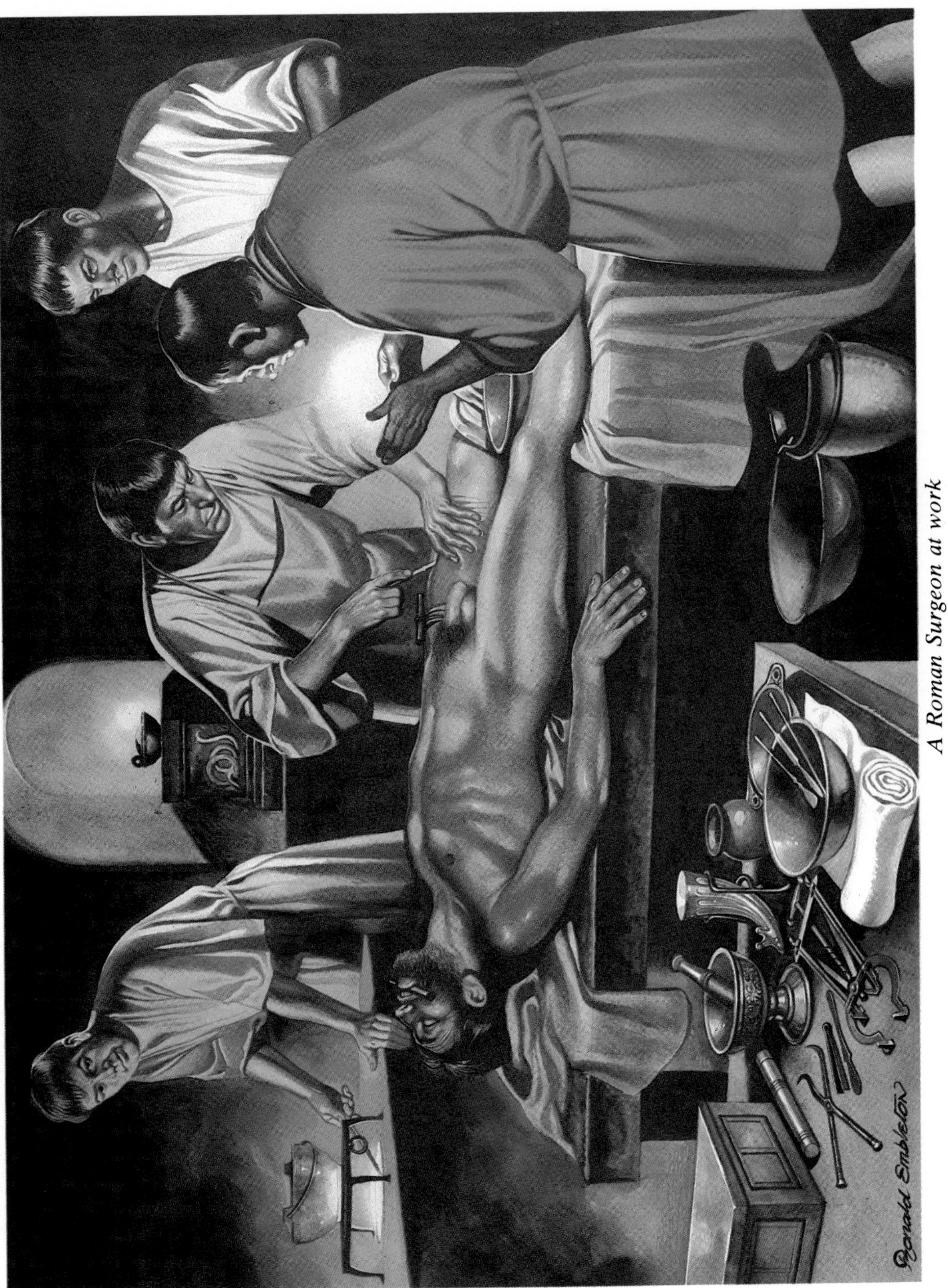

A Roman Surgeon at work

*Opposite. The Bridge at Newcastle*

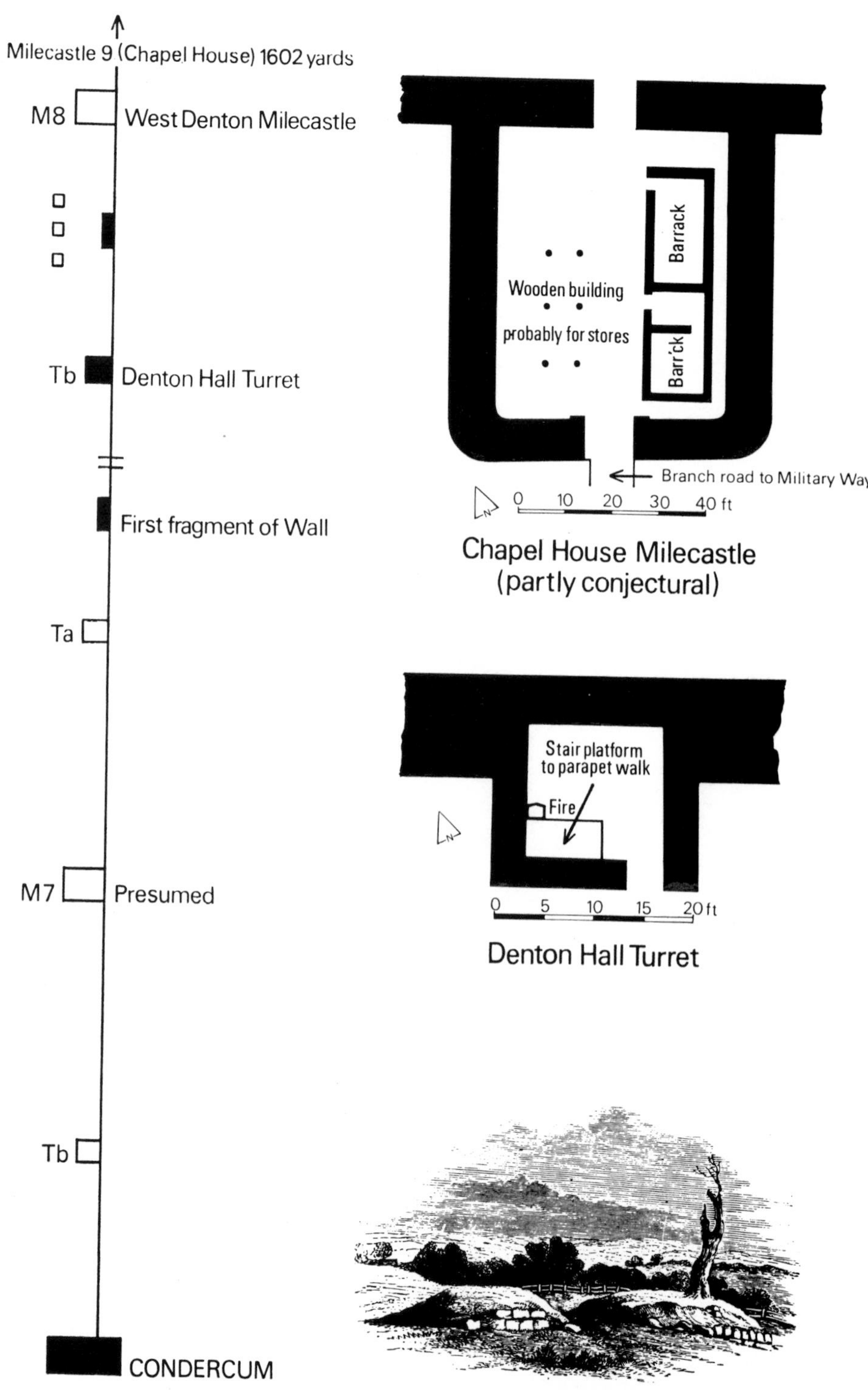


Chapel House Milecastle
(partly conjectural)

Denton Hall Turret

First fragment of Wall at Denton Burn
as drawn in 1845

## BENWELL TO CHESTERS

Just over two miles west of Benwell Fort the modern traveller gets his first glimpse of the Roman Wall in situ. Two stretches are visible on his left as he goes up Denton Bank.

Where the wall crossed Denton Burn there could still be seen in Bruce's day a Roman culvert which he described and illustrated.

"The circular arch is the drain which was formed when the road was made. The Roman channel is beneath. It consists of two lines of massive stones laid parallel to each other, about two feet apart. The top was covered overby other large blocks, giving the conduit a height equivalent to its breadth. This seems to have been the usual way of allowing brooks to pass the Wall".

## CENTURIAL STONES FROM THE VALLUM

West of Denton Burn in 1936 six centurial stones were discovered in the Vallum when a new road was being built. They were set in the mounds to the north and south and looked on to the berms. They were all alike, thin slabs about three inches thick in which the *centuria* had inscribed its official title. This was the first discovery to show that the Vallum as well as the Wall had centurial stones. From the discoveries near Denton Burn we now know that the Vallum was built in sections about 100 yards long, the work being done by centuries, from the auxiliaries as well as the legionaries. Each century was entirely responsible for its section and marked the completion of its task by two identical inscriptions on the north and south mounds. At Denton the work was done by centuries of the Second Legion and the First Cohort of Dacians. The most interesting stone is the one shown on our drawing. It reads:— COH.T DACOR(UM) (CENTURIA) AEL(I) DIDA(E) — *First Cohort of Dacians, century of Aelius Dida.*

The second element of the centurion's name DIDA is thought to be Dacian. The name Aelius is from the praenomen of the emperor Hadrian during whose reign Dida must have received his Roman citizenship.

*Centurial stone near Denton Burn*

*The Works at Heddon-on-the-Wall*

Between Denton and Heddon-on-the-Wall little is to be seen today, but at Heddon we encounter the Military Road, a work of immense importance to the Wall, since its construction led to the overthrow of a large section of the mural barrier.

The history of the Military Road is well known.

During the Jacobite revolt of 1745 the Pretender's forces advanced down the west coast. General Wade, stationed at Newcastle, was unable to advance on Carlisle because there was no good road along which he could transport his artillery, and the city was lost. To avoid a similar contingency in the future the "Military Road" was built and a large section of the Roman Wall was destroyed.

The Northumberland section was started in 1752 and completed five years later.

From Heddon the Military Road runs east in an almost straight line. The older road to Corbridge (A69) turns off to the south and follows a winding course. Travelling along the Military Road today one can see, for long stretches, the wall ditch to the north and the Vallum to the south. The road generally runs on the Wall foundations.

Milecastle 13 which is the nearest to Vindobala (Rudchester) is visible.

Towards the end of the occupation of the Wall one can imagine the troops at Vindobala were in a state of nervousness expecting an attack any day. At some point the fort commander must have decided to hide some of the cohort's money in case the fort was overrun. Beneath the floor of the nearest milecastle the money was hid temporarily (or so it was thought) and almost fourteen hundred years later the hoard was uncovered. *See page 80.*

*In the castellum nearest to VINDOBALA, on the east, two poor labourers, in 1766, found a small urn full of gold and silver coins, 'almost a complete series of those of the higher empire: among them several others: most of them in fine preservation'. At first a quantity of them were dispersed about Newcastle; but Mr. Archdeacon, the proprietor of the estate and mesne lord of the manor 'claimed them as treasure trove, and recovered nearly five hundred silver and sixteen gold coins'; though he in turn, after proceedings at law, was compelled to deliver them up in the court of Ovingham to the Duke of Northumberland, the chief lord of the fee.*

**RUDCHESTER FORT (Vindobala)**

Rudchester, the fourth fort from the eastern end of the Wall, lies 6¾ miles from Benwell. It was garrisoned in the fourth century by the First Cohort of Frisiavones, the name of a tribe from what is now the Netherlands. In the *Notitia* it is called *Vindobala,* in the *Ravenna* List *Vindovala.* In the second century the garrison was probably cavalry, the fort having been built by Hadrian for a *cohors quingenaria equitata.* Towards the end of the second century it was burnt down but shortly afterwards rebuilt. A century later it was abandoned for reasons unknown, and about 370 A.D. it was re-occupied and restored and continued in occupation for a long time.

Apart from brief mention by Camden the first description of the fort is by Robert Smith (1708):

*On the south side of the Wall, are visible ruins of a very large square Roman Castle, with foundations of several houses in the middle of the area: the square, as*

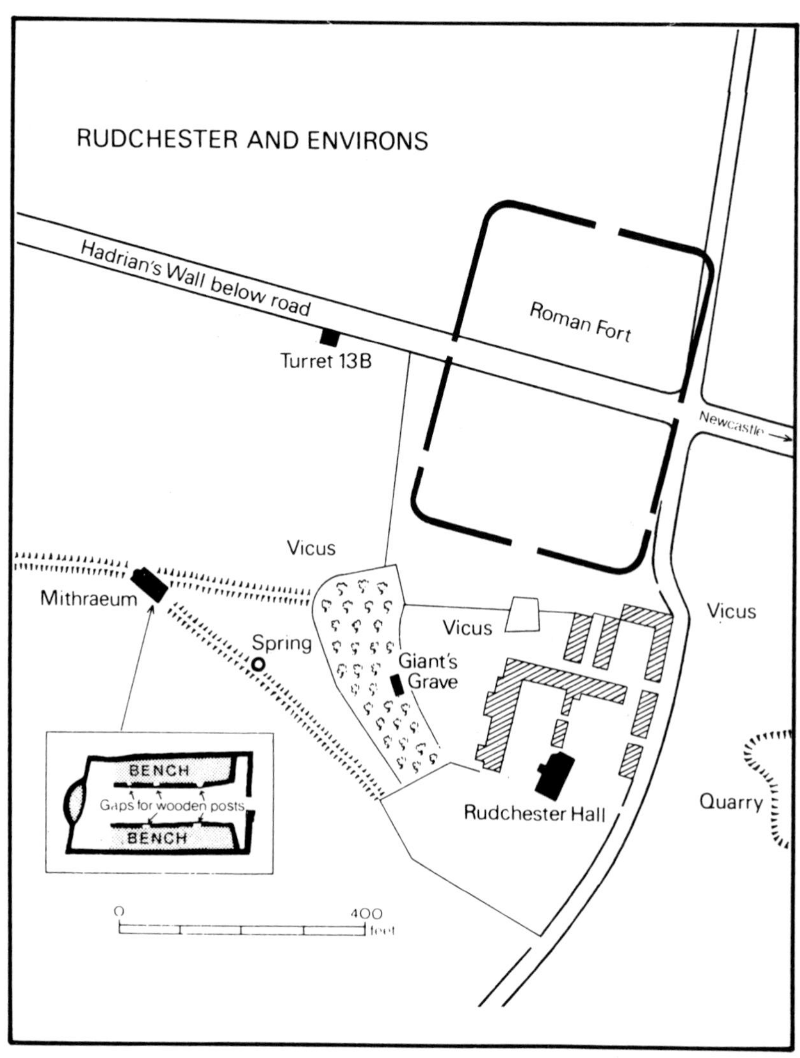


*nigh as I can guess, may be about one hundred and fifty yards; and at the west part of the square are three or four plots of ground in the very Wall (which seems to have been five or six feet thick) for little Towers. This has also a Vallum round it, and joins close to the Wall.*

The last account of Rudchester before the military road was built is from Horsley's *Britannia Romana,* 1732.

"This fort has been very considerable, as the ruins of it at present are very remarkable. On the north side there have been six turrets, one at each corner, one on each side of the gate, and one between each corner and those adjoining to the gate. On the east and west sides there is also a tower between the gate and the angle, in that part of the fort that is on the north side of the wall; but 'tis doubtful whether there has been the same number of towers in that part that lies within the wall. At present however they are not so distinct.

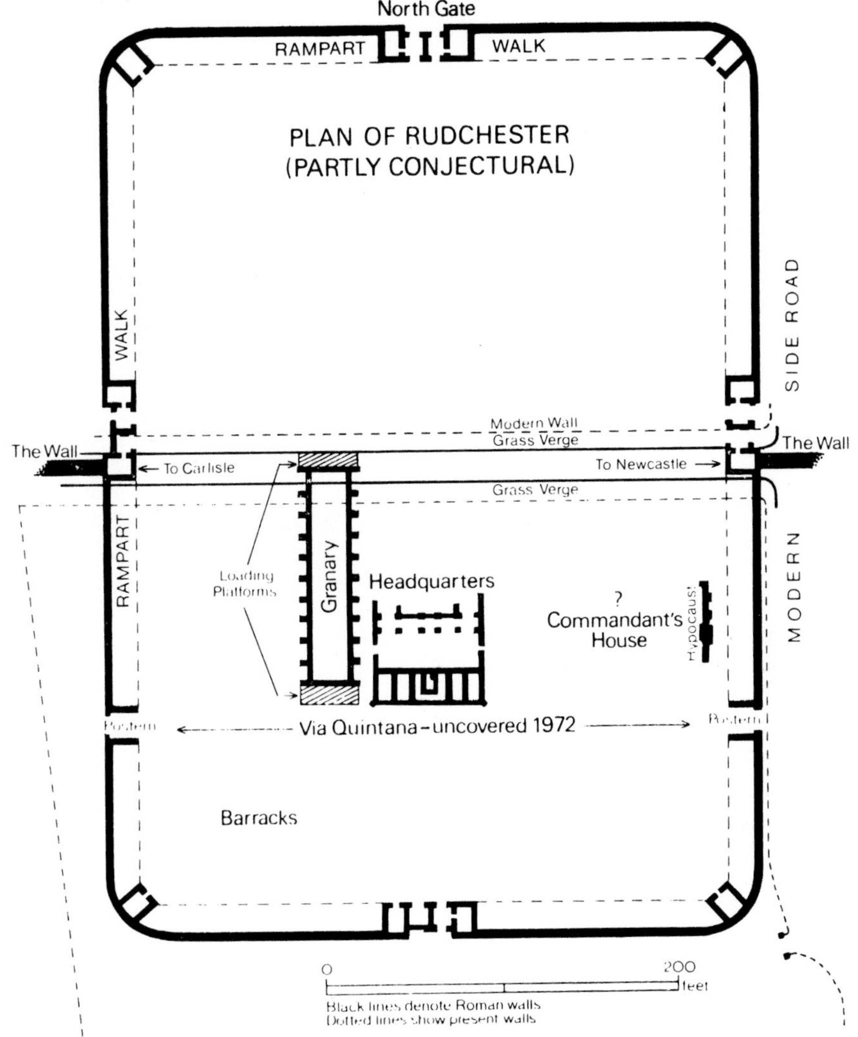


The ramparts of this fort are still very visible, being in the second degree or more on everyside. The ditch is but feint, and scarce discernible on the east side, being levelled in the highway. On the other three sides it is visible. The ruins within the fort plainly appear, and the entries into it may be distinguished. If there has been a town without, which there can scarce be any doubt of; it has been as usual on the south, where the village of *Rutchester* now stands, and covers its ruins".

William Hutton (1801) describes how:

*What remains is a close, joining the road, of five acres, now in grass, and eminently situated, carries the strong marks of former buildings, and still stronger of its ramparts. The platform of this grand Station is complete. I have all along inquired for turrets; but might as well have inquired among the stars. I was given to understand, that part of one was remaining here.*

*Fireplace at Rudchester Hall*

*The farmer was not helpful and made a jingle in his honour.*

*I saw old Sir at dinner sit,*
*Who ne'er said, "Stranger, take a bit",*
*Yet might, although a Poet said it,*
*Have sav'd his beef, and rais'd his credit.*

The fort measures 515 by 385 feet and covers 4½ acres. Little is to be seen apart from mounds to the south of the Military Road marking the west and south ramparts.

The building of the Military Road and the growth of agriculture in the eighteenth and nineteenth centuries led to systematic despoliation of the fort for its stone. The farm and house to the south and many field walls are built of Roman stones.

The first real exploration of the fort was carried out in 1924 and later in 1962. Two of the main gateways were excavated, a large granary and part of the principia were revealed, and a hypocaust belonging to the Commandant's house was discovered.

The Wall joined the fort at the main east and west gates leaving the gate passages to the north. The Wall Ditch existed before the fort was built. The west gateway which led on to the berm of the Wall was walled up but the date is uncertain. The thresholds show no sign of wear but since it was rarely used by wheeled traffic the closure might have been late in the Wall's history.

The south gate had an unusual arrangement. The west guard chamber was entered from the north and faced into the fort, probably to control traffic going out. The other guard chamber had its door leading onto the gate passage as was normal. Early on the west portal was blocked and changed into a guard chamber.

At the same time the east portal was furnished with two inner gates.

When the Headquarter's building was excavated the wide middle chamber contained the usual strong room. Coloured plaster showed the room had once been decorated. The site marked hypocaust was probably the Commandant's house and bath-house. The wall shown has large buttresses.

The Vallum passes some 240 yards to the south of the fort while the *vicus* lay to the south and south-west. The "Giant's Grave" 95 yards south of the south-west angle of the fort is probably connected with a military bath-house not yet revealed.

Five altars (one of them uninscribed) were found to the west of the Giant's Grave. Four are here reproduced. They belonged to the Mithraeum which was

Size, 4 ft. 1 in. by 1 ft. 6 in.

DEO
L(VCIVS) SENTIVS
CASTVS
LEG. VI. D(ECVRIO)? P(OSVIT)?

To the god (Mithras)
Lucius Sentius
Castus
A decurion of the sixth legion erected
(this).

DEO INVICTO
MYTRAE P. AEL(IVS)
FLAVINVS PRAE
V. S. LL. M.

To the invincible god
Mithras Publius Aelius
Flavinus the praefect
most willingly
and fittingly discharges his vow.

Size, 3 ft. 6 in. by 1 ft. 8 in.

Size, 3 ft. 4 in. by 1 ft. 7 in.

DEO SOLI INVIC(TO)
TIB. CL. DECIMVS
CORNEL(IA) ANTO-
NIVS PRAEF(ECTVS)
TEMPLE(VM) RESTIT(VIT)

To the god the sun unconquerable
Tiberius Claudius Decimus
Antonius of the Cornelian tribe
the prefect
this temple restored.

SOLI
APOLLINI
ANICERO

To the sun
Apollo
. . . .

Size, 3 ft. 7 in. by 1 ft. 5 in.

completely excavated in 1924. Two buildings were revealed, both in the traditional style and shape. The date of the second building can probably be dated shortly after the destruction of Hadrian's Wall in 197 A.D.

The present Rudchester Hall is to outward appearance eighteenth century and the remains of the medeival tower can only be distinguished by the thickness of the walls. In the house is a remarkable fireplace here illustrated. The inner fireplace with stone lintel and carved jambs has at the bottom a Roman Cohort and Centurial Stone from the Roman Wall which recorded the work done by the Fourth Cohort of the Century of Pedius Quintus.

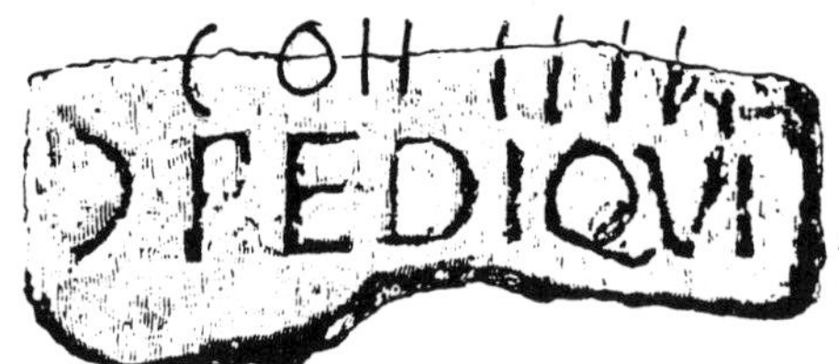


*A centurial stone found at Rudchester. It reads COH IIII C PEDI QVI – "the century of Pedius Quintus of the fourth cohort"*

Size, 1 ft. 6 in. by 7 in.

## RUDCHESTER TO HALTONCHESTERS

From Rudchester to Haltonchesters the Wall was practically destroyed by the builders of the Military Road. The Reverend William Stukeley in *Carausius* (1757-59) was incensed at the destruction wrought by "these senseless animals" as he called them:—.

*The overseers and workmen employed by Act of Parliament, to make a new road across the kingdom . . . demolish the Wall, and beat the stones in pieces, to make the road withal. Every carving, inscription altar, milestone, pillar, etc., undergoes the same vile havoc, from the hands of these wretches.**

About half a mile beyond Rudchester we notice some old buildings on the south of the road.

Here was once an inn, of which only the outbuildings survive, called "The Iron Sign". It was built almost entirely of Roman stones. The Centurial and sculptured stones (here reproduced from Bruce) which were in a wall of the building are now in the Museum of Antiquities, Newcastle upon Tyne.

**Landowners actually complained that more Roman stones were used than was necessary "whereby several parts of the road are higher than should be, and very few, if any, stones are left for making any fence from the new road".*

*Opposite. General Wade's Army advancing along the old "Heeway" to Hexham in 1745.*

Although difficult to read the first is COH VIII, the second C HOS(TILI) LUPI, and the third is C(ENTURIA) ( ) ISI VERI.

When we reach the Whittledean Reservoirs at the crossroads to the south stands Welton Tower, a fifteenth century pele built almost entirely of Roman stones. The manor house attached to it has the date 1614 and the initials W.W. (Will of Welton) over the door. Nearly opposite Welton Hall, close behind the wall on the Military Way was found a Roman milestone, now destroyed, whose inscription was preserved in a drawing by John Hodgson. The text is restored by Eric Birley (A.A.4.16). It was set up by the Emperor Antoninus, known as Caracalla, in A.D. 213.

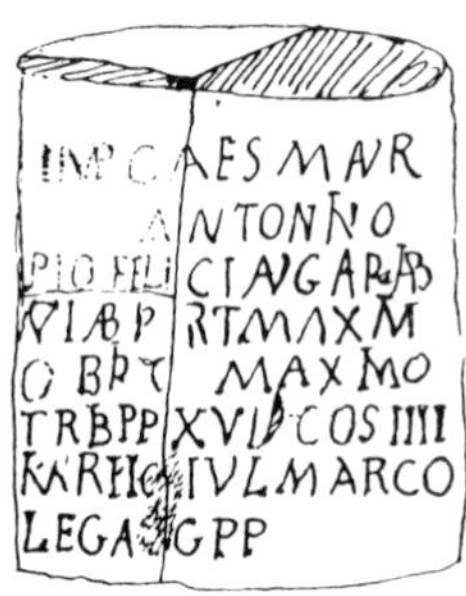

**IMP CAES M AVR**
**[ELIO] ANTONINO**
**PIO FELICI AVG ARAB**
**ADIAB P[A]RT. MAXIM**
**O BRIT MAXIMO**
**TRIB P[OT] XVI COS IIII**
**IMP II C IVL MARCO**
**LEG A[V]G P[R] P[R]**

As we proceed west little can be seen today and the traveller in Roman times would have seen nothing unusual. As he travelled past the spot where the Robin Hood Inn now stands he would have noted Milecastle 18 which now appears as a low platform south of the road, 150 yards west of Rudchester burn.

## RECONSTRUCTION OF A TURRET

Turret 18a (Wallhouses East) was excavated in 1931 and was found to be well preserved with its ladder platform intact. We have attempted a detailed restoration of this turret. There were a number of problems. The first question needing an answer was whether the doors opened inwards or outwards. Roman doors were not hinged like ours, but pivot hung. In the turrets at any rate it seems that doors opened outwards.

How many windows were there in a turret? Since the turret was placed at the back of the wall they didn't need to be strong militarily. They were designed for temporary residence. On the ground floor was a hearth where cooking took place. There was no chimney so windows were necessary to allow the smoke to escape and to provide light. A small water tank was set into the soil on the ground floor. The two ground floor windows were unglazed. The window glass which has been found in turrets undoubtedly came from the windows on the first floor. It has been suggested that the first floor was built of wood, an unlikely assumption since the Romans built their military works to last.

Access to the first floor was by a trap door. Originally there was no stair landing (all the stair landings found were later additions) so access must have been by

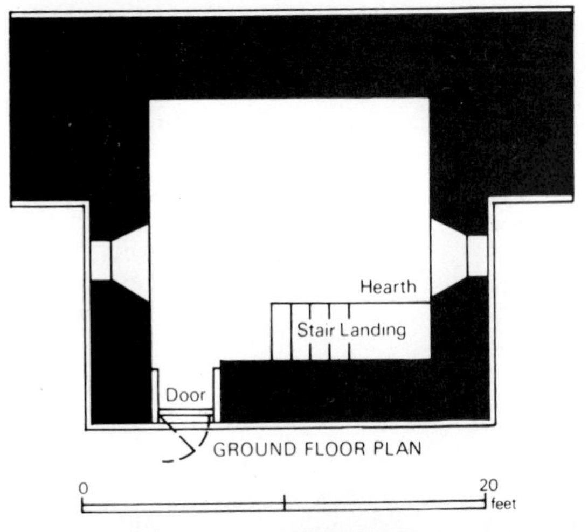


ladder against the Wall. Later (perhaps for military security reasons) the fixed ladder was replaced by a moveable one. Without the stair landing the ladder would have had to be about 15 feet long, difficult to raise and store away on the first floor which was only 15 feet from east to west. With the stair landing a shorter ladder of 11 to 12 feet would have been sufficient and easier to store.

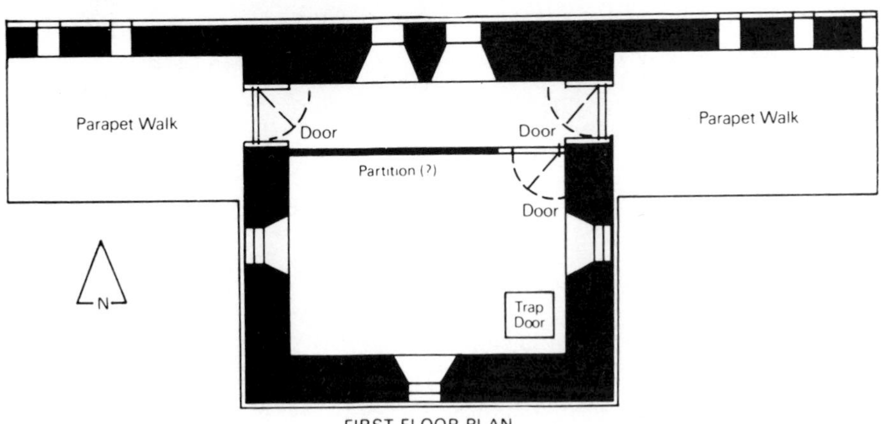


The ground floor was 15 feet high, the same as the parapet walk, but the first floor chamber was probably only 10 feet. Besides windows in the east and west walls there was probably one in the south. Since it had access to the parapet walk on both sides it would have been abnormally draughty. This would probably have been avoided by a wooden partition forming a corridor. On the north side of the corridor unglazed windows would have given a view to the north, a great boon for the guards in inclement weather.

Although the upper structure of the turrets and the Wall is entirely conjectural, we can assume in the weather prevailing in the north that there was a gabled roof. A flat crenellated top would have been unsuitable for a northern climate. It has been suggested that in the gabled roof there would be a small window in the north gable which would provide a high and wide view to the north.

We do not know how many soldiers were stationed at a turret. The ground floor was undoubtedly used for cooking and the first floor probably provided limited sleeping facilities.

(This section is partly based on an article by Parker Brewis in *Archaeologia Aeliana,* 1932).

*William Hutton is "welcomed" at Rudchester Hall*

*Opposite. The interior of Turret 18a at Wallhouses East*

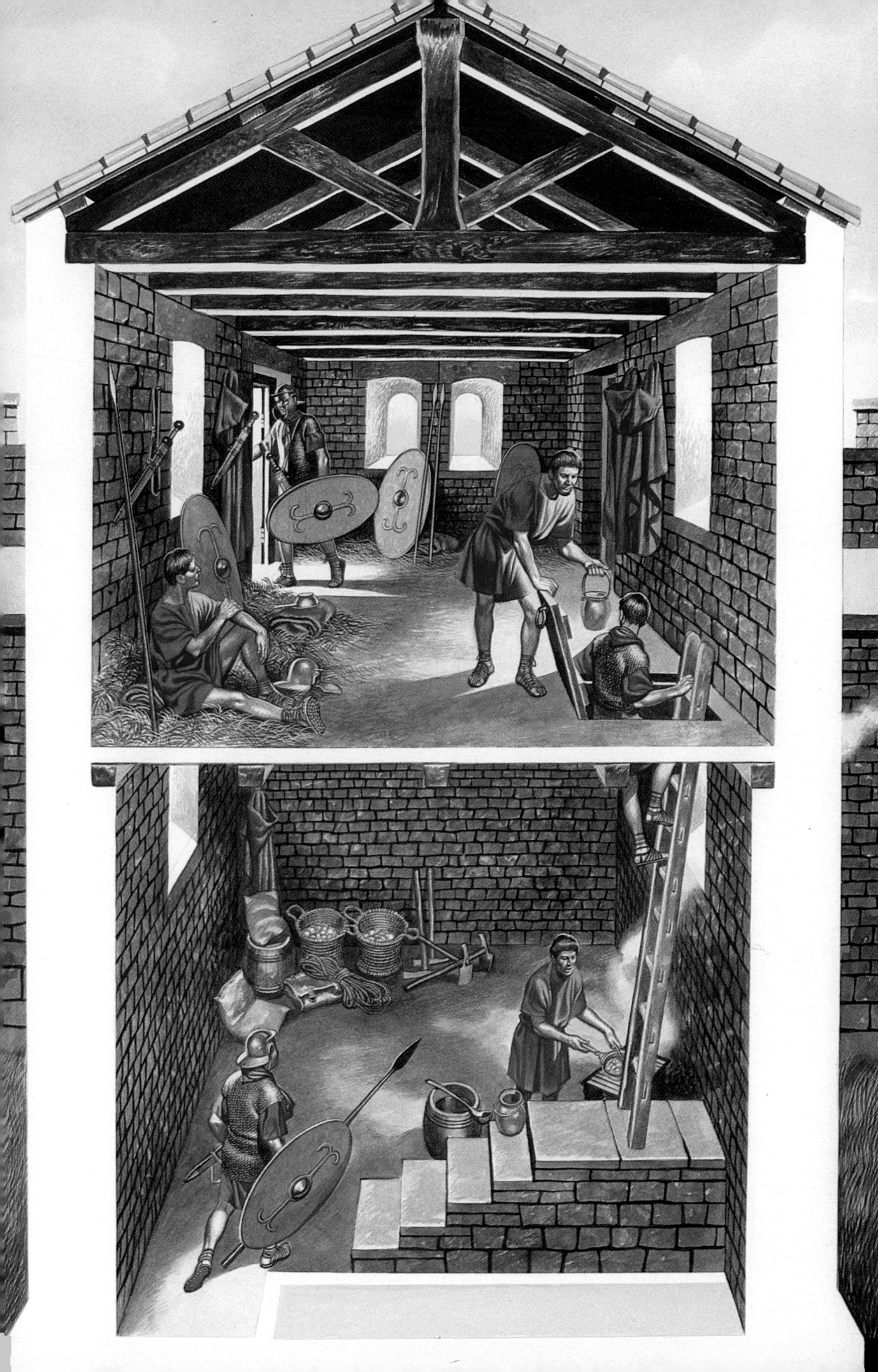

The next Milecastle (19) was also excavated in the same year and an interesting altar discovered (here reproduced). It is 2 feet 6 inches high and one foot square. On the left and right are the customary axe and cleaver. The inscription is as follows (quoted from A.A. 1932 Eric Birley).

*Matrib(us) templ(um) cum ara vex(illatio)coh(ortis) I Vard(ullorum), instante P(ublio) D(omitio) V(...)v(otum)s(olvit)l(ibens)m(erito).*

"To the Mothers, a vexillation of the first cohort of Vardulli, under Publius Domitius V(ictor) (has erected) a temple with an altar in willing payment of a vow.".

The presence of a vexillation from the First Cohort of the Vardulli raises the question of who garrisoned the milecastles and turret since the Vardulli cannot be traced either at Rudchester or Haltonchesters forts. It is usually assumed that the fort garrisons looked after the milecastles. However there are problems in this assumption. Here is one Roman Wall controversy which has not yet been settled.

With a mile to go to Haltonchesters our Roman traveller would have noticed how on Down Hill the Vallum makes a dramatic turn south to avoid the hill which the Wall crosses.

H. Burden Richardson's drawing highlights this change.

**HALTONCHESTERS FORT (Onno)**

The Roman fort near Halton is called Haltonchesters (in Roman times ONNO). It covers five acres and is divided in two by the modern road. It was garrisoned by a cavalry regiment called the Ala Sabiniana. From Corstopitum it is distant about two and a half miles. It guards Watling Street which traverses the valley immediately beneath it. A portion of a monumental slab, now at Trinity College, Cambridge, refers to the fort and its garrison. It is probably a third century inscription. The fort was built between 122 A.D. and 126 A.D.

*The Vallum at Down Hill*

This tombstone was found in the centre of Haltonchesters fort. It is interesting because it depicts a family group, father, mother and child: such groups are uncommon in the north. There are two names on the tombstone, Vitalis and Virilis, which is rather confusing. In the panel above is a large pine-cone, a funerary symbol popular in the region of Hadrian's Wall.

*Tombstone from Haltonchesters Fort*

*Roman soldiers burying money*

*Opposite. Hadrian surveys a site for the Wall*

The original Wall and ditch had already been built before the fort had been decided upon. Turret 21a was built 80 yards to the east and turret 21b a similar distance to the west placing them in the unusual position between Milecastles 21 and 22. As soon as the curtain wall was completed a decision to build the fort was taken. The ditch was filled in and turned into a street connecting the east and west gates whose north portals were built on the ditch. A building inscription discovered at the West Gate records the date of the fort.

Dedication slab from West Gate at Haltonchesters Fort:—
IMP. CAES. Tra Hadriani
AUG. LEG. VI Victrix p.f.
A. PLATORIO Nopate
LEG. AUG. pr. pr.

"To the Emperor Caesar Trajan Hadrian, the Sixth Legion Loyal and Victorious, under Aulus Platorius Nepos, the Emperor's propraetorian Legate". A Platorius Nepos was Imperial Legate in Britain from 122 to C.125.

At a later date (probably in the time of Severus) an extension was built on to the south west side giving the fort an unusual L plan.

When in 1827 the field north of the road (called the "Brunt-ha-penny" field) was first ploughed, a fine bath house was discovered. Large internal bath-houses are rare in the Wall forts. In the south part of Hunnum (called Silverhill, probably from the discovery of Roman silver coins) an elaborate slab in Antonine style was discovered. It is here reproduced. The bath-house belongs to the reconstruction under Constantius Chlorus at the end of the third century, when the Severan bath house in the extension was demolished.

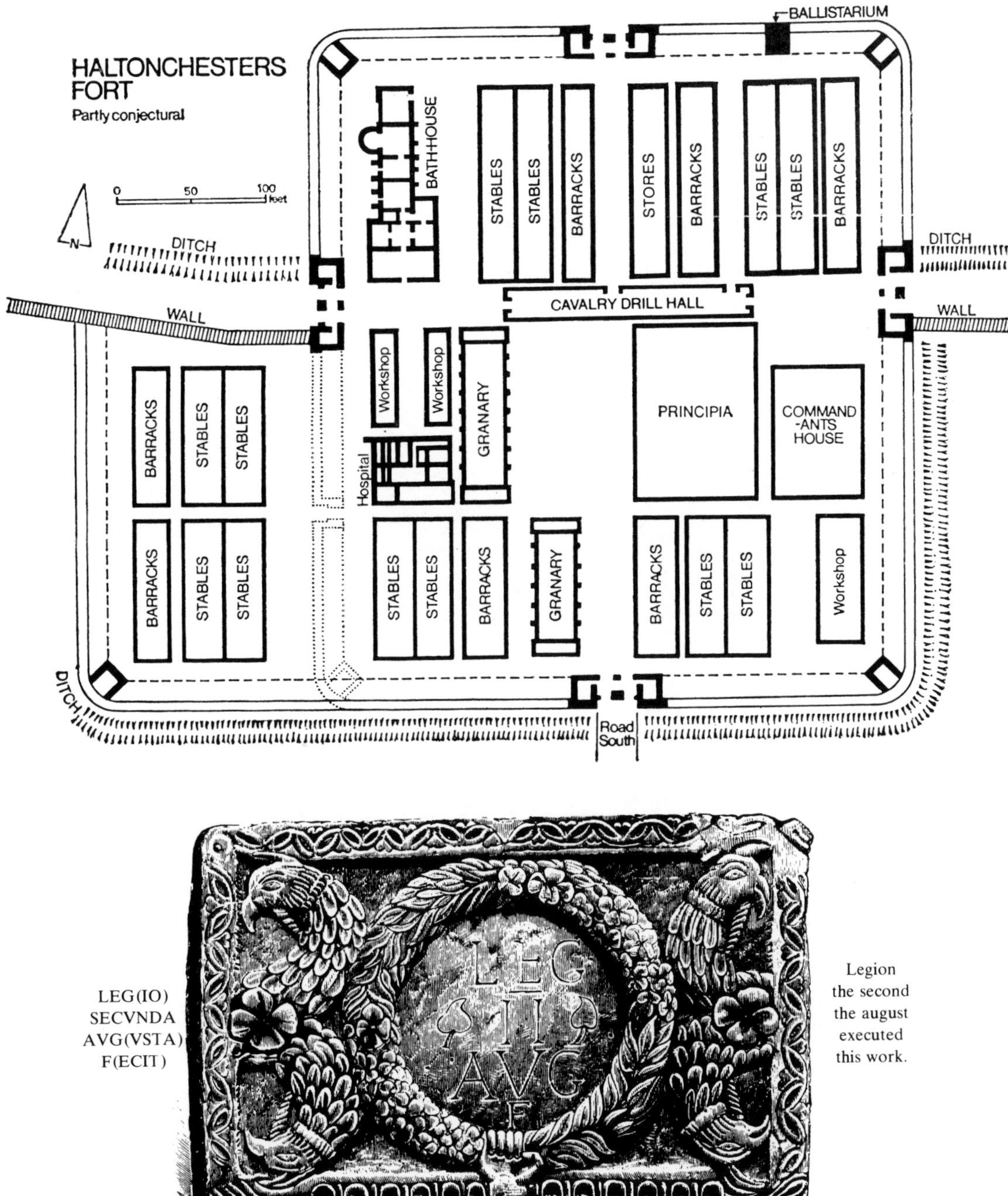


LEG(IO)
SECVNDA
AVG(VSTA)
F(ECIT)

Legion
the second
the august
executed
this work.

The vicus extended for three or five hundred yards south of the fort and it has been suggested that the road from the south gate continued south to join Dere Street to the north of Corbridge.

*Decurion and troopers of a cavalry* ala, *3rd century A.D.*

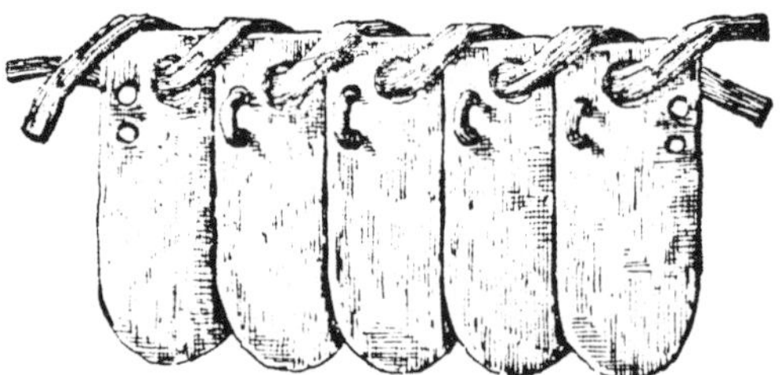

*Armour Scales showing method of lacing*

**PRESENTING MILITARY DIPLOMAS**

In the 1st century A.D., shortly after the invasion of Britain, the system was introduced in auxiliary units of granting citizenship to all men who completed twenty-five years service. In addition they were given the rights of marriage *Ius connubi)* which was made retrospective so that their children became citizens also (in A.D. 140 however, children born during military service lost this privilege).

These rights were recorded on two tablets of bronze which are today called diplomas. The tablets contained not only the recipients name but those of all others who were discharged in that year, either in Britain or the area in which they were serving. These tablets are valuable archaeological sources.

A special review of the trophy in the area was probably held at which these diplomas were presented, since they were considered of great importance to the discharged soldier and were a reward to which all the other soldiers in the unit could look forward. Our painting reconstructs such a presentation.

Ronald Embleton

Many inscriptions, tombstones and sculptures have been found at Haltonchesters. In 1803 a massive gold signet ring was found in the north part of the fort. The woodcut shows its actual size. Its bezel contained a small artificial blue stone on which was engraved a female figure. Probably it belonged to one of the officers who was entitled to wear it. The stone was stolen long ago, and its whereabouts are now unknown.

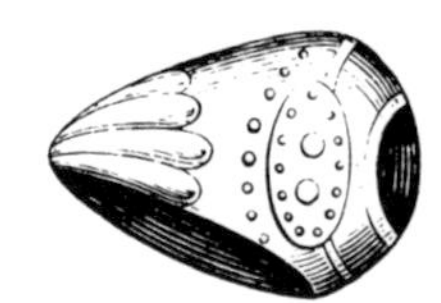

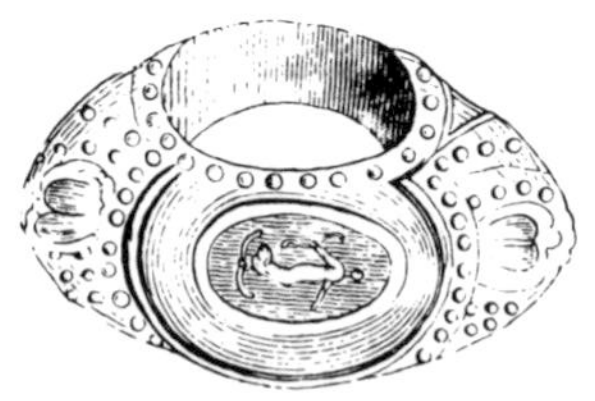

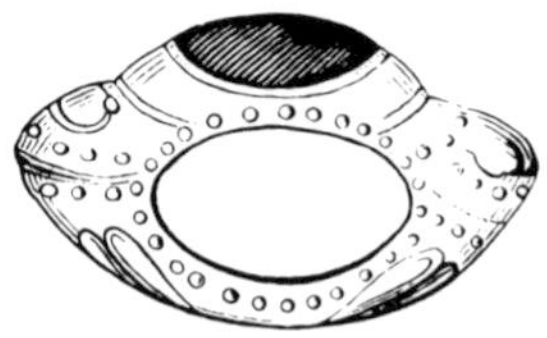

One of the most interesting buildings discovered at Haltonchesters was a cavalry drill hall. It was 160 feet long and 30 feet wide and spanned the street in front of the Principia. This monumental building was probably built early in the 3rd century. A similar building is recorded at Netherby. We haven't the slightest information about its internal arrangement but can assume it was like a large barn with some lighting in the upper part.

Slavery was a normal feature, in fact the basis of Roman society. Epigraphic evidence for their existence is of course rare, since few slaves or their families could afford the expense of a tombstone. This makes the following, found at Haltonchesters, of great interest. It comes from the monument to the slave Hardalio, and was set up by the "guild of his fellow slaves", *collegium conser (vorum).* Hardalio is a typical slave name meaning "busybody", and he probably belonged to one of the soldiers stationed there.

Size, 1 foot 8 inches by 1 foot 6 inches.

(D · M · )
HARDALIO
NIS ·
COLLEGIVM
CONSER
B · M · P

(Diis Manibus)
Hardalio-
nis
Collegium
conservo
bene merenti posuit

How many officers and soldiers had slaves we do not know but probably there were many. We have a number of references to slaves on the Wall. One famous tombstone from South Shields commemorates Regina, the freedwoman and wife of Barates of Palmyre and from the same location we have the fine tombstone to the freedman Victor who was by nationality a Moor but belonged to a cavalryman called Numereanus who came from southern Spain. He was probably bought at one of the slave markets in Britain. The north would be an important source for slaves. In the frequent fighting north of the Wall any prisoners taken would almost certainly be sold into slavery.

*Mourners at a Roman Funeral*

*A Cavalry Drill Hall*

*Opposite. The Roman gate at Portgate*

## HALTONCHESTERS TO CHESTERS

On leaving Haltonchesters we cross the Fence burn and climb the hill which brings us to Milecastle 22. Its north gate was blocked towards the end of the 2nd century because the gate at Portgate served the same purpose. At Portgate, 260 yards farther on, Dere Street crossed the Wall. It was first described by Horsley as a "square structure half within and half without the Wall". It lies south west of the new Errington Arms roundabout just north of the old road before the roundabout was built.

CHO · VIII
CAECILI
CLIME

Cohortis octavae
centuria Caecilii
Clementis

Size, 1 foot 3 inches by 9 inches.

*A centurial stone in the front of the farmhouse at St. Oswald's Hill Head. It reads:– "the century of Caecilius Clemens of the eighth cohort"*

## ROMAN FAIR

At Stagshaw Bank between Corbridge and the Roman Wall on Dere Street was once held a great fair whose origins are shrouded in antiquity. Today it is difficult to visualize the bustle of this great fair with the great multitude which attended. It is very likely this cattle fair had its origins in Roman times. About one mile west of Haltonchesters the Roman road Dere Street crossed the Wall at Portgate. Dere Street was a military road but was also used by traders since it passed through the whole of Northumberland and into Scotland and it would have been ideal for the movement of cattle. The Roman Wall garrison and the thousands of civilians who lived in the vicinity along the Wall would provide a ready market for any surplus cattle reared in the native settlements of which there were many in the relatively peaceful hills and plains of Northumberland.

So a fair would have been an ideal place where the agricultural products of the north could be exchanged for the various products of the more civilised south, such as pottery, metal work, leather goods and clothes.

Two hundred yards beyond Portgate near Turret 22A the slab here illustrated was found.

The inscription FVLGVR. DIVO(RV)M meaning the *lightning of the Gods,* suggests some soldier was here hit by a lightning bolt. When passing the superstitious Roman soldier or traveller would make some religious sign to ward off from himself any such calamity.

Five hundred yards further on we find the Vallum in a remarkable state of preservation.

Hutton's description of these earthworks has often been quoted:

*I now travel over a large common, still upon the Wall, with its trench nearly complete. But what was my surprise when I beheld, thirty yards on my left, the united works of Agricola and Hadrian, almost perfect! I climbed over a stone wall to examine the wonder; measured the whole in every direction; surveyed them with surprise, with delight; was fascinated, and unable to proceed; forgot I was upon a wild common, a stranger, and the evening approaching. I had the grandest works under my eye of the greatest men of the age in which they lived, and of the most eminent nation then existing; all of which had suffered but little during the long course of sixteen hundred years. Even hunger and fatigue were lost in the grandeur before me. If a man writes a book upon a turnpike-road, he cannot be expected to move quick; but, lost in astonishment, I was not able to move at all.*

South of Milecastle 24 is a Roman quarry, one of several found near the Wall. Here on Fallowfield Fell was the famous Written Rock carved on a large ridge of sandstone, carrying in deeply chiselled letters the inscription PETRA FLAVI(I) CARANTINI. It is thought that Flavius Carantinus may have been the foreman of the gang who were quarrying stones for the Wall.

There are other rocks inscribed by soldiers working in the Wall quarries but this one is the most famous and to preserve it from vandals it has been removed to Chesters Museum.

*The Turret at Brunton*

*The Wall at Brunton*

Our Roman traveller approaching Chesters in his day wouldn't have noticed anything special, but today our Wall pilgrim for the first time since Heddon-on-the-Wall would see part of the Wall still standing, a very fine section indeed, which owes its preservation to William Hutton who almost two centuries ago arrived as the farmer was demolishing it. Due to Hutton's remonstrances part was left standing.

Here also today we can visit Brunton Turret, one of the best preserved on the line of the Wall, standing fourteen courses high. Here we can see the change in the width of the Wall.

At Brunton Turret the Wall is 9 feet 3 inches thick but there is no abrupt expansion but a gradual thickening of the Wall as it reaches the turret. About 50 yards west of the turret the Wall is 7 feet 10 inches thick. This increase in the width of the Wall near the turret bears some relation to the passage of the rampart walk over the lower chamber of the turret. It also effects the upper structure of the turret which of course has now gone. The core of the Wall is now mortared for preservation but originally was set in puddled clay which was still resilient when uncovered in 1950. In front of the Wall the ditch is very bold.

From Brunton Turret the Wall ran in a straight line to the North Tyne where the soldiers crossed by the magnificent stone bridge at which our Roman traveller would have been amazed as we are by the Humber and the Forth bridges. For its time the bridge at Chesters was probably a greater feat of engineering.

*Receiving the password*

## WILLIAM HUTTON AT PLANETREES

When we visit the Roman Wall today we find that large sections have been demolished. Most of the demolition was deliberate. The stone was needed for road construction and farm buildings. The greatest destruction took place in the 19th century. When William Hutton visited the Wall in 1801 he saw the process taking place. When he came to Planetrees, a mile east of Chester, he intervened to try and halt the removal of a fine section. Ronald Embleton has tried to recapture this famous incident as described by William Hutton.

"At the twentieth milestone I should have seen a piece of Severus's Wall 7½ feet high and 224 yards long, a sight not to be found in the whole line: but the proprietor, Henry Tulip, esq., is now taking it down to erect a farm house with the materials. Ninety-five yards are already destroyed, and the stones fit for building removed. Then we come to 13 yards, which are standing and overgrown on the top with brambles. The next 40 yards were just demolished, and the stones, of all sizes from 1 pound to 2 cwt., lying in one continued heap, none removed; the next 40 yards are standing 7 feet high.

Then follows the last division, consisting of 36 yards, which is sacrificed by the mattock, the largest stones selected and the small left. The facing stones remain on both sides. This grand exhibition must be seen no more. How little we value what is daily under the eye.

Here was a fine opportunity for measuring. The foundation was, in fact, below the surface of the ground and consisted of two courses of stones, each 6 inches thick, extending to the width of 6½ feet. The second course set off 3 inches on each side, which reduced the foundation to 6 feet, and the third 3 inches of a side more, reducing the wall to 5½ feet, its real thickness here.

The foundation is laid in the native earth, the bed is cemented with mortar. The soil being afterwards thrown up on each side of the Wall 2 feet high caused the foundation to be 3 feet deep.

I desired the servant, with whom I conversed, to give my compliments to Mr. Tulip and request him to desist, or he would wound the whole body of antiquaries. As he was putting an end to the most noble monument of antiquity in the whole island, they would feel every stroke. If the wall was of *no* estimation he must have a mean opinion of me, who would travel 600 miles to see it; and if it *was* he could never merit my thanks for destroying it. Should he reply 'The property is mine and I have a right to direct it as I please', it is an argument I can regret but not refute."

## CHESTERS FORT — CILURNUM

The name Chesters is found frequently in Northumberland applying to fortified sites especially those of Roman origin. Symeon in 1104-8 calls the place *Scytlescester juxta murum.* If we have the correct place Allen Mawer says the modern name should be Shittleschester and the original owner would be one *Scytel.* The Roman site here is of great interest. Beside the fort itself we have the finest military bath-house in Britain, remarkable remains of a Roman bridge and a museum with an outstanding collection of Roman antiquities discovered at various places on the Wall. With a few exceptions the museum is the work of John Clayton (1792-1890), a wealthy man who was deeply interested in the Roman remains to be seen in the neighbourhood of his home. The Reverend Thomas Machell in 1691 was the first writer to record the fort. Hutchinson (1778) says this was the first station in his tour "where the direct appearance of regular streets was observed", the place being "crowded with the ruins of stone buildings". He also recorded many ruins to the south of the fort and some to the north. The *Notitia Dignitatum* gives us the Roman name of Cilurnum.

Cilurnum was garrisoned by a cavalry regiment *ala II asturum,* the Second Asturian Horse — 500 strong. Benwell, a similar fort, was occupied by the First *ala,* The fort measures north to south 582 feet and east to west 434 feet, covering 5¾ acres. It is the customary rectangle with rounded corners and six gates. The wall is 5 feet thick backed by an earthern mound and fronted by a ditch.

At Chesters the northern rampart does not coincide with the Wall as at Housesteads. It lies across it just as at Benwell (Condercum) and Rudchester (Vindobala). This was normal in cavalry forts.

### The Gateways

The gateways at Chesters were all of the same type. Our reconstructions of the main gateway, the *porta decumana* (page 103), shows what they were like. The double gate has towers on either side with guard chambers. The *spina* separating the two portals is built of massive masonry. The rest is in stone similar to the wall itself. The doors would be of oak reinforced with iron. The doorways of the guard rooms opened into the gate-passage.

### North Gate (Porta Praetoria)

The visitor enters the fort by this gateway. It is a double portal gateway but its west portal was blocked very early since its threshold is almost unworn. Its east portal however is of great interest since the stone channel of an aqueduct enters here, fed by one of the springs to the north of the fort.

### Main West Gate (Porta Principilas Sinistra)

This also has twin portals and guard chambers. However, both sills are unworn suggesting the gate was walled up at an early date. The northern guard chamber has a large stone storage tank fed by an aqueduct to the west. Whether there were one or two aqueducts we don't know, but the bringing of water (aqua adducta) is recorded in an inscription (to be seen in the Museum), probably of the early third century when the governor was Ulpius Marcellus. The Narrow Wall on a broad base comes up to the south tower. Originally the wall crossed the fort and in 1945 Turret 27a was found near the north east corner of the headquarters building.

### Smaller West Gate (Porta Quintana Sinistra)

About 50 yards to the south is a single portal gateway with little to be seen. Travelling round the fort we meet traces of the angle tower and half-way between the angle and the south gate is a fine interval tower. The doorway at the back led onto the street called the *Intervallum.* The gutter can still be seen. There were eight interval and four angle towers at Chesters. They were all probably raised 10 feet above the rampart walk like the gate towers.

### South Gate (Porta Decumana)

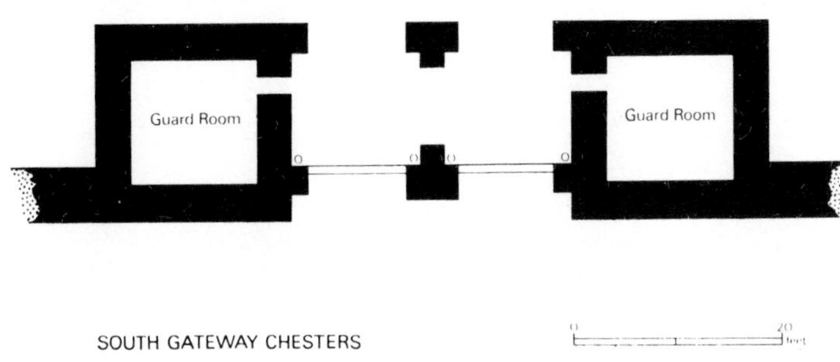


Has the usual twin portals and towers. The western portal was blocked when still new. The eastern portal was restored on more than one occasion, after the fort had been overrun, so the level of the portal is much higher.

In the east guard chamber of this gate a remarkable bronze tablet of 146 A.D. was found. It is a *diploma* or *tabula honestae missionis.* (see page 23).

This was given to an auxiliary soldier when he had served for twenty-five years and received an honourable discharge. It legalised his marriage past or future. The original is in the British Museum but a copy can be seen in the Chesters Museum.

*The strongroom (aerarium). Woodcut showing its aspect when discovered*

*Chesters Roman Camp Reconstruction*

*Opposite. Soldiers inside their sleeping quarters*

**Smaller West Gate (Porta Quintana Dextra)**

Of the eastern wall only the gateways can be seen. This gate is a single portal and the Military Way, leading from the bridge across the Tyne, enters the fort here.

**Main East Gate (Porta Principalis Dextra)**

In a fine state of preservation with walls standing twelve courses high. It was never used by wheeled traffic and was walled up about 300 A.D. Each portal had an arch at back and front and the south near pier still has the slots on top of the upper course which held the shuttering for the arch.

**Headquarters (Principia)**

This is the most important building in the fort, almost twice the size of that at Housesteads, and the finest on the line of the Wall. It was the nerve centre of the fort. Here in the various rooms all the business of the regiment was transacted. The entrance was on the north through a monumental gateway (although there are two side entrances as well) into an open courtyard. From here the visitor could look straight ahead through the Cross Hall to the chapel. The courtyard was paved with a veranda on three sides whose supporting columns can still be seen. In the north-west corner is a well and nearby on one of the paving stones is a large phallus. From the courtyard the spacious Cross Hall is entered. The south side is occupied by five rooms. The central one is the *sacellum* which housed the regimental colours and a statue of the emperor. The chapel gave access to the strongroom which was under one of the rooms of the standard bearers. It was used for the money and valuables of the regiment. The two rooms to the west of the chapel were the offices of the adjutant who controlled the regimental records. The two rooms to the east were used by the standard bearers who looked after the company records and the individual savings of the soldiers. The strongroom *(aerarium)* is illustrated here from an old woodcut. It was found by accident in 1803 but only excavated in 1840. We are told that "a tradition existed in the country that the station had been occupied by a cavalry regiment and that the stables, which were capable of accommodating 500 horses, were underground. The rustics when they came upon this vault naturally enough thought that the latter part of the legend was about to be verified and that they would soon enter the stables; it was not to be so, however. An oaken door, bound and studded with iron, closed the entrance into the chamber, but it fell to pieces shortly after being exposed. On the floor were found a number of base denarii, chiefly of the reign of Severus. The roof of the apartment is peculiar. It consists of three separate arches, the intervals between them being filled up by the process called 'stepping over'.".

**Commandant's House**

This building is very confusing but was obviously an elaborate and luxurious house with the normal Roman central heating and a private bath-house attached. The commander of the cavalry unit *(praefectus equitum)* was a man of importance in the Roman army.

There were probably two granaries to the west of the headquarters but the area has not been excavated. The fragments of a large building to the south of the Commandant's house probably contained the regimental hospital.

The civil settlement was to the south and east of the fort. Excavations have not been carried out but aerial photography suggests there was a large population here with several important houses. Excavations at some future date will probably provide valuable information about civilian life on the frontier. The *vicus* here was almost a military town.

*Reconstruction of the main gateway . . . Porta Decumana*

*The east gateway at Chesters in the 19th century*

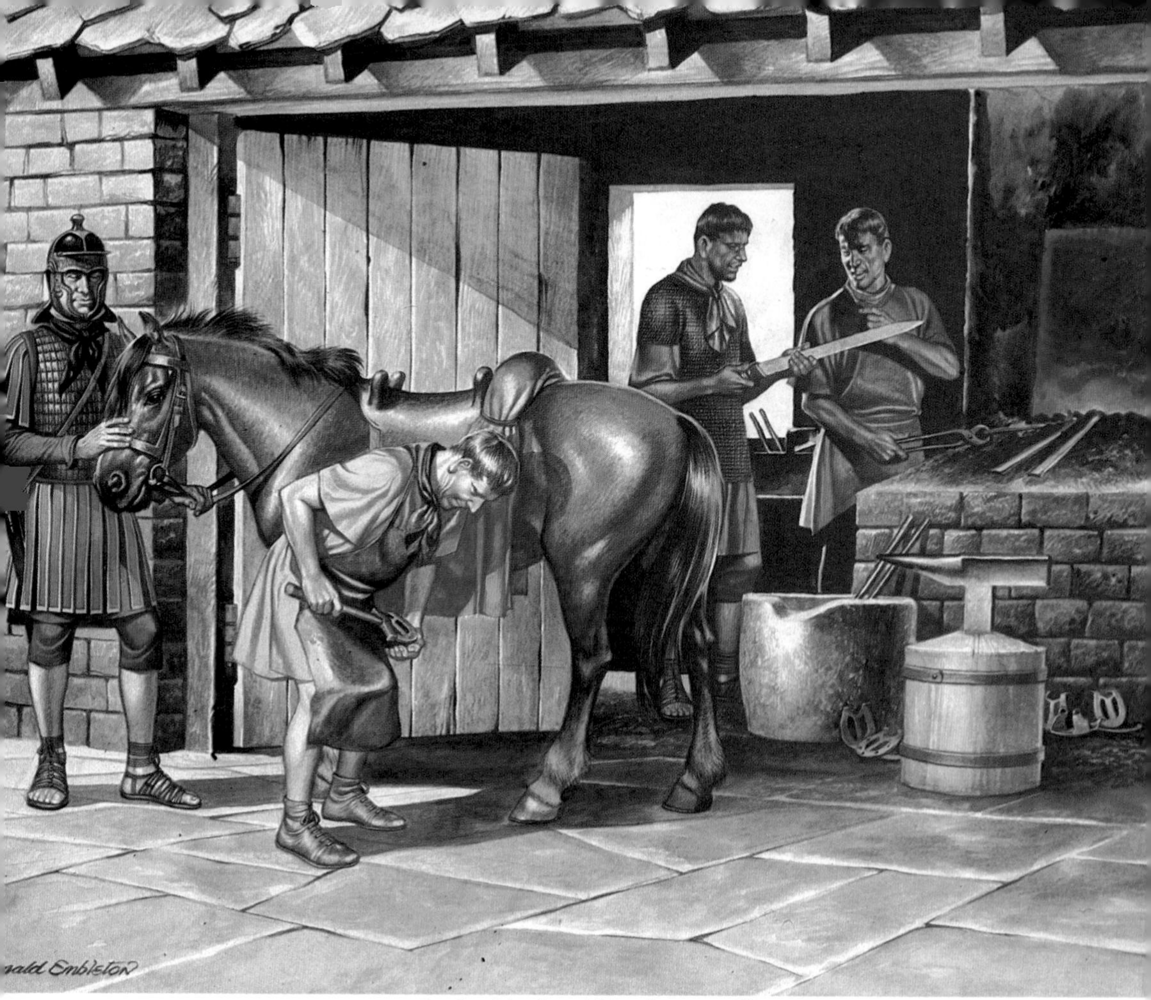

*At the blacksmith's shop at Chesters*

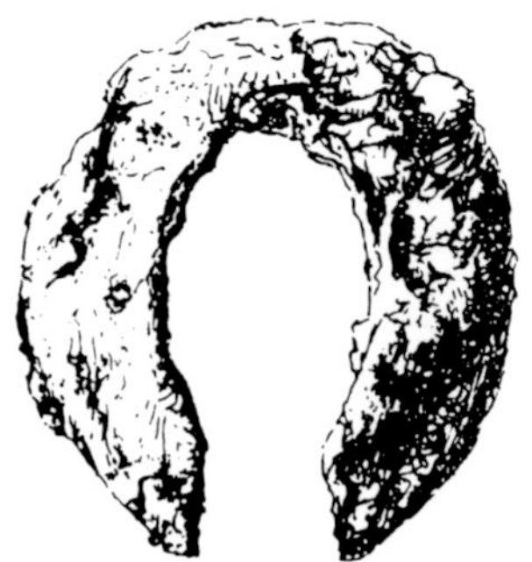

*Roman horseshoe.*
*This rare specimen was found at Condercum. There are also examples in the Museum at Chesters*

*Wooden bucket from Newstead*

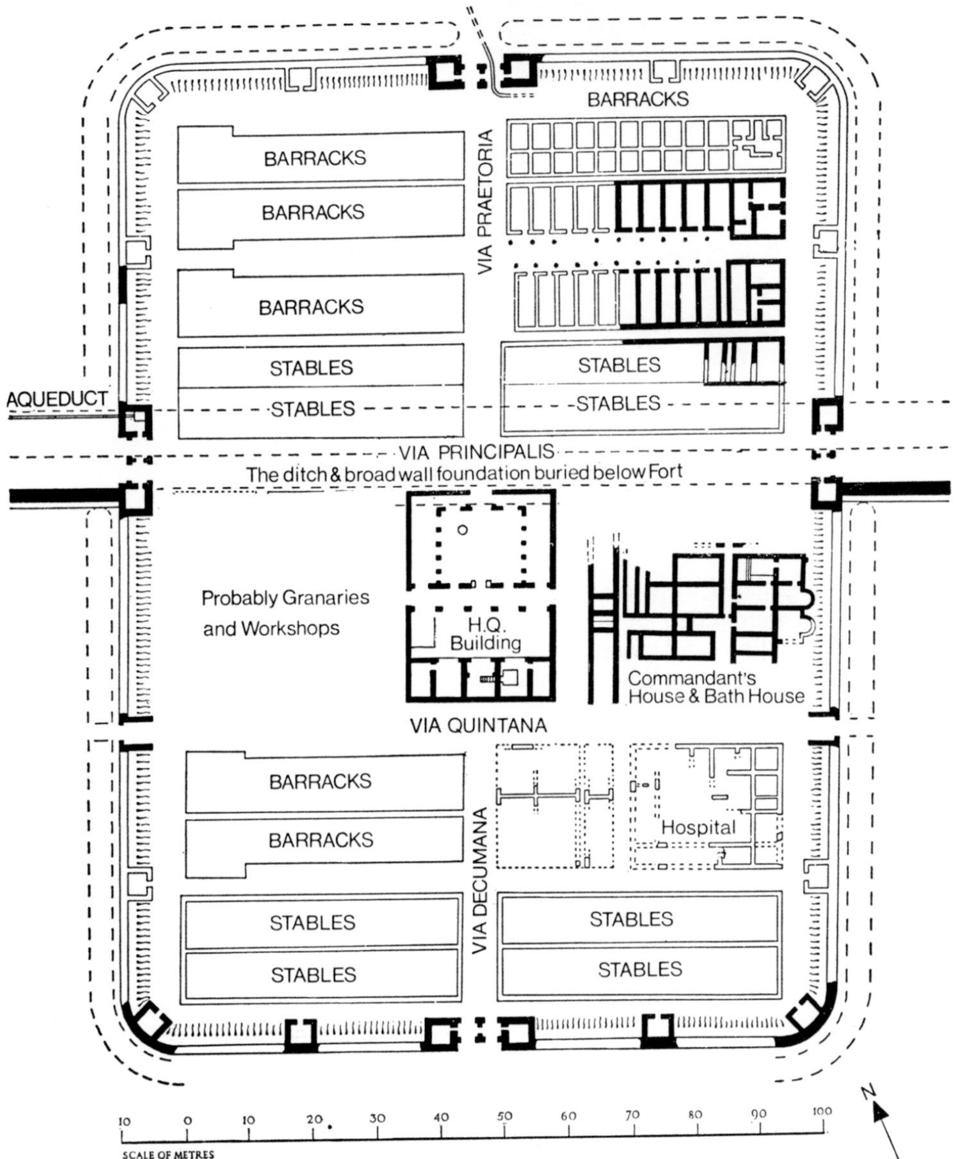


## The Blacksmith's Shop

A blacksmith's shop would be essential in any Roman fort, especially one used for cavalry. There would be the day to day repair of armour and weapons and the shoeing of the horses. Horse shoes were used by Roman cavalry but samples are not often found. We have therefore had to use a sample from the cavalry fort at Benwell.

**The Stables and Barracks**

Cavalry regiments were divided into 16 units called *turmae* and each consisted of 30 men commanded by a decurion, and two N.C.O.'s. Ronald Embleton's reconstruction (page 84) shows a decurion with two troopers of an *Ala* in the third century. Almost nothing is known of the stables at Chesters apart from their sites which are partially conjectural. Since there were at least 500 horses in the fort and since in the winter they would consume large quantities of hay and straw, it is difficult to visualize how they could have been accommodated in the eight blocks suggested for stabling. (It is noteworthy that the cavalry fort of Hunnum had to be increased in size).

Some of the barracks can, however, be seen. Cavalry were given more ample accommodation than infantrymen, probably because they kept their harness and equipment where they slept. There were eight barrack blocks. Each housed two *turmae* and at the ends near the fort walls were the rooms of the unit commanders. The 60 men were probably equally divided among the remaining ten rooms. The barracks had a veranda on which the cooking was done. Some of the pillars which supported this veranda can be seen.

When Ronald Embleton painted the interior of one of the barrack rooms he was faced with many questions — Were there racks for weapons? Did the Roman cavalryman store his saddle and bridle in the stables or did he keep them with his belongings in the barrack room? Cloak, mail shirt, tunic, breeches, eating utensils, helmet — there had to be a place for all these articles. How did the Roman soldier sleep? Wrapped in his cloak? Did he have a mattress, blankets? Did he have single beds or two-tiered bunks? Was the barrack room cluttered and squalid or was it rigidly organised?

Archaeological discoveries have provided NO answers to any of these questions. There was no hard evidence, only conjecture. The drawing of the barrack interior is the most important in the book. Imagination based on common sense has furnished us with an intelligent answer to the questions that were posed.

**Bath-house**

The large military bath-house outside the fort is one of the sights of Chesters. Due to the damp air and changes of heat bath-houses needed constant attention to prevent deterioration. The bath-house at Chesters has undergone several alterations. So today it is difficult to follow exactly the route the bathers would take through the various rooms.

They entered by a flight of steps from the military way leading to a porch which gave access to the Dressing Room. This was the largest room in the baths as was customary. Going to the baths was a social function where you met friends and had a chat, almost like a club, so this main room needed to be substantial. In the west wall are seven niches. Their use is a matter for argument. Alcoves for statues, for clothes, for ointments, etc., have all been suggested. To the east of the changing room was a latrine. Leaving the main room the bather entered the vestibule. From here three rooms opened. On the left was the cold room with a washing basin in the centre. To the right were two rooms for dry heat, the inner one being the hottest. Straight ahead were the warm and hot rooms with moist heat. Off the hot room was a room containing a hot bath. This room was lighted by a window, the broken glass of which was discovered when excavating. Parallel with the *tepidarium* and *caldarium* are two extra warm rooms entered from the cold room to the north.

The rooms were heated by a complicated system of hot air channels, which ran under the floors and through the walls, the heat being provided by three stoke holes.

To keep in the heat the various warm rooms had barrel vaulted ceilings composed of blocks of tufa, which were light and so avoided the necessity of heavy buttresses on the walls. The rest of the baths had the conventional roof of red tiles.

*In the baths at Chesters*

*Milking a goat*

We do not know to what extent the Roman soldiers on the Wall grew some of their own food. Land near the fort had to be used for the horses and pack animals of even infantry units. We can be certain that the soldiers responsible for feeding them would also keep other animals. Roman soldiers were never allowed to waste their time so a certain amount of farming would be a useful way of keeping them busy. It would also be an economic advantage.

*Making Charcoal*

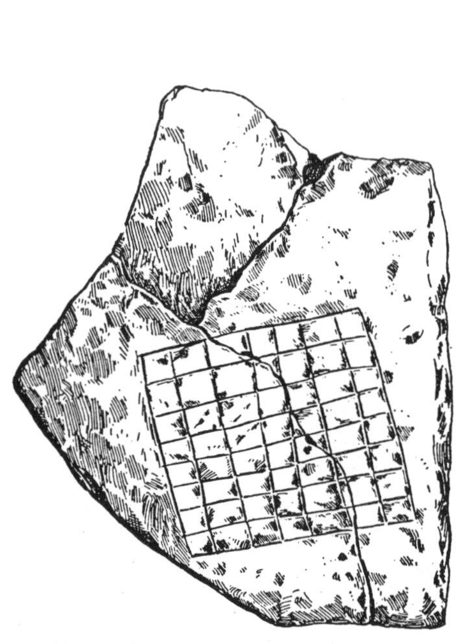

*'Draught Board' from Corbridge*

*Roman cart wheel from Newstead*

**Roman Bridge**

The remains of the Roman bridge at Chesters are an outstanding example of Roman civil engineering. The bridge had stone piers with a wooden superstructure. There have been two bridges on the site. The first was a narrow bridge arched in stone carrying only the Wall across the river. The second was wider and carried the Military Way. On the next page we show an early reconstruction by Paul Brown. Today his drawing would be changed in many ways (for example the drawbridge at the two ends would not be included), but Paul Brown was a pioneer in showing the Wall as it once was when the Romans were still here.

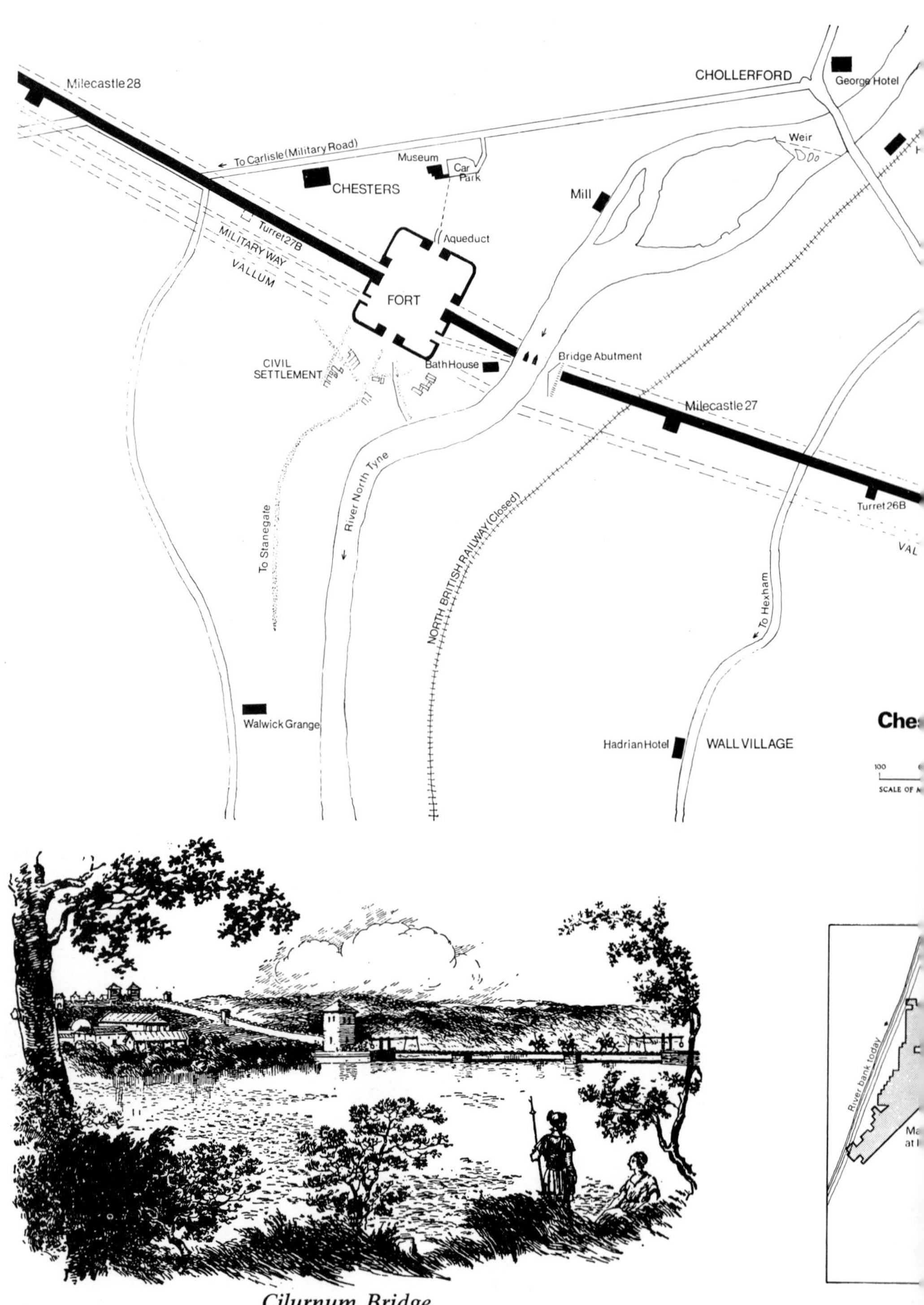

Milecastle 28
CHOLLERFORD
George Hotel
To Carlisle (Military Road)
Museum
Car Park
CHESTERS
Weir
Mill
Turret 27B
MILITARY WAY
VALLUM
Aqueduct
FORT
CIVIL SETTLEMENT
Bath House
Bridge Abutment
Milecastle 27
River North Tyne
NORTH BRITISH RAILWAY (Closed)
To Stanegate
Turret 26B
To Hexham
Walwick Grange
Hadrian Hotel
WALL VILLAGE
River bank today

*Cilurnum Bridge*

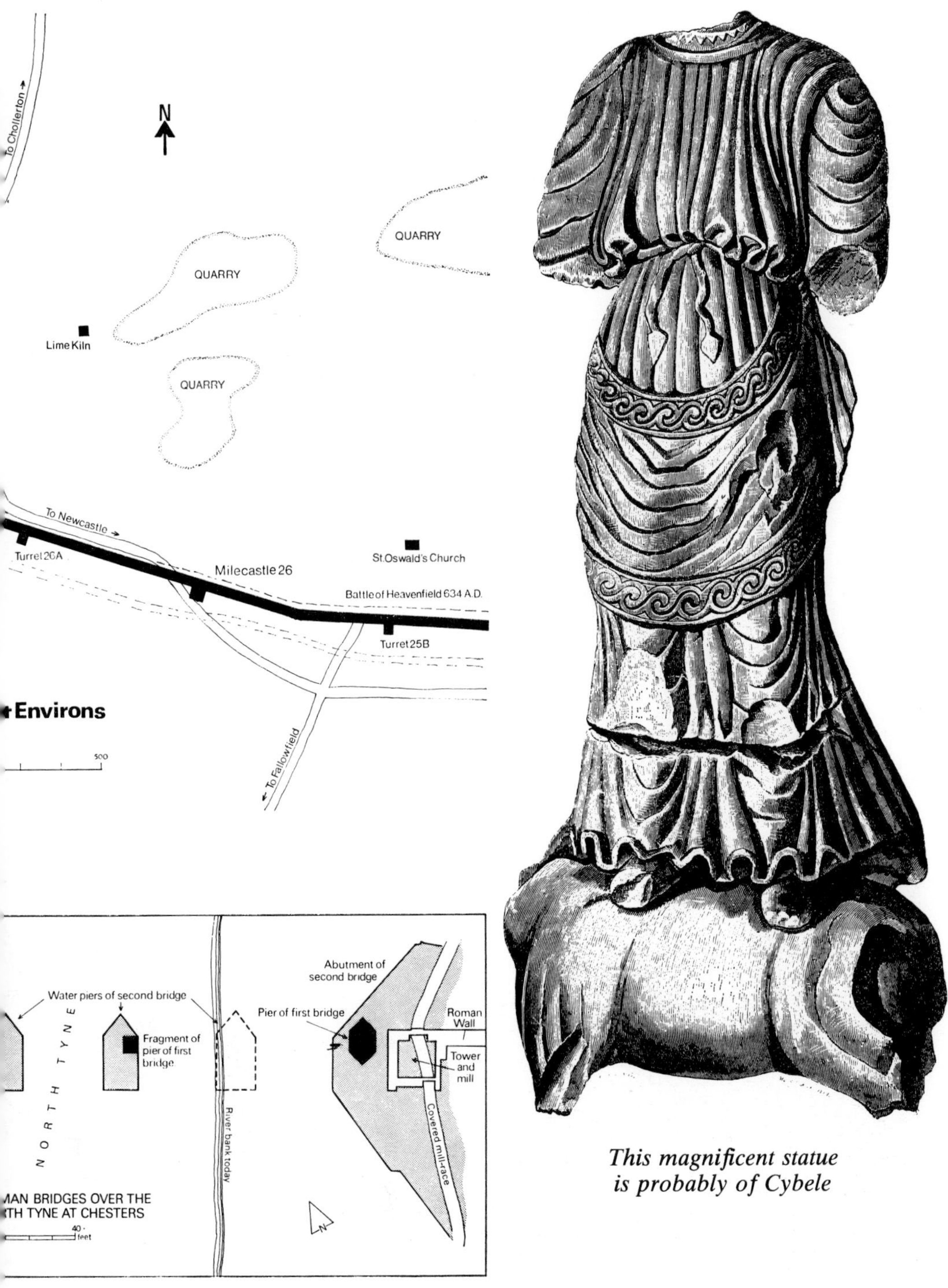


*This magnificent statue is probably of Cybele*

## FROM CHESTERS TO CARRAWBURGH

From Chesters fort the Wall passes through the private grounds of Chesters then up the hill to Walwick Hall. Six hundred yards further on brings us in sight of Limestone Bank.

As we climb the hill at Limestone Bank three fine stretches of the Wall can be seen on the right at Blackcarts Farm. It has recently been restored by the Ministry of the Environment. Included in this stretch is turret 29a of which we here reproduce a woodcut from Bruce (1884).

*Mural turret on Blackcarts Farm*

Internally it measures eleven feet ten inches by eleven feet four inches. The wing walls to fit the Broad Wall can be clearly seen on the engraving. The stretch of Wall is broken by the Hen Gap through which the Simonburn branch road passes. The next stretch of the Wall is shown in our etching of 1884. The facing stones here are larger than usual.

As we ascend the hill the Vallum is cut out of the rock all the way up. Most of the rock excavated was broken and packed into the mounds but four huge rocks can be seen on the south berm as they were taken out of the ditch. One of these blocks has holes for the chain-grips that were used to lift it.

Near the summit of Limestone Bank (where there is a small lay-by) fifty yards downhill on the right several things need to be noted. Milecastle 30 lies where the field walls on the summit join. Here the military way can be seen (with difficulty) for the first time leading to and from the milecastle. It passes under the modern road and occupies the north mound of the Vallum almost as far as Procolitia. One hundred yards south of the milecastle is a temporary camp probably used by the builders who struggled here on the rock. Except for a crossing leading to the milecastle the Vallum on top of the hill was completed, because for the Romans the Vallum was more important that the Wall ditch.

Our lithograph shows the striking works here to be seen. The wall ditch however was never completed. Finding the work so difficult the officers probably decided it was not vital. Perhaps the soldiers went on strike. The drawing by R. Embleton (page 128) suggests they got fed up with their almost impossible task.

The gigantic works here have always attracted attention. In his *Handbook to the Roman Wall* (1884) Bruce writes:

*The fosse both of Wall and Vallum may next be examined; a grander sight Britain can hardly afford us. In each case it has been cut through the basalt which forms the summit of the hill, and the excavated masses lie upon the brink. How the Romans managed to dislodge such large blocks of this tough material without the*

*The Fosse of the Vallum, Limestone Bank*

*aid of gunpowder is a marvel. Dr. Lingard, in his MS "Tourification of the Wall", says:– "It is a most astonishing sight". The fosse of the Wall is specially curious. On its northern margin lies a stone, now split into three pieces by the frosts of winter, which when laid upon its present bed must have been one block, weighing not less than thirteen tons. In the fosse itself will be seen a mass of stone which has not been dislodged from its bed; on its upper surface may be noticed a number of holes intended for the insertion of wedges. For some reason the wedges were not inserted or not driven home and the mass of rock remains unmoved to this day. It will be observed that the wedge holes are all inserted in the thin veins of quartz which intersect the basalt and which when the wedges were driven in would aid the cleavage. Perhaps wooden wedges were used, in which case they would be expanded by having water poured upon them.*

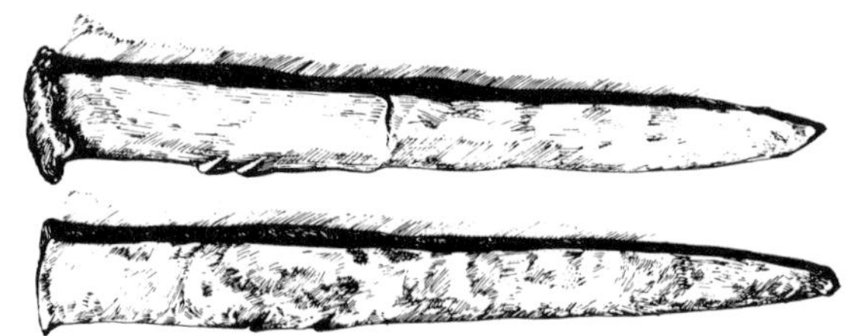

*Steel wedges found near Planetrees Farm, Brunton Bank. Length 10½ inches*

A mile along the road brings us to the fort of Carrawburgh (Brocolitia).

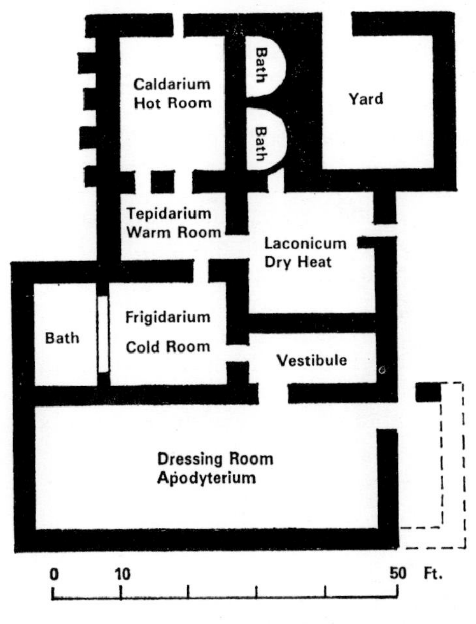


**BATH-HOUSE AT CARRAWBURGH**

Excavated by Clayton in 1873

## CARRAWBURGH (Brocolitia)

Little can be seen of the fort here which stands on a bare flat moor. The north rampart and the wall are covered by the road while the east, west and south ramparts are only mounds in the fields. It covers about three and a half acres. In the second century the garrison was the first cohort of Aquitanians, later the first cohort of the Cugernians and in the third and fourth centuries the first cohort of Batavians. Little excavation has taken place here although the walls would be impressive if cleared of debris. The position of the Vallum is of great interest. It can be seen as though passing through the fort.

Clearly the fort was built later than the Vallum and was built over it. This makes Brocolitia either contemporary with or later than the Narrow Wall which formed the north rampart.

The western and southern slopes outside the fort were occupied by the *vicus* in which was a bath-house excavated by Clayton in 1873. In plan it was similar to the one at Chesters. Nothing can be seen of it today.

Outside the south west corner of the fort in boggy ground are the remains of the most important Mithraic temple to be found in Britain. It was discovered in 1949 during a very dry summer. Three altars to Mithras, still standing in position, were seen protruding through the grass. The following year it was completely excavated. Building was early in the third century and alterations were carried out several times before its destruction in 297 A.D. It was rebuilt shortly afterwards but before many years had passed it was demolished early in the fourth century, probably by Christians.

The pilgrim entered the ante chapel (Nathex) by a door in the south wall. On his left was the hearth where food was prepared and nearby was the ordeal pit. To the right, in front of the wickerwork screen, is the statuette of a mother goddess. On entering the nave raised benches could be seen on either side. Here were four small altars, especially the twin statues representing on the east CAUTES (torch upright to represent the rising sun), and on the west CAUTOPATES (torch downwards to represent the setting sun). At the far end was the sanctuary with its three main altars dedicated by officers from the fort. The western one depicts Mithras as charioteer of the sun (dedicated to Marcus Simplicius Simplex), the central altar is dedicated by Lucius·Antonius Proculus, and the eastern altar is dedicated by Aulus Cluentius Habitus. Behind the altars in a recess would have been a relief showing Mithras slaying the bull, but it was probably destroyed by Christians. (The altars to be seen in the Temple are replicas. The originals are in the Museum of Antiquities at Newcastle University). North west of the Mithraeum on the edge of the Vallum is Coventina's Well. It was discovered in 1876 but had been recorded by Horsley in 1726.

"They discovered a well. It is a good spring, and the receptacle for the water is about seven foot square within, and built on all sides, with hewn stone; the depth could not be known when I saw it, because it was almost filled up with rubbish. There had also been a wall about it, or an house built over it, and some of the great stones belonging to it were yet lying there. The people called it a cold bath, and rightly judged it to be *Roman*".

Here was found the richest collection of Roman coins and altars ever discovered on the frontier. There were 13,487 coins (apart from many carried away in a raid upon the site) and numerous altars and native objects now to be seen in the Chesters Museum. The water goddess worshipped here was the Celtic *Coventina.* The whole shrine measured forty feet square internally with the sacred spring in the centre. Among the coins found were over three hundred brass *"as"* of Antoninus Pius. They commemorated the pacification of northern Britain after the revolt of 155. They show Britannia sad and disconsolate with her head bowed unlike her usual portraiture.

**Shrine of the Nymphs and the Genius Loci**

The shrine was discovered in 1957 and excavated by Dr. D. J. Smith in 1960. The remains consist of a sandstone altar standing on a pedestal, a well and an apsidal stone structure. The altar is inscribed on back and front with the same

words suggesting it stood in the centre of an open shrine to be read on both sides. The text is as follows:—

nymphis )e)T G(E)N(IO)
LOCI · M · HISP(A)N(IV)S
MODESTINVS · P(R)AE(F)
COH · T · BAT · P(R)O SE
ET SVIS · L · M

The translation could be "To the Nymphs and the Genius Loci, Marcus Hispanius Modestinus, Prefect of the First Cohort of Batavians, willingly (dedicated this altar) on behalf of himself and family".

The side of the altar has a ladle and pole-axe carved on it. The apse is a problem since it is unlikely that it supported a roof. The *nymphaeum* was probably open to the air. The well itself, unlike that of Coventina, unfortunately contained no treasures.

The nymphaeum abuts on the mithraeum. The date of its construction is uncertain but it fell into disuse early in the 4th century.

(Article and reconstruction based on report by D. J. Smith in *Archaeologia Aeliana* 4.XL. 1962).

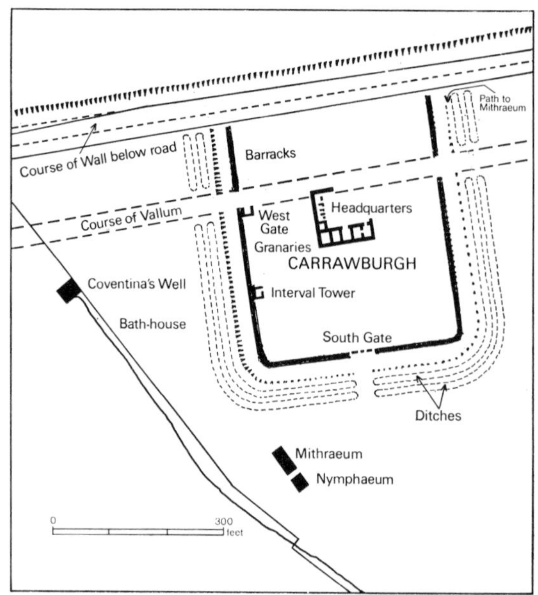


*JEWELLERY WORN AT CILURNUM*

*Gem engraved with a scene representing a chariot race*

*Engraved carnelian bezel of a ring. The seated figure is thought to be Jupiter*

*Soldier stops to ask the way to Chesters*

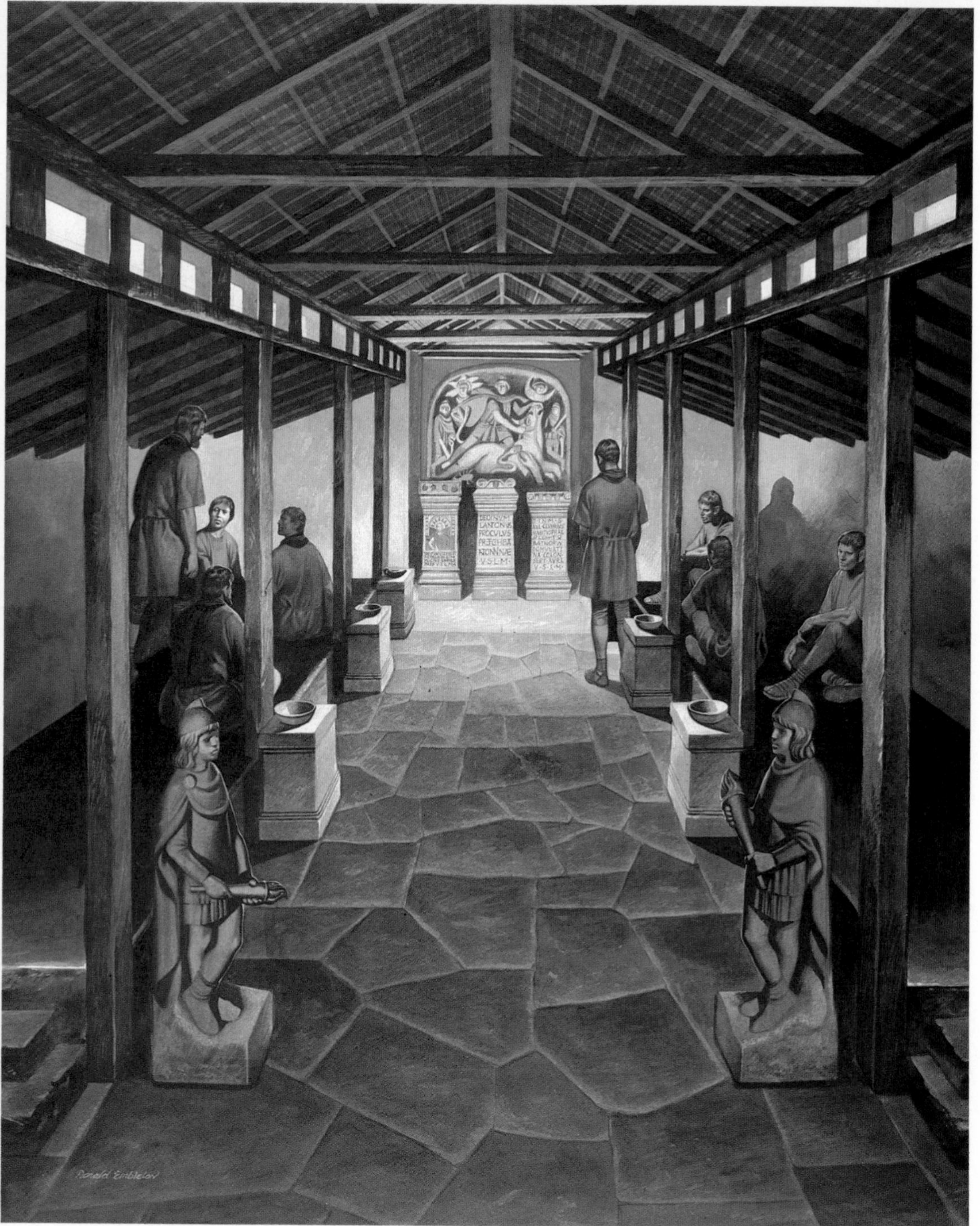


## THE TEMPLE OF MITHRAS AT CARRAWBURGH

Little can be seen of the Roman fort of Brocolitia but the religious remains are of great importance. So much has been found that it could almost be described as a religious centre although most Roman forts probably had as many temples but they have either not survived or have not yet been found. The most important temple found is the one to Mithras.

The climate on Hadrian's Wall is probably the same today as during Roman times. During winter therefore the troops would have had a problem in keeping warm. The barracks seem to have been unheated. Extra warm clothing would have been a necessity. A cloak, resembling a large blanket, was worn over the regular uniform and a warm hat was used as head gear. The "Pannonian" hat is the best known.

*Head showing the Pannonian cap*

**CARRAWBURGH TO HOUSESTEADS**

Leaving Carrawburgh we reach the farmhouse of Carraw in about half a mile. This was once the grange or rural retreat of the Priors of Hexham. Shortly after passing Carraw the site of Milecastle 32 is visible south of the road. Half a mile to the south west are two temporary Roman camps. One is hardly visible, but the other, called Brown Dikes, crowns a small hill with a wide prospect. It is furnished with traverses. Three hundred yards beyond Milecastle 32 is the site of turret 32a. From here the Vallum and Wall ditch are well developed and very close to each other. The Vallum continues in a straight line but the Wall turns slightly northwards to maintain possession of the crown of the hill. The modern road keeps to the south parallel with the Vallum. Shortly after the diversion Milecastle 33 (Shield-on-the-Wall) appears. Its north wall and gate and southern entrance can be seen. We soon reach on the left of the road the deserted cottage of Shield-on-the-Wall with the reservoir beyond it which once supplied water to the Settlingstones lead mine.

The great basaltic ridge of the Whin Sill now comes into view. "We quit", as Hutton remarked, "the beautiful scenes of cultivation, and enter upon the rude of nature, and the wreck of antiquity". Four successive mountain crests are before us which seem to chase each other to the north. Passing turret 33a the road and the Wall part company at a rivulet called the Coesike. The Vallum and Wall also separate. The Wall naturally follows the precipitous edge of the hill and the Vallum takes the lower ground which was more easily excavated. The Wall itself has been completely robbed of stones but for a third of a mile the ditch can clearly be seen to Milecastle 34 (Grindon) where it ends, being no longer necessary because of the steep cliffs. The Military Way leaves the north mound of the Vallum and runs between it and the Wall, following the most convenient route, bearing in mind the position of the milecastles which it supplied. It can now be traced for the rest of the way in Northumberland. At the fieldwall beyond Milecastle 34 is turret 34a which was discovered in 1913 and a short distance brings us to Sewingshields.

The farmhouse of Sewingshields is built entirely of stone from the Wall. The name is Old English meaning *shiels of Sigewine.* Turret 34b lies among the farm buildings and a centurial stone is preserved in the farm inscribed "The century of Gellius Philippus". West of the farmhouse on the north side of the Wall once stood Sewingshields Castle. When Dr. Lingard visited it in 1800 or 1807 its walls were five feet high, but a farmer later removed the vaults and the area was ploughed over. Hodgson tells us that in his time only a square lumpy mass of ruins overgrown with nettles could be seen near Broomlee Lough. In 1266 a manor house at Sewingshields belonged to Sir John de Holton but only in 1415 it is described as a castle in the hands of Robert Ogle. The list of 1541 says the old "tower" belonged to John Heron of Chipchase but was roofless and waste.

When Sir Cuthbert Radcliffe was Deputy-Warden of the East Marches he appointed two watchmen to stand at the *Sewynge sheralls cragge from sonne sett untyll the sonne aryse* in order to give warning of any bands of raiders. In the sixth canto of *Harold the Dauntless* by Sir Walter Scott the old tower is referred to as *The Castle of the Seven Shields.* Here is his description:—

"... No towers are seen
On the wild heath, but those that Fancy builds,
And, save a fosse that tracks the moor with green,
It nought remains to tell of what may there have been".

But a fine legend has been preserved by Hodgson in his *History of Northumberland.* "Immemorial tradition has asserted that King Arthur, his queen Guenever, court of lords and ladies, and his hounds, were enchanted in some cave of the crags, or in a hall below the Castle of Sewingshields, and would continue entranced there till some one should blow a bugle-horn that laid on a table near the entrance into the hall, and then, with 'the sword of the stone', cut a garter also placed there beside it. But none had ever heard where the entrance to this enchanted hall was, till the farmer at Sewingshields, about fifty years since, was sitting knitting on the ruins of the castle, and his clew fell, and ran downwards through a rush of briars and nettles, as he supposed, into a deep subterranean passage. Full in the faith, that the entrance to King Arthur's hall was now discovered, he cleared the briary portal of its weeds and rubbish, and entered a vaulted passage, followed, in his darkling way, the thread of his clew. The floor was infested with toads and lizards: and the dark wing of bats, disturbed by his unhallowed intrusion, flitted fearfully around him. At length his sinking faith was strengthened by a dim, distant light, which, as he advanced, grew gradually brighter, till all at once, he entered a vast and vaulted hall, in the centre of which a fire without fuel, from a broad crevice in the floor, blazed with a high and lambent flame, that showed all the carved walls, and fretted roofs, and the monarch, and his queen and court, reposing around in a theatre of thrones and costly couches. On the floor, beyond the fire, lay the faithful and deep-toned pack of thirty couple of hounds; and on a table before it the spell-dissolving horn, sword and garter. The shepherd reverently but firmly grasped the sword, and as he drew it leisurely from its rusty scabbard, the eyes of the monarch and his courtiers began to open, and they rose until they sat upright. He cut the garter; and, as the sword was

*King Arthur's Cave*

*Relief of a signifer or standard bearer of the early 3rd century from the fort at Carrawburgh.*
Clayton Museum, Chesters fort

*(From the book 'What the Soldiers Wore on Hadrian's Wall' by Russell Robinson)*

*The coloured plate shows the equipment of the soldier reconstructed*

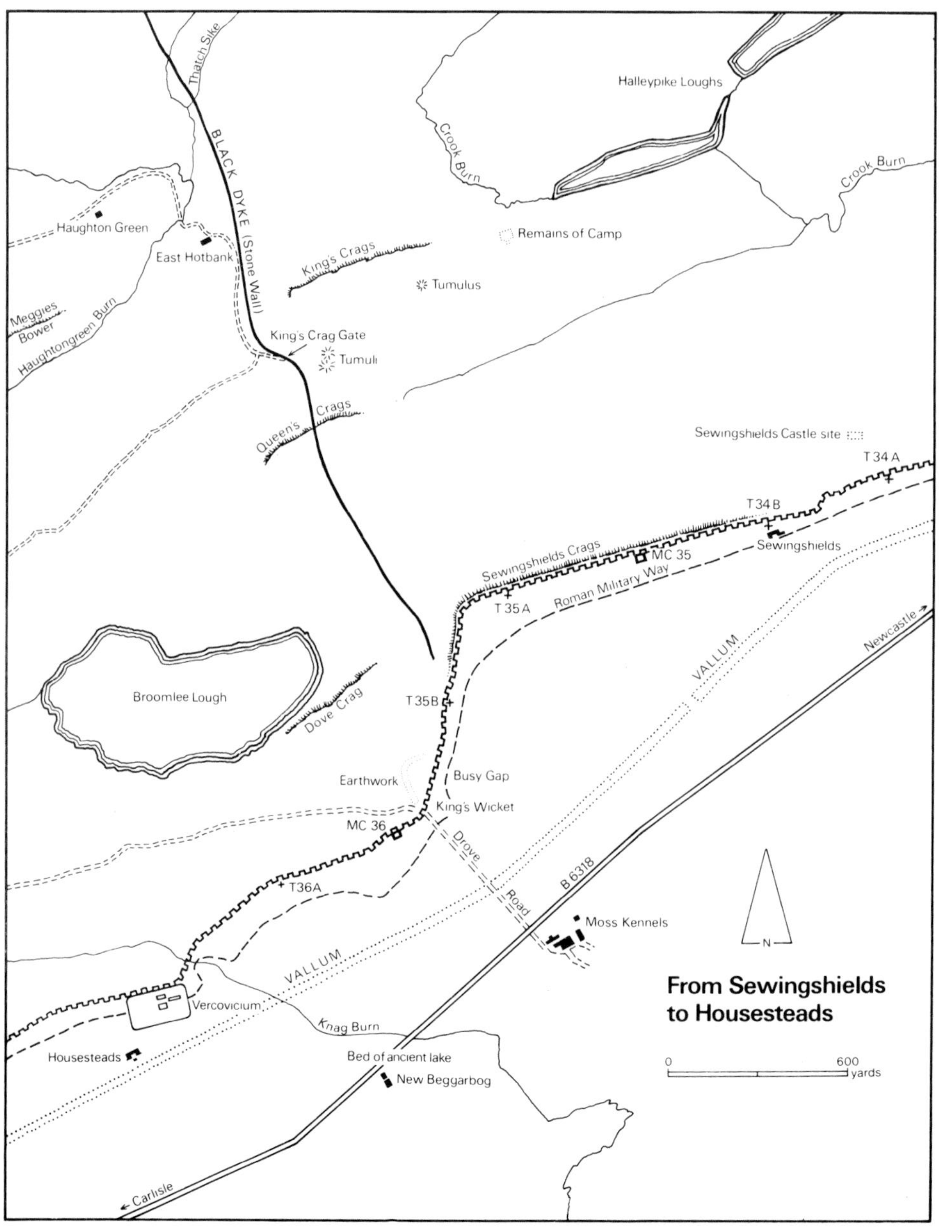
Thatch Sike
Halleypike Loughs
Crook Burn
Crook Burn
BLACK DYKE (Stone Wall)
Haughton Green
East Hotbank
Remains of Camp
King's Crags
Tumulus
Meggies Bower
Haughtongreen Burn
King's Crag Gate
Tumuli
Queen's Crags
Sewingshields Castle site
T 34 A
T 34 B
Sewingshields
Sewingshields Crags
MC 35
Roman Military Way
T 35 A
VALLUM
Newcastle
Broomlee Lough
Dove Crag
T 35B
Earthwork
Busy Gap
King's Wicket
MC 36
Drove Road
T36A
B 6318
Moss Kennels
N
From Sewingshields to Housesteads
VALLUM
Vercovicium
Knag Burn
Housesteads
Bed of ancient lake
New Beggarbog
0
600
yards
Carlisle

slowly being sheathed, the spell assumed its ancient power, and they all gradually sunk to rest; but not before the monarch had lifted up his eyes and hands, and exclaimed,

"O woe betide that evil day,
On which this witless wight was born,
Who drew the sword — the garter cut,
But never blew the bugle-horn!".

. . . Terror brought on loss of memory, and he was unable to give any correct account of his adventure, or the place where it occurred".

Half a mile north west of Sewingshields are two high points called the King's and Queen's Crag. Another local tradition is told about them.

"King Arthur, seated on the farthest rock, was talking with his queen, who, meanwhile, was engaged in arranging her 'back hair'. Some expression of the queen's having offended his majesty, he seized a rock which lay near to him, and with an exertion of strength for which the Picts were proverbial, threw it at her, a distance of about quarter of a mile! The queen, with great dexterity, caught it upon her comb, and thus warded off the blow; the stone fell about midway between them, where it lies to this very day, with the marks of the comb upon it, to attest the truth of the story. The stone probably weighs about twenty tons!".

North east of Sewingshields farmhouse is Fozley Moss. On an island in the swamp was once a prehistoric settlement.

At Sewingshields farmhouse a centurial stone is preserved and a walling stone from this locality is to be seen at Newcastle upon Tyne.

C CENTVRIA GELLI(I)
PHILIPP(I)
The century of Gellius
Philippus
LEG. II.
AVG.
The second Legion the August

Proceeding uphill west from Sewingshields, we come to Cats' Gate, a narrow chasm in the rocks through which, according to local tradition, a Scots crept under the Wall. A little over a quarter of a mile west is Milecastle 35 (Sewingshields). Just before the summit (which is 960 feet above sea level), we reach turret 35a. This turret was originally 20 feet square and recessed into the Wall with a door in the east corner. Later when it was abandoned, the Wall was strengthened where the recess had been. Broomlee Lough now comes into view to the north of the Wall and the smaller Grindon Lough can be seen to the south of the Newcastle road. Before we descend to Busy Gap we must notice the famous Saxon boundary earthwork called the Black Dyke. It consists of a ditch with the earth thrown out from it on the east side. Old maps show it running from the northern part of Northumberland to Allenheads in Durham. Today it runs from the North Tyne at Tarset to the South Tyne at Moralee. The point where it crossed the Wall is not clear but it was probably near Busy Gap. Nothing remains of turret 35b which precedes Busy Gap. Here the Wall ditch reappears as it always does when the precipitous escarpment is broken.

The name *Busy Gap* was probably originally *bushy-gap,* that is a gap with plenty of bushes. A drove road passes through here. The spot was much frequented by the mosstroopers and thieves of the Middle Ages. When Camden and Cotton visited here in 1599 they dared not go to Busy Gap. "The Wall", Camden wrote, "goeth forward more aslope by Iverton, Forster, and Chester-in-the-Wall, near to Busy Gap — a place infamous for thieving and robbing; where stood some castles (Chesters they call them) as I heard, but I could not with safety take the full survey of it, for the rank robbers thereabouts".

The term a "Busy Gap Rogue" was one of abuse down to the seventeenth century.

The triangular earthwork to the north of Busy Gap is post-Roman but the reason for its construction is a mystery. Climbing again we come to a gate called the King's Wicket through which a drove road passes. It may once have been Roman. This old engraving shows the view in 1884.

Soon we reach Milecastle 36 (King's Hill) which is remarkable because it stands on a slope of about one in five. It was a long-axis milecastle and its north gate was rebuilt as a postern but later blocked. Near the milecastle was discovered the centurial stone shown here. The perculiarity of it is that it seems to show the number of paces built by this unit.

Ↄ FLORINI
P(ASSVS) XXII

The century of Florinus
(built) twenty-two paces

We next pass two narrow and steep gaps and cross Kennel Crags. Nothing of the Wall can be seen here nor turret 36a, which stood on the summit. Descending the valley of the Knag Burn we come to the Knag Burn Gateway and Housesteads — Camden's *Chester-in-the-Wall.*

*Left. A "Strike" on the Wall*

## HOUSESTEADS FORT

Today most people who visit the Roman Wall call at Housesteads which is the fort from which the most dramatic views of the Roman Wall can be seen. Unless the visit is made during the few warm weeks of summer one cannot but feel sorry for the Roman troops who spent most of their life in such a bleak, cold and inhospitable place. The illustration on page 164 has been chosen to emphasize this point.

However we are not sure what the climate of northern Britain was like in Roman times. It was probably warmer, especially in the summer, but even so the winter months must have been a trying time. The vegetation was probably more varied with a fair number of trees but no large forests. Wild animals and game appear to have been abundant.

In the present book we have tried to show what life was like when Housesteads was filled with soldiers and the adjacent village was a busy commercial and agricultural centre. We must remember however that Housesteads was occupied for almost 300 years and the fort and *vicus* underwent many changes during this period. The most flourishing time was the third century. We have ignored the changes of the years and have not tried to show Housesteads at a particular point in time but have selected material which applied to most periods of its history.

Julius Agricola, governor of Britain (77-84), was the founder of the Roman defences in North Britain. He built the Stanegate, the Roman road which ran from Corbridge to Carlisle, passing a mile south of Housesteads. A few years after his recall to Rome several forts were established along the Stanegate to make it the effectual frontier of Roman Britain. The fort at Vindolanda was the most important in the area while at Housesteads a mere turret, probably to be used as a watch tower, was built. About 120 A.D. Hadrian decided to build a wall right along the frontier, but the forts along the Stanegate were to garrison the soldiers. The Wall itself was to have only turrets and milecastles. But before the work was completed a decision was taken to build forts on the Wall itself. The newly built fort at Housesteads superseded that at Vindolanda. It would have taken a number of years to build and the Second Legion was probably responsible for the work. We do not know who were the first garrison. In fact the early history of Housesteads is very confused. It was destroyed three times, in A.D. 197, 296 and 367. The first rebuilding was by Severus soon after 200 A.D., and a permanent garrison, the First Cohort of Tungrians (who came from what is now Belgium), 1,000 strong, was stationed here. They were reinforced in later years by the *cuneus Frisiorum,* a detachment of irregular troops, and in the fourth century by Anglo-Saxons. By A.D. 400 the garrison had declined to two or three hundred. The headquarters building was then used as an armoury and a smith was turning out arrow heads when sudden destruction came to Housesteads. The illustration on page 150 shows the final onslaught on the fort.

Most Roman stations had civilian settlements attached to them in which the wives and children of the soldiers lived. Many of the troops when they retired after twenty five years service would also settle here. Merchants, craftsmen, farmworkers and others would make up what was one of the largest civilian settlements attached to a Wall fort. The village was most prosperous and extensive in the late 3rd and early 4th century. The size and prosperity of the Housesteads settlement was probably helped by the gateway in the Wall at the Knag Burn which encouraged trade across the frontier.

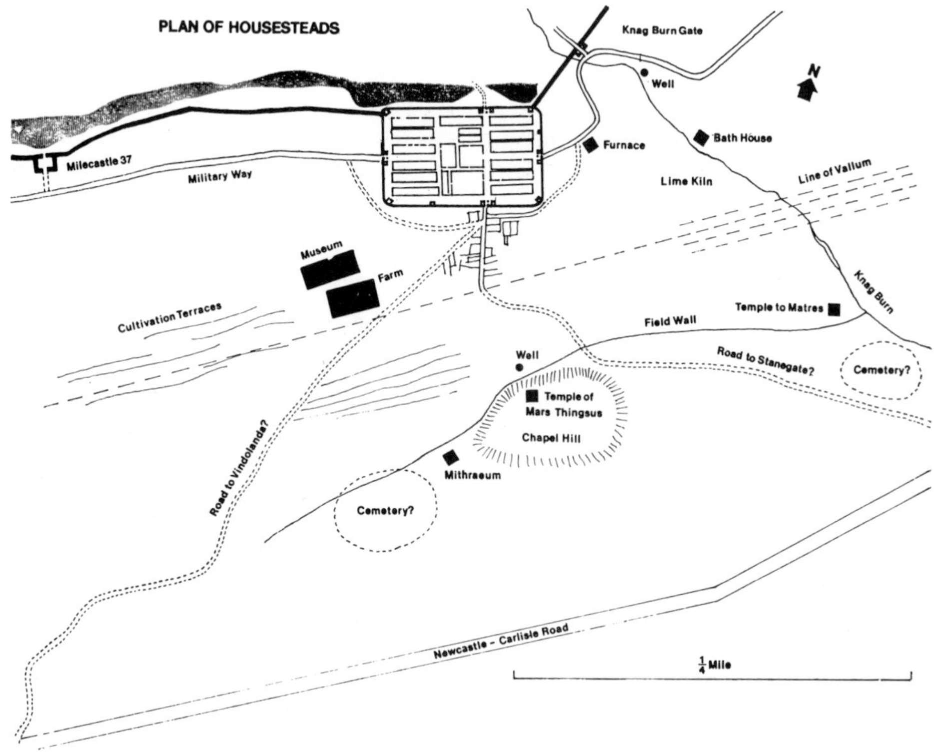


For long periods life at Housesteads must have been peaceful and secure. The civilian settlement spread out from the walls of the fort in all directions and no attempts were made to provide it with defences. The Vallum it is true cut it off from the south, but in other directions it was open to sudden raiding parties. Clearly the *Pax Romana* prevailed at Housesteads for many generations.

After the third destruction of 367 the northern frontier was restored by Count Theodosuis. At Housesteads the civilian settlement was abandoned and the dependants of the garrison moved inside the walls. Many of the buildings were modified and altered for their reception.

We do not know the history of Housesteads after the fort was finally overrun. There is slight evidence that it became an Anglian Christian settlement. Cuddy's Crag nearby is said to have received its name from St. Cuthbert on one of his visits, and fragments of a possible small Christian church have been found.

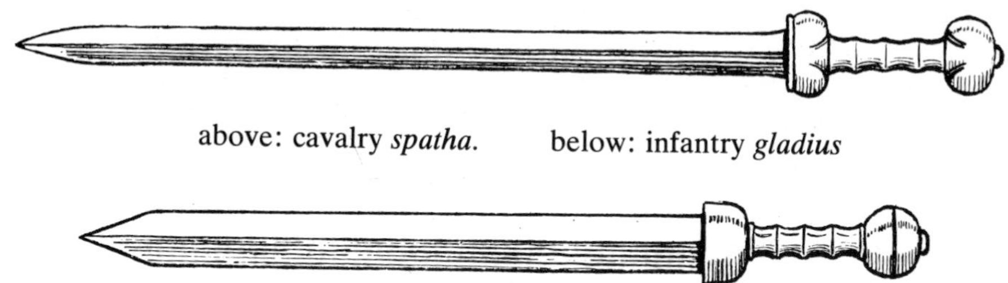

above: cavalry *spatha*. below: infantry *gladius*

In the Middle Ages the site was occupied by mosstroopers. Camden, the famous topographer, visited the area about 1600 and wrote — "I could not with safety take the full survey of it, for the rank robbers thereabouts". The mosstroopers made alterations to the south gate, turning part of it into a bastle house, inserting a corn drying kiln and extra accommodation. Although a danger to travellers the mosstroopers indirectly helped to preserve Housesteads. They kept genuine farmers at bay so the fort was not plundered so early for stones for farm buildings and field walls.

Housesteads of course was not the Roman name of the fort. The Roman name without any authority was often given as BORCOVICUS. The *Notitia Dignitatum* (5th century) suggests BORCOVICIUM, while the Ravenna list (7th century) gives VELURTION. An inscription from the site starts with the letters VER and hence VERCOVICIUM (the "hilly place") has been suggested. Perhaps we had better keep the name of the 18th century farmhouse of HOUSESTEADS.

## COMMANDANT'S HOUSE

The house was built on sloping ground with a stone slated roof. The main entrance was from the *via principalis.* On the left was the reception room, with the kitchens on the right. The dining room was in the North wing. There were 19 rooms (apart from possible upstairs rooms in the South wing), but their uses are difficult to interprete. Those that are heated can be seen from the chimneys shown in the roof. It is a typical courtyard house of Mediterranean type, probably unsuitable for the climatic conditions at Housesteads. The South East corner of the house seems to have been used as stabling, and an exit for cattle and horses is shown on the drawing. There was provision for a small bath (but not a full suite) and a latrine. Whether there were two storeys is uncertain but the South wing was probably so in order to provide privacy, so that the courtyard couldn't be overlooked by soldiers on the fort wall.

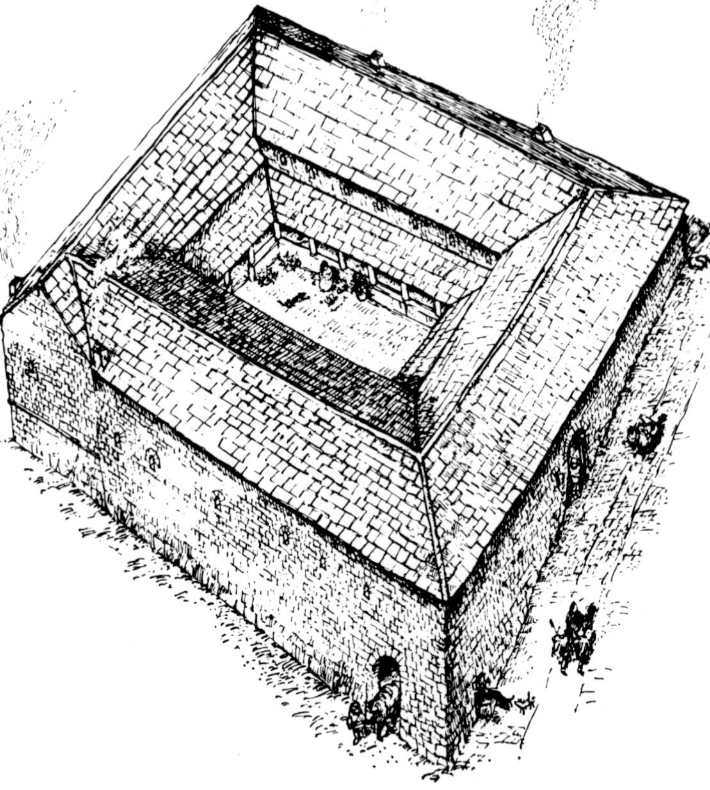

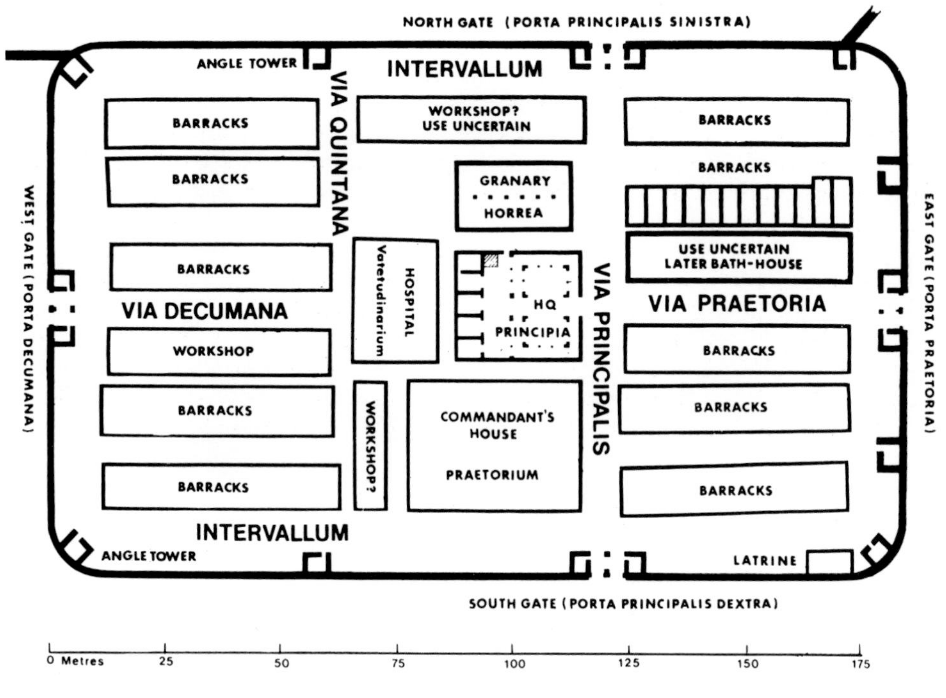


**HOUSESTEADS FORT** (CONJECTURAL EARLY PLAN)

## BARRACKS

The early plan shows ten long buildings which were used as barracks. Each block accommodated 100 men, the garrison at Housesteads being a battalion a thousand strong. The plan was descended from that of the tented camp. In this eight tents, each holding ten men (two groups would always be on guard duty), were placed side by side with a larger tent at the end for the centurion. We have divided up one of the barrack blocks showing how this division was carried out. The two larger rooms at the end were for the centurions and N.C.O.'s. Each room would be divided by a partition leaving a large room for sleeping and a smaller one for equipment. All the rooms would probably be connected by a veranda. The floors appear to have been of clay. No traces of bunks or beds have been found so mattresses were probably laid on the floor at night. Strange to record we do not know where the men cooked or ate their food. There was certainly no central cookhouse. Ovens for baking were sometimes placed at the back of the fort ramparts but at Housesteads no traces have been discovered.None of the barracks at Housesteads have been completely excavated and they have at times been extensively remodelled making it difficult to have a clear picture of their internal arrangements. When the barracks were finally remodelled here they were split into eight instead of ten rooms and each room was separated by a small space. Clearly they wanted to provide more commodious living accommodation for whatever soldiers occupied them. The centurion's room at the end was also enlarged. (Our plan has been based on the one in *The Army of Hadrian's Wall* by B. Dobson and D. Breeze, 1972).

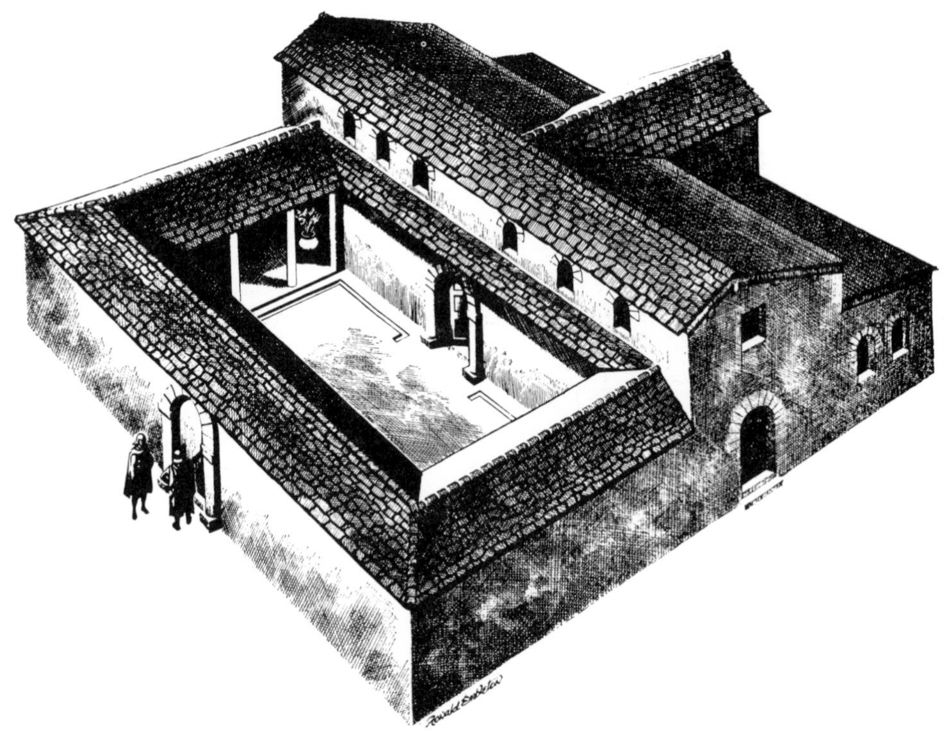

*Headquarters Building*

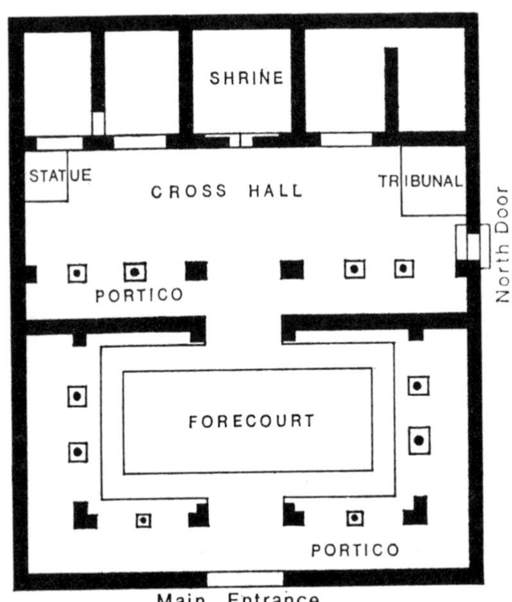


## HEADQUARTERS (Principia)

The *principia* or headquarters building was, as is normal, in the centre of the fort. It was the finest building at Housesteads and was the administrative and spiritual centre of the fort. It was entered from the main street by a large arched and projecting gate.

On entering the soldier came into a paved courtyard surrounded originally on four sides by a colonnaded veranda (later on the north, east and south only). From this forecourt another arched doorway led to the great hall which could also originally be entered from the two side streets but later only the north entrance was available. This mighty basilica was roofed in, the roof being supported by a row of columns which ran the length of the hall. In the north west corner is a large block of masonry called the *tribunal* where the fort commandant took his seat on ceremonial or public occasions. In the opposite corner was another raised platform probably occupied by a statue. The hall was the highest building in the fort and would be lit by upper clerestory windows as in a church.

Farthest from the entrance lay a range of rooms, five in all. The central one was the *aedes* or shrine where were kept the standards of the regiment, the statue of the emperor, and possibly other altars. It was guarded day and night. This central shrine could be seen as soon as one entered the main entrance. In the *aedes* was usually an underground strongroom where the regimental treasures and money were kept, but because of the hard whinstone it does not feature at Housesteads. The two rooms to the north of the shrine were occupied by the adjutant *(cornicularius)* and his clerks who were responsible for the administration of the unit. The two rooms on the south were used by the standard bearers *(signiferi)* who were responsible for the pay and savings of the troops. Originally the three central rooms had wide arched entrances. The cross hall was the place where the commandant issued his orders, heard complaints, dealt out punishments and received visitors. It would also be used for a variety of meetings, especially of the centurions.

In later years drastic changes were made to the *Principia.* The forecourt was changed into living accommodation, the hall became a kitchen and mess room, and the adjutant's office became an armoury. As danger threatened the Wall only the barest of administration was maintained.

## VIA QUINTANA

The *via quintana* ran parallel to the main *via principalis.* It was a minor road giving access to the barracks and also to the granaries. It is joined in the middle by the *via decumana.* Both these roads are named after divisions in the larger legionary camps. The *via quintana (quintus-fifth)* divided the fifth maniple from the sixth. The *via decumana (decimus-tenth)* was the area occupied by the 10th Cohort.

## VIA PRINCIPALIS

The *via principalis* passed between the two gates in the side walls. The area to the east was known as the *praetentura* (front portion), and was normally used exclusively for barracks. On the left starting from the bottom of the picture are the Commandant's House, the Headquarter's Building, the granary and the last building whose use was uncertain but was probably used as a workshop. The *via principalis* terminated in the massive north gate. Visitors often think this must have never been used because of the sharp drop to the north. But originally there was an inclined road here which was removed during excavations.

**Plan of Hospital**

SURGICAL WARD
ENTRANCE
ENTRANCE
ENTRANCE HALL
VERANDA
COURTYARD
VERANDA
1
2
3
4
5
6
7
Use unknown STORES?
Use unknown STORES?
ENTRANCE
ENTRANCE
10
9
8
LATRINE
Bath & washing arrangements
DRAIN
0 2 4 6 8 10
Metres
N

## THE HOSPITAL

Behind the headquarters building stands a courtyard type of building. Although little of medical significance was found during the two excavations (1898 and 1972), the building was undoubtedly the fort hospital. Analogy from other Roman forts makes this supposition almost certain. It has four ranges of rooms including an operating theatre, rooms for patients, latrines, baths and medical stores. It was a stone building with tiled roof; and no heating arrangements, and unless the rooms marked *use unknown* were used for that purpose it had no kitchen. Food would be brought in from the main kitchens. The building was altered many times and in the 3rd and 4th centuries was probably used for workshops. Our plan tries to show the building in its original form.

*(See article by Miss D. Charlesworth in A.A. 5th Series, Volume IV).*

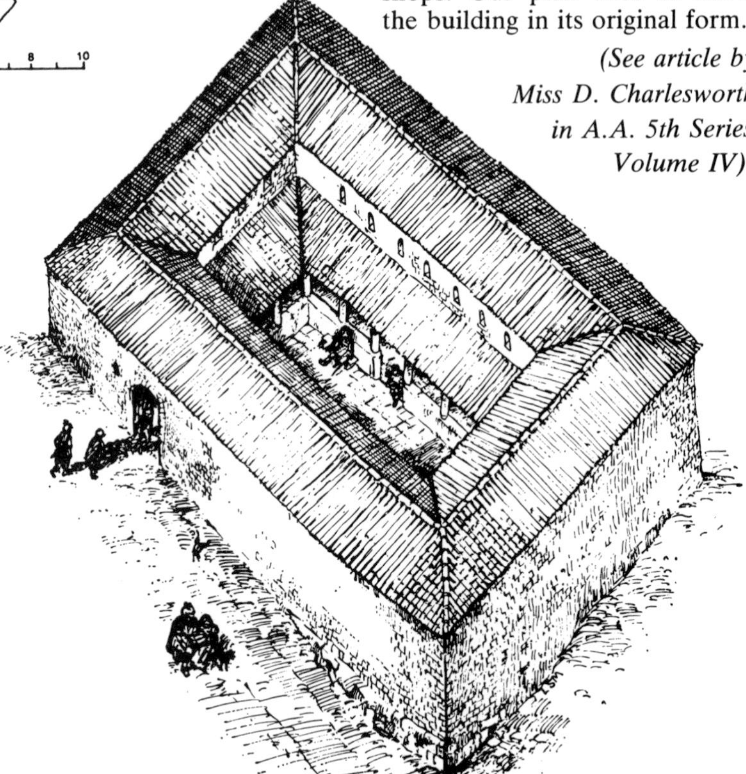

## THE BUTCHER'S SHOP

The village of Housesteads would certainly have had a butcher's shop to serve the needs of the civilian population. Meat was important in the diet of Roman soldiers. The granaries also probably stored salted meat. However the diet of the civilians would depend upon their income. Research at Vindolanda suggests that beef, mutton and pork (in that order) were the most popular meats; but goats, venison and all manner of birds were also eaten. The steelyard, chopping block and methods of hanging meat from hooks are all shown on Roman carvings which have survived. Besides the knife here illustrated the butcher also used a chopper similar to those used today. The scales here shown were used in the first century A.D. Meat placed in the pan was weighed by moving the sculptured weights along the horizontal bar.

Fish was popular among the Romans and could probably be bought at the butcher's in Housesteads.

*Bird's eye view of Housesteads Fort*

## THE GATEWAYS

All the gateways at Housesteads were built to the same plan and were more elaborate than in the other wall forts. Each gate was flanked on either side by a guard-room which opened onto the gate passage, closed at both ends by double doors. The gatehouse extended over both the passages as well as the guard rooms. The outside of the south gate is illustrated on page 139. In the spandrel of the gate arches can be seen an inscription recording the Emperor Hadrian, his legate Aulus Platorius Nepos and the legion which built the fort. One of the portals is shown as built-up to conserve manpower. The large room which ran the whole length of the massive gateway was lit by round-headed windows, fragments of which have been found. The roof was probably flat and used as a fighting platform, the rain water draining off into a tank. The gateway was almost certainly crenellated.

The *West Gate* is the best preserved in the fort, the west impost still standing at full height with bolt holes for the doors still to be seen. In the 4th century the gateway was blocked and the guard chambers turned into heated rooms.

The *North Gate* has twin portals divided by two piers with flanking guardchambers opening onto the roadway. The gate is well built of large stones and opened onto a causeway (which has now been removed). The large water-tank near the gate was used to collect water from the roof. Even before it was completed the north gate had one of its portals blocked. Its inside is shown on page 146.

The *East Gate* also had twin portals. It was the main entrance to the fort. The south passageway was blocked after 297 A.D. to strengthen the fort defences.

The *South Gate* which is here reconstructed was probably rarely used for wheeled traffic because the gradient inside was too steep. It was considerably altered in post-Roman times, being for many years converted into a pele tower.

*The South Gate at Housesteads*

## THE KITCHEN

Commanders of auxiliary units were men of importance in the Roman army and when posted to frontier forts would bring their wives and families with them. They would expect some of the comforts they were accustomed to at home. Our artist shows a meal being prepared in the kitchen of the commandant's house. Most of the cooking was done in earthenware jars or bronze pans supported on tripods over burning charcoal or wood. One of the cooks is using a heavy bowl *(mortaria)* to pound some food with a pestle. The young woman is using a hand rotary quern for grinding some corn. Around the walls are a variety of cooking utensils and from the ceiling hangs an oil lamp. An interior pump supplies water from a storage tank.

## THE TEMPLE TO MITHRAS

Many altars have been discovered at Housesteads showing that several deities were worshipped but the most important was the Persian sun-god Mithras whose temple stood in the valley below the farmhouse. Nothing can now be seen but when excavated valuable sculptures and inscriptions were found. Mithraic temples were all very similar and were dark to suggest the cave where Mithras slew the bull. The altars found at Housesteads were all dedicated by fort commanders of the third century when the worship of Mithras flourished. A few miles away at Carrawburgh the remains of a remarkable Mithraic temple can be seen.

## HAMIAN ARCHER FROM HOUSESTEADS

The garrison of Housesteads in the third and fourth centuries was the first cohort of Tungrians, an infantry battalion from the area on the continent now called Belgium. Before that period the garrison is unknown. In the third century the garrison seems to have been reinforced by a unit of irregulars called the *cuneus Hnaudifridi,* named after its commander Hnaudifridus. The Frisian cavalry mentioned about the same time *(cunus Frisiorum)* may be the same detachment under a different name. For the early second century we have a gravestone of a Hamian archer *(cohors Hamiorum Sagittariorum)* which suggests they were at Housesteads at that time. Our reconstruction is based on information supplied by Russell Robinson. From his tombstone: "the soldier is in a conical helmet and probably wearing a mail shirt. On his back is slung a quiver of arrows and on his waist-belt, at the right side, hangs a large knife. His bow, of a recurved composite type, is in his left hand and a small axe is in his right". The Hamians were a Syrian tribe.

*Reconstruction of Latrines – Housesteads Fort*

**THE LATRINE**

Sanitation and cleanliness were given much attention in the building of Roman forts. At Housesteads the latrine is found in the south east corner. The latrine is probably the most famous building to be seen here; only a few are known on the Wall. The drawing by Ronald Embleton is his most famous and most popular.

The wooden seating was arranged along two of the walls and fresh water flowed along two channels in which the soldiers could wash their sponges (used like paper today). Each soldier carried an individual sponge which was attached to the end of a stick. There seems to have been a small hole in the floor in front of each seat into which the soldier could stand his individual sponge. The water from the two floor channels emptied into a lower one which flushed under the seats.

In Roman times the walls would have been covered with plaster (and probably *graffiti)* and the stone would not have been visible as in the drawing.

The external sewer passed beneath the fort wall near the corner and surfaced one hundred yards to the south on one of the terraces. The sewage was probably used as manure.

A very large military latrine has been found at Piercebridge which could accommodate thirty soldiers. It was built on the Intervallum road.

The word latrine is derived from the Roman work *lavatrina,* the Roman word lavare meaning "to wash". Latrines were always found in bath houses.

**THE GRANARIES**

The granary was an important part of a Roman fort. They were usually placed near the centre to be as far away as possible from incendiary missiles. Here was stored corn and possibly other food to last the garrison for several months. Originally there seems to have been a single granary at Housesteads, as shown on the plan, with a line of columns supporting the massive roof. The line of columns was later replaced by a partition wall and later by two walls so two granaries were formed with a narrow space between.

These were typical granaries built according to a standard military pattern. They had heavy fire-proof roofs of stone slabs with massive external buttresses at intervals. They were intended not only to take the extra weight but also to allow the roof to project so that water did not run down the walls and cause damp. The upper part of the wall between the buttresses was louvred for ventilation, (louvres were overlapping boards so arranged as to admit air but exclude rain), and near the bottom of the wall were ventilators which allowed free passage of air beneath the floor. The floor was supported on short pillars. Across them ran beams with their inner ends let into the partition walls. On these beams rested lengthwise planks or sometimes flagging (our reconstruction shows short thick planks). This arrangement must not be confused with the hypocaust system which used hot air circulating beneath the floor to warm the room above. The granary entrances were at the west end where there was an open space for carts so they did not interfere with the movement of troops and traffic on the *Via Principalis.* Both granaries had a projection which acted as a loading bay. The southern granary also had an entrance on the east with steps leading up to the door as illustrated on the drawing. (This was probably because at some stage this granary was divided internally). The space between the southern granary and the headquarters building was quite narrow but for artistic reasons this is not shown.

We do not know whether grain was stored in bulk or in barrels. Our artist has used wooden bins which are now considered the most likely method. Each bin would probably be allocated to an individual unit in the camp to assist in the equal rationing of supplies. We are uncertain whether other kinds of food such as meat and oil were stored here as well. In the last days of the occupation the granaries were used for living accommodation. The floors were made solid and flagged over.

*View on the VIA PRINCIPALIS showing the granaries on the left*

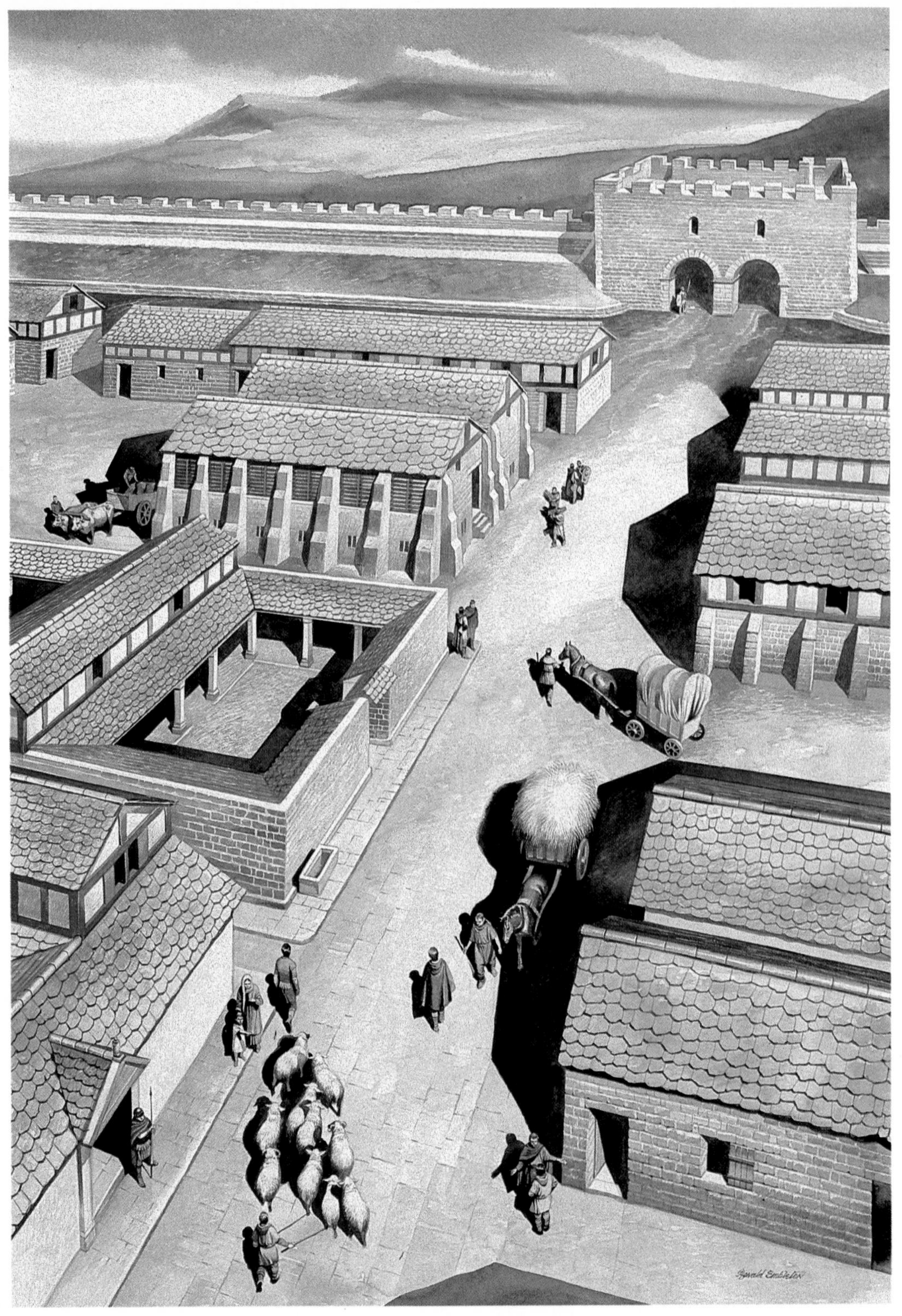

*Main Street (Via Principalis)*

*Opposite: Joinery Shop*

Ronald Embleton

## MURDER HOUSE

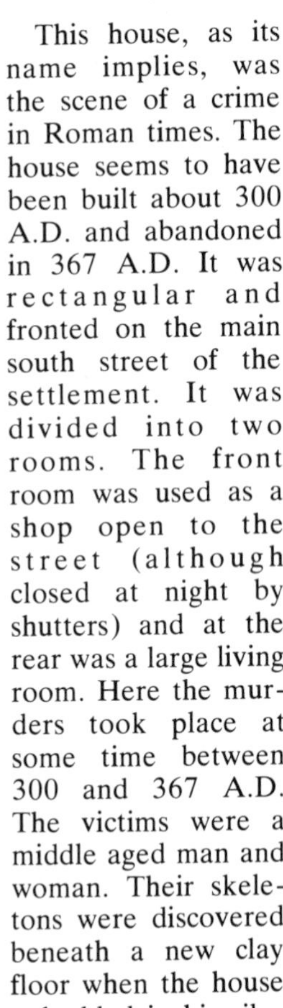

This house, as its name implies, was the scene of a crime in Roman times. The house seems to have been built about 300 A.D. and abandoned in 367 A.D. It was rectangular and fronted on the main south street of the settlement. It was divided into two rooms. The front room was used as a shop open to the street (although closed at night by shutters) and at the rear was a large living room. Here the murders took place at some time between 300 and 367 A.D. The victims were a middle aged man and woman. Their skeletons were discovered beneath a new clay floor when the house was excavated in 1932, the man having a broken sword embedded in his ribs. Burial within a settlement was forbidden in Roman law so the burial had taken place secretly and care taken to hide the grave. Our artist has tried to reconstruct the scene. One of the corpses lies covered in a toga and the two accomplices have paused to listen to some noise or movement outside. There is here a fine subject for a story, an early 'whodunit'. Since we know nothing about the murderers, the victims or the motives there is ample scope for imagination.

## JOINERY SHOP

The Roman forts were probably self-sufficient regarding repairs to buildings, clothing and military equipment, so there would be a number of workshops either in the fort or the *vicus*. The joinery shop on page 147 shows in detail the variety of tools used by the Romans. Large quantities of such tools have been discovered at various sites on the Wall.

## CULTIVATION TERRACES

To the south of the fort are numerous terraces formed for the purpose of cultivation. Many prehistoric hill forts in Northumberland have them. Those at Housesteads were almost certainly built by local people who lived in the *vicus*. Food production was one of the most important economic activities of the *vicus*.

## CEMETERIES

Imperial regulations forbade burial within civilian settlements. Two possible cemeteries are shown on our map but insufficient excavations have been carried out to confirm their size and contents. The people who lived along the Wall believed in an after-life of various kinds and so correct burial was important. In the first and second centuries the dead were usually cremated and the ashes buried in an urn usually along with some grave goods. From the second half of the second century onwards inhumation gradually replaced cremation.

## WATER SUPPLY

Unlike Chesters and Vindolanda there was no well at Housesteads since the fort is built upon whinstone, one of the hardest rocks to be found. Because of its height Housesteads could not be supplied by an aqueduct so elaborate arrangements had to be made to collect water from the roofs. Since rainfall at Housesteads was probably as high in the times of the Romans as today there would be a plentiful supply available. When necessary, perhaps in the summer, the supply could be supplemented by water from the Knag Burn although it is very unlikely that the water was pumped to the fort (the Romans had the technical knowledge to do this if they wanted). When needed, the water would have been transported in containers on the backs of mules.

The water tank which collected rain water from the roof of the north gateway can still be seen. The sides are worn, but not by Romans sharpening their swords as is often suggested, but probably by farmers many centuries later who sharpened their agricultural instruments here. As can be expected there was a large tank near the latrines which collected water from the angle tower.

The well near the south gate of the fort is fairly modern.

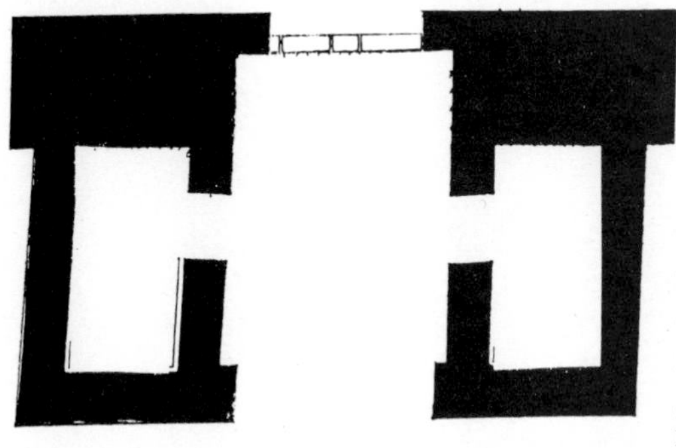

## KNAG BURN GATEWAY

This gateway, along with another which once stood at Portgate, is one of the rare gateways through the Wall used for civilian purposes. It was closed by double gates with a guard room on each side entered from the gate passage. The gateway is not original and was probably built after 300 A.D. when the civilian settlement was flourishing and trade was expanding. Lying on a drove road it was clearly intended to regulate traffic and levy necessary tolls. Custom tolls were collected by a Roman official called a *beneficiarius* and we know there was one stationed at Housesteads. The existence of this gateway probably led to the establishment of an important market at Housesteads.

*Above. A Roman sacrifice*

*Opposite. The destruction of Housesteads*

## HOUSESTEADS TO GREATCHESTERS

This section of the Roman Wall is the best visited part because it has magnificent scenery. History and scenic beauty are uniquely combined. To the Roman soldier it appeared otherwise, since it was the most isolated and rugged section, exposed to storms for more than half the year. The units here must have cursed their misfortune, looking with envy on those guarding the Tyne Valley below as at Chesters where the climate was more equable and the countryside more welcoming.

Probably the most noticeable characteristic in Roman times was that everyone, civilians and soldiers, wore the *paenula* or hooded cloak at all times apart from a few summer months.

The weather was probably the same as today with slightly warmer summers. The land was unproductive with cattle, especially sheep and goats, as the main source of wealth. Only in a small area near the forts and scattered Celtic villages would a limited amount of cultivation be carried on.

During the winter months there would be little movement in this sector of the Wall. It would be safe from any attacks from the north since the weather would make campaigning difficult and the Roman soldiers would spend most of their time in the comparative warmth of the forts and milecastles. It would be a period of hibernation for man and beast.

*Drawing of paenula or hooded cloak*

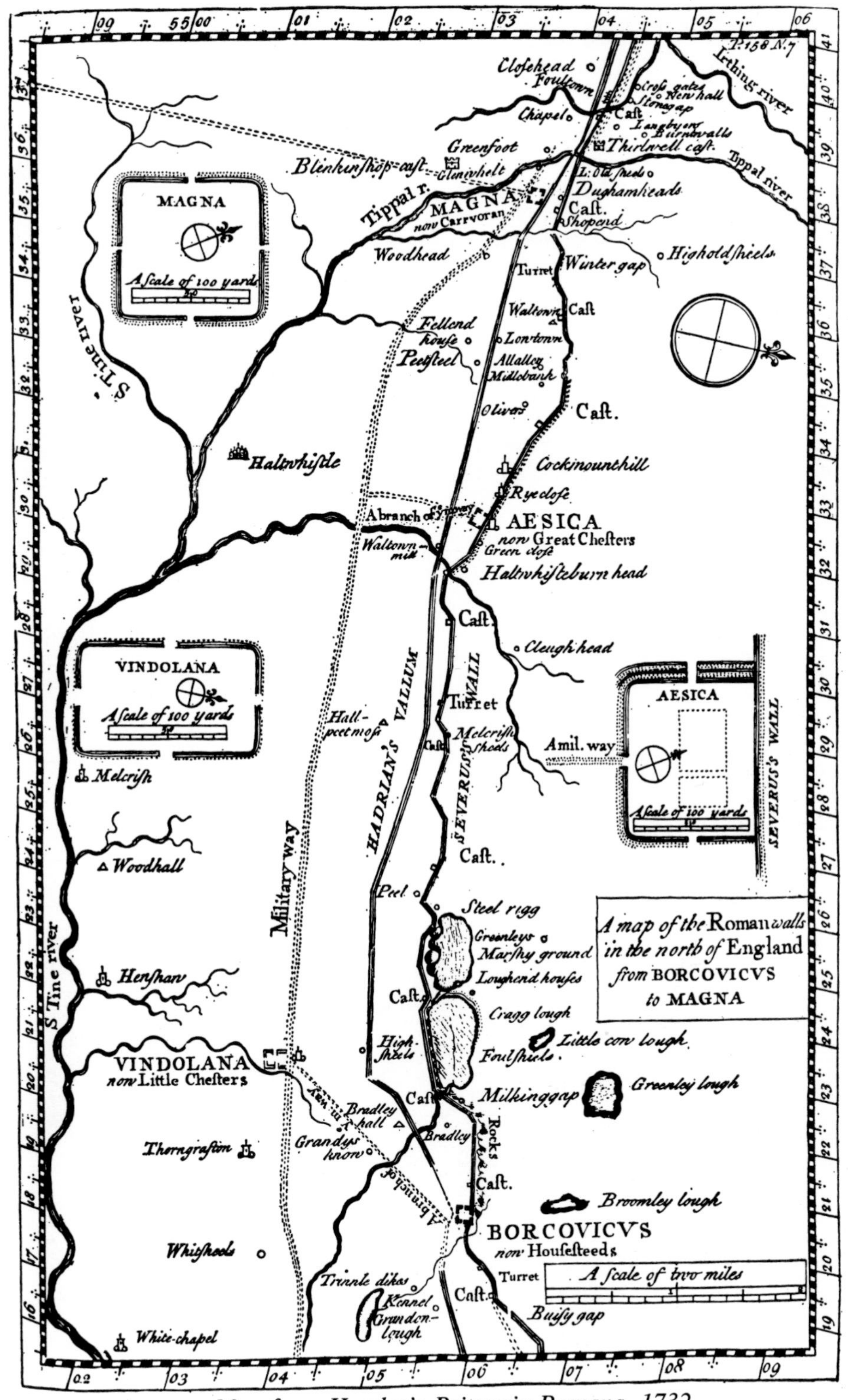


Map from Horsley's Britannia Romana, 1732

Westwards from Housesteads we can go along the Wall itself or take the Roman Military Way which runs behind the Wall for several miles in this section. It can be followed easily because most of the field-gates are placed on it. Bruce's *Handbook* (2nd Edition, 1884) tells us:

*This military way was in use as a public road not very long ago. The family of Wright were hereditary carriers between Newcastle and Carlisle for more than 100 years, and so continued till driven off the road by the railway. The representative of the family at the time the first edition of this book was prepared was tenant of the Housesteads farm. He stated that the tradition in the family was, that the traffic from east to west was originally conducted on pack-horses, and that the carriers, in the central part of their journey between Newcastle and Carlisle, were accustomed to resort to the Roman way. In certain parts of their journey they had to camp out all night, and one of their camping places was opposite 'Twice-Brewed Ale', a carriers' inn contemporaneous with the turnpike road, which is now abandoned as a place of public entertainment.*

The Vallum along this part of the Wall is clearly visible in the valley below at a considerable distance from the Wall. Those who are walking along the Wall itself will have a magnificent view.

*The walk along the cliffs is exceedingly beautiful, and the Wall for the most part is in excellent condition, all the way to Hot Bank. The traveller will notice, too, that it differs in width in different places, as is shown by the offsets and insets which occasionally occur. No doubt different gangs of workmen wrought simultaneously on different parts of the line, and the superintendent of each was allowed to exercise, within certain limits, his own judgement as to the width of the Wall. On the north face of the Wall the line is continuous. (Bruce).*

*Sketch of the interior of Milecastle 37, as excavated by John Clayton in 1852*

## MILECASTLE 37

450 yards west of Housesteads we come to milecastle 37 which is here reconstructed. It measures internally 57 feet 6 inches from east to west and 49 feet 6 inches from north to south, with side walls nine feet thick. A building inscription

informs us that it was built by the Second Legion in the governorship of Aulus Platorius Nepos who came to Britain in A.D. 122. The milecastle is of the normal type with the Wall acting as a north side. The southern corners are rounded externally but squared on the inside. It was approached by a branch road leading from the Military Way and entered by a gateway in the centre of the south side. A road led north to a similar gateway through the Wall. Inside on the east side was a store building probably used as a barracks by the garrison of perhaps twenty men. Between it and the north wall were ovens. On the west side stood timber buildings used for stores and equipment and probably horses as well. The stone steps leading up to the ramparts of the Wall were probably in the north west corner not as shown by our artist in the north east. Ronald Embelton has shown this milecastle covered with winter snow, a typical scene, since we must remember that the inclement weather was one of the problems the Wall garrison had to face.

*Part of Dedication Slab from Milecastle 37 commemorating the original building*

A hundred yards further on brings us to the gap between Housesteads Gap and Cuddy's Crag. It will be noticed that here for a short distance the Wall ditch reappears. After Cuddy's Crag comes Rapishaw Gap and then Hot Bank Crags. Turrets 37a and 37b can no longer be seen. From Hot Bank Crags the view is magnificent. Here is Bruce's description (2nd edition).

*The view from the summit is very extensive and fine. All the four loughs — Broomlee, Greenlee, Crag Lough and Grindon, are in sight. Not far from the western margin of Greenlee is Bonnyrig, a shooting-box belonging to Sir Edward Blackett, Bart. The course of the crags in this vicinity will be viewed with interest. Beyond the waste to the north-east are the Simonside Hills, and beyond them is the Cheviot range. The heather-clad hill immediately to the south of us is Borcum now*

*The former Carrier's Inn on the Military Road (see page 161)*

*called Barcombe, from which the Romans procured much of their stone, and from which the name of the station BORCOVICUS is no doubt derived. The defile leading by its western flank to the Tyne will be noticed, and the propriety of guarding it by a stationary camp perceived. The platform of the station of VINDOLANDA may be distinguished by its perculiarly verdant surface. On the south side of the Tyne, Langley Castle may be noticed — near the angle of a large plantation; beyond it are the chimneys of the smelt-mills. The valley of the river Allen is seen joining that of the Tyne; and near the confluence of the two rivers, may be discerned the ruins of Staward Peel. In the distance, to the south-west of us, are the lofty summits of Cross-fell, Skiddaw, and Saddleback.*

After passing the site of turret 37b the famous Crag Lough comes into view. Water-hens nest in the reeds and wild ducks and swans often resort here. Descending past Hot Bank Farm we reach Milking Gap.

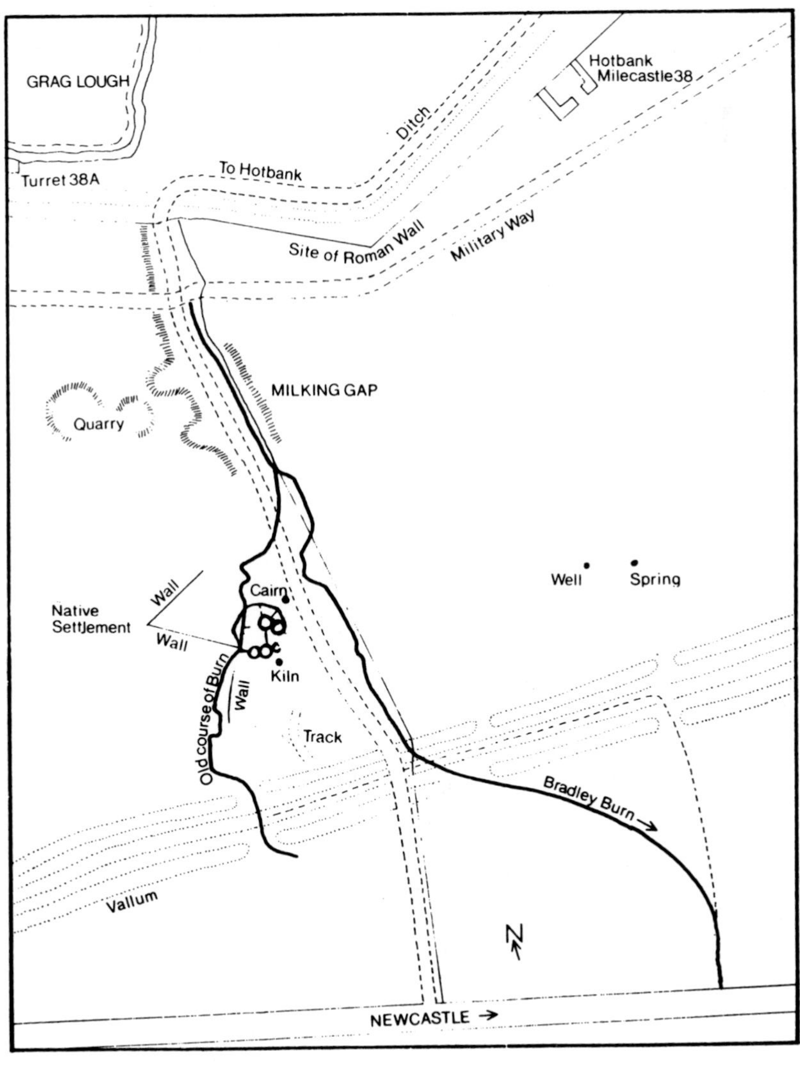

## MILKING GAP

The break in the basaltic ridge opposite the farm house of Hot Bank is called Milking Gap. This gap affords easy access to the area north of the Wall. Through it runs the Bradley Burn which drains Crag Lough to the north of the ridge. Here the remains of a native settlement can be traced. It consists of five round stones enclosed by a turf wall, on a stone foundation but not really fortified. The central house is the most important. All the houses were built of uncut stone and rubble to the height of about five feet and the roof was supported on internal wooden posts placed near the outer wall. The entrance was closed by a plaited wattle door. The roof would be thatched, probably with reeds from the lough.

Although the few dated remains found on the site suggest it was occupied between 120 A.D. and 180 A.D., it is now accepted that the inhabitants of this village were expelled when the Vallum was built, since a native settlement within a military zone was unthinkable.

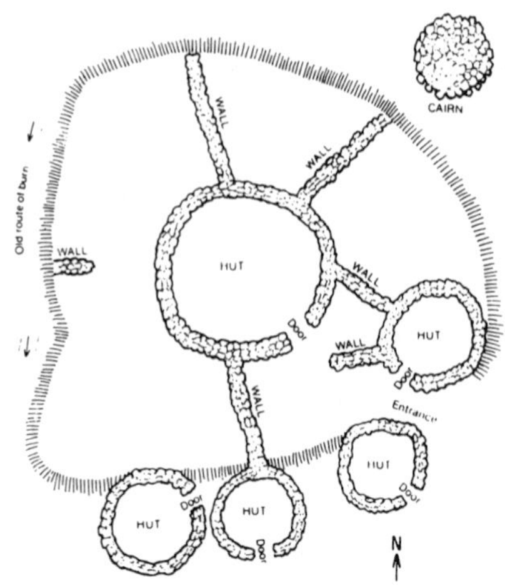


*Milking Gap Native Settlement*

Hot Bank Milecastle (38) here was excavated in 1935. The broken inscribed stone here shown was found at this milecastle.

The inscription reads — IMP CAES TRAIAN HADRIANI AVG LEG II AVG A PLATORIO NEPOTE LEG PR PR. (In honour of the Emperor Caesar Trajanus Hadrianus Augustus the second legion (styled) the august (erected this by command of) Aulus Platorius Nepos, legate and propraetor). It records building by the Second Legion under Aulus Platorius Nepos who was governor of Britain from 122 to 126 A.D. Part of the stone is at Durham, the other half at Newcastle. However, a second and more perfect inscription (wrongly ascribed by Bruce to Castle Nick Milecastle) almost certainly came from Hot Bank.

Scale, 1¼ inch to the foot.

Size—3 feet 2 inches by 2 feet.

*Dedication Slab from Milecastle 38, now at the Museum of Antiquities, Newcastle upon Tyne*

This shows that an identical inscription was placed above both the north and south gates.

West of Milking Gap on the majestic cliffs overlooking Crag Lough are turrets 38a and 38b. From High Shield Crag the Wall drops down to Castle Nick Milecastle (39).

## CASTLE NICK MILECASTLE

Castle Nick receives its name from Milecastle 39. The milecastle measures internally 50 feet from east to west and 65 feet north to south. Its well-preserved walls are seven feet thick. On the west side the foundations can be traced.

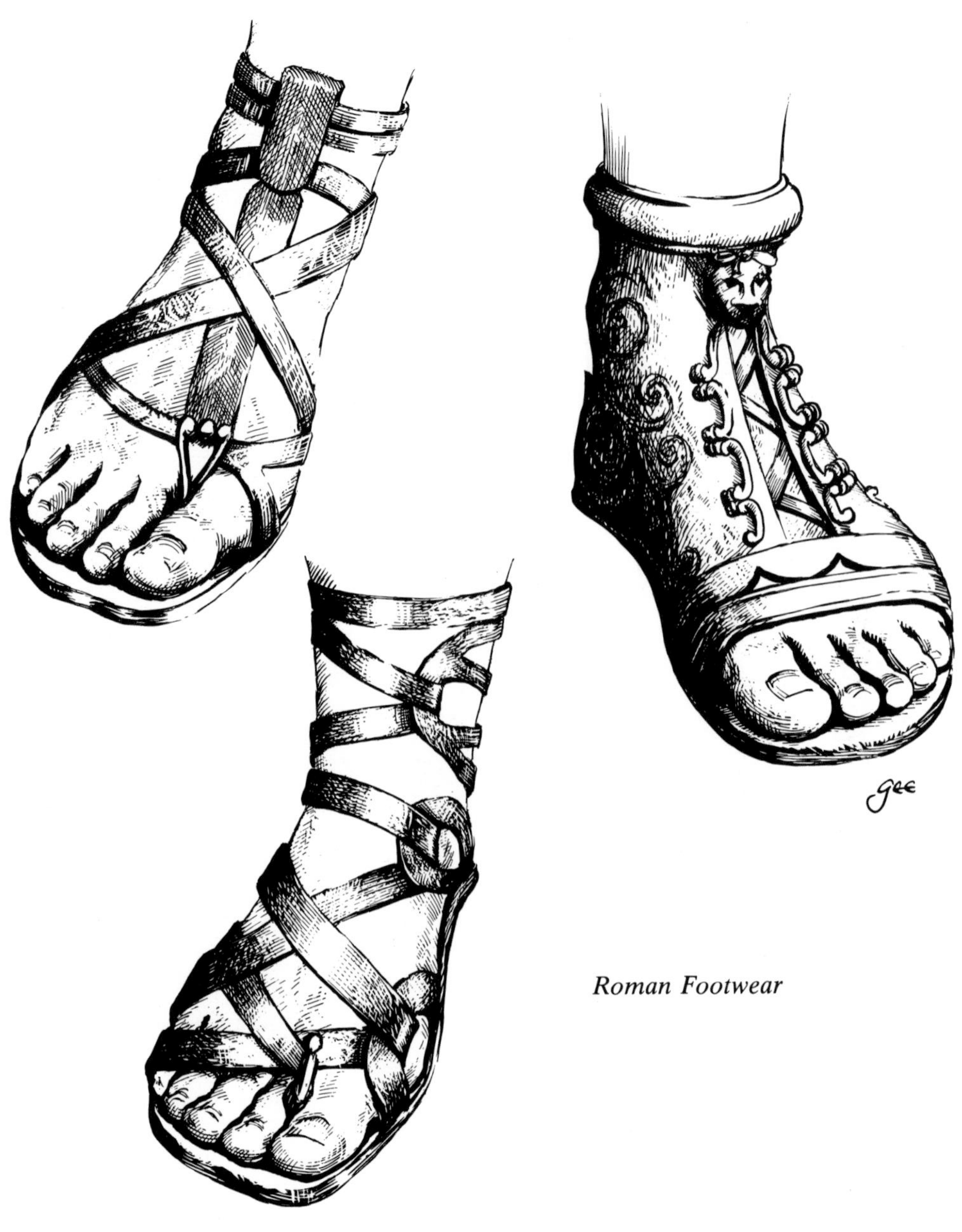

*Roman Footwear*

William Hutton, in the year 1801, at the age of 78 travelled the whole length of the Roman Wall and wrote an account of his journey. Here is his amusing description of the Twice Brewed:—

> "As the evening was approaching, and nature called loudly for support and rest, neither of which could be found among the rocks; I was obliged to retreat into the military road, to the only public house, at three miles distance, known by no other name than that of Twice Brewed.

'Can you favour me with a bed?'
'I cannot tell till the company comes.'
'What, is it club-night?'
'Yes, a club of carriers.'

A pudding was then turned out, about as big as a peck measure; and a piece of beef out of the copper, perhaps equal to half a calf.

Having supped, fifteen carriers approached, each with a one-horse cart, and sat down to the pudding and beef, which I soon perceived were not too large. I was the only one admitted; and watched them with attention, being highly diverted. Every piece went down as if there was no barricade in the throat. One of those pieces was more than I have seen eaten at a meal by a moderate person. They convinced me that eating was the 'chief end of man'. The tankard too, like a bowl ladling water out of a well, was often emptied, often filled."

*Castle Nick Milecastle* *Lithograph by J. T. Kell*

Examination of the south gateway shows that in the Severan reconstruction it was reduced to a postern. Both gateways were built of small masonry perhaps because it was difficult to transport large blocks to such a difficult site. The Military Way can be seen here very clearly, in some cases both kerbstones are visible. The terra-cotta lamp here reproduced was found in the Milecastle.

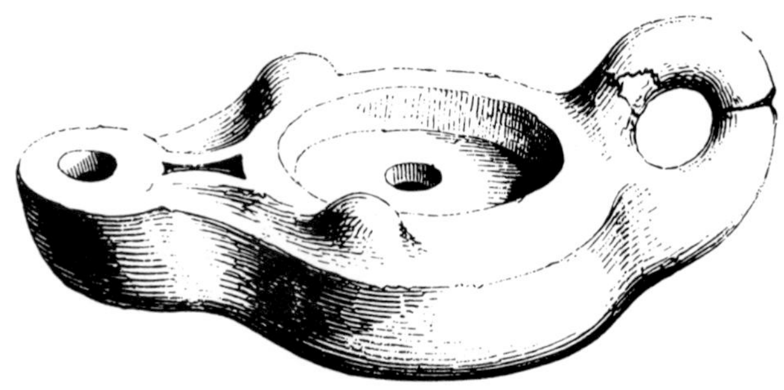

*Terra-cotta Lamp, 4 inches in length, discovered in the Milecastle, Castle Nick*

Beyond Castle Nick Milecastle a minor depression in the basaltic ridge is called *Cat's Stairs.*

*Cats' Stairs, from the North*

On Peel Crag the Wall is in fine condition, the Narrow Wall on narrow foundations. Turret 39a was excavated in 1911. It had been demolished in the second period of Wall building and the recess in the Wall was built up. At Peel Gap the Wall ditch reappears and continues as far as Whinshields Milecastle. Here on both sides of the gap the Wall bends sharply to the south forming a re-entrant. Nearby once stood the farm house of Steel-rig. The minor road passing through the gap leads to Kielder and by a mere track into Scotland. To the south it leads to the Once Brewed Youth Hostel with the modern Twice Brewed Inn a little to the west. However, before the building of the Newcastle to Carlisle Railway, the inn was at the farm of East Twice Brewed, a few hundred yards to the east on the Military Road. (See our book *Tynedale* for Hutton's adventures here).

From turret 39a to Milecastle 40 the Wall is very narrow, at some points only 5½ feet. The reason can only be conjectured. The Wall is now no longer on the basaltic crags but runs along a sandstone ridge. After turret 39b (excavated in 1911) we come to Milecastle 40 (Winshields). Winshields is the highest point on

*The Wall on Winshields*

Ronald Embleton

the Wall (1,230 feet above sea level) with an extensive prospect in every direction. The distances between Milecastle 39, 40 and 41 are unusually long (over an English mile). Perhaps the natural strength of the Wall did not need a very large garrison. South of the Wall near turret 40a is a sheltered spot called *Green Slack* where MacLaughlan saw foundations of British hut-circles. A little further at the deep valley of *Lodham Slack* he saw traces of a British camp. Nothing can be seen of these British remains today. No traces of turret 40b (Melkridge) are visible. A gentle descent brings us to the short-axis Milecastle 41 (Shield on the Wall). Shortly afterwards we come to a bold gap called *Bogle Hole* which popular tradition says was the abode of evil spirits. The next defile is Caw Gap. Here the Wall has the usual re-entrant for a weak spot. A road passes through the gap, north and south. "Northwards is a solitatary house, called Burn Deviot (now gone), which was once the resort of smugglers and sheep stealers. Lights, as the shepherds believe, are still to be seen at night flickering about the windows, the spirits of those who have been murdered in it." (Bruce). For some distance after Caw Gap the Wall has been uprooted. Turret 41a (excavated 1967) was dismantled and the Wall built across its recess in the second stage of the Wall. In front the ditch reappears for a short distance. To the south are two standing stones known as the *Mare and Foal* just north of the Stanegate.

One more is marked on Armstrong's *Map of Northumberland;* the three probably formed part of a neolithic stone circle. After Bloody Gap and Thorney Doors was turret 41b (discovered in 1912) of which no definite signs remain today. Crossing Cawfield Crags we come to Hole Gap on the east side of which is Milecastle 42 (Cawfields).

*Milecastle near Caw-Fields.* *Old print from a painting by H. B. Richardson*

This milecastle stands about a mile east of Greatchesters Fort. It is well preserved with the walls standing seven or eight courses. Internally it measures 63 feet from east to west, and 49 feet from north to south with walls 8 feet thick. Both gates are of massive masonry. The pivot holes and bolt holes can still be seen in the south gateway. It was built by the Second Legion. The milecastle is built in broad gauge although the Wall itself is narrow gauge.

When he excavated the milecastle in 1848 Clayton discovered two inscribed stones. One of them, a mere fragment, is a repetition of those found at Milecastles 37 and 38. The other was a monumental slab cut down to serve as a hearth-stone. It read as follows: D.M. DAGV.ALDA MI(LES) PAN(NONIAE) VIXIT AN(NOS) PUSINNA (CONIV)X TITVL(VM) (POSUIT), which informs us that his wife Pusinna erected this tombstone in memory of her husband called Dagvalda who belonged to the Cohort of Pannonians. We reproduce one of these stones.

Size, 2 feet in diameter

D. M.
DAGVALDS(VS) MI(LES)
PAN(NONIAE) VIXIT AN(NOS)
PVSINNA
CONIV)X TITVL(VM) (POSUIT)

To the divine Manes.
Dagualdus a soldier
of Pannonia lived years —
Pusinna
his wife placed this memorial.

South of Cawfields Milecastle on the Roman Military Way three milestones have been found. The one of Severus Alexander (A.D. 222-226) is here reproduced, the second was of Numerian (A.D. 283-284). Both are now in the Chesters Museum. The third, uninscribed, is still in situ.

This milestone belongs to a series along the Military Way. The nearest junction to which the 18 Roman miles refers seems to be Portgate, 20 Roman miles to the East.

Because of the shape not all the lettering on the milestone can be shown. Here is the full text and translation:

*Imp(eratori) Caes(ari) M(arco) Aurel(io) / Seuer(o) Alexandro / Pi(o) Fel(ici) Aug(usto) p(ontifici) m(aximo) tr(ibuniciae) p(otestatis) II / co(n)s(uli) p(atri) p(atriae) cur(ante) Cl(audio) Xenephon/te leg(ato) Aug(usti) pr(o) pr/aet(ore) m(ilia) p(assuum) XVIII.*

'For the Emperor Caesar Marcus Aurelius Severus Alexander Pius Felix Augustus, pontifex maximus, in his second year of tribunician power, consul, father of his country, under the charge of Claudius Xenephon, emperor's propraetorian legate, 18 miles'.

A few yards south of the Vallum, near to a spring, an altar to Apollo dedicated by a soldier from Upper Germany was found. It is here reproduced. Turret 42a has been destroyed by quarrying and 42b stood just south of a large temporary Roman camp at the point where the Wall turns westwards for Greatchesters. But, before these two turrets we should look at the series of fortlets in the valley of the Haltwhistle Burn.

## HALTWHISTLE BURN FORT

This Roman fortlet was thoroughly excavated in 1908. It stands in a strong position covering an area of ¾ acres and measuring 210 by 170 feet. The rampart is faced with stone and there are stone buildings inside. The two gateways on the east and south have single portals. The postern on the west was later blocked. The fort is surrounded by deep ditches. The stone buildings inside were only suitable for a small garrison. Perhaps the fort was mainly for administration purposes. The two buildings in the north of the fort are barracks. The large buttressed building in the south is a granary. The other two buildings were probably offices.

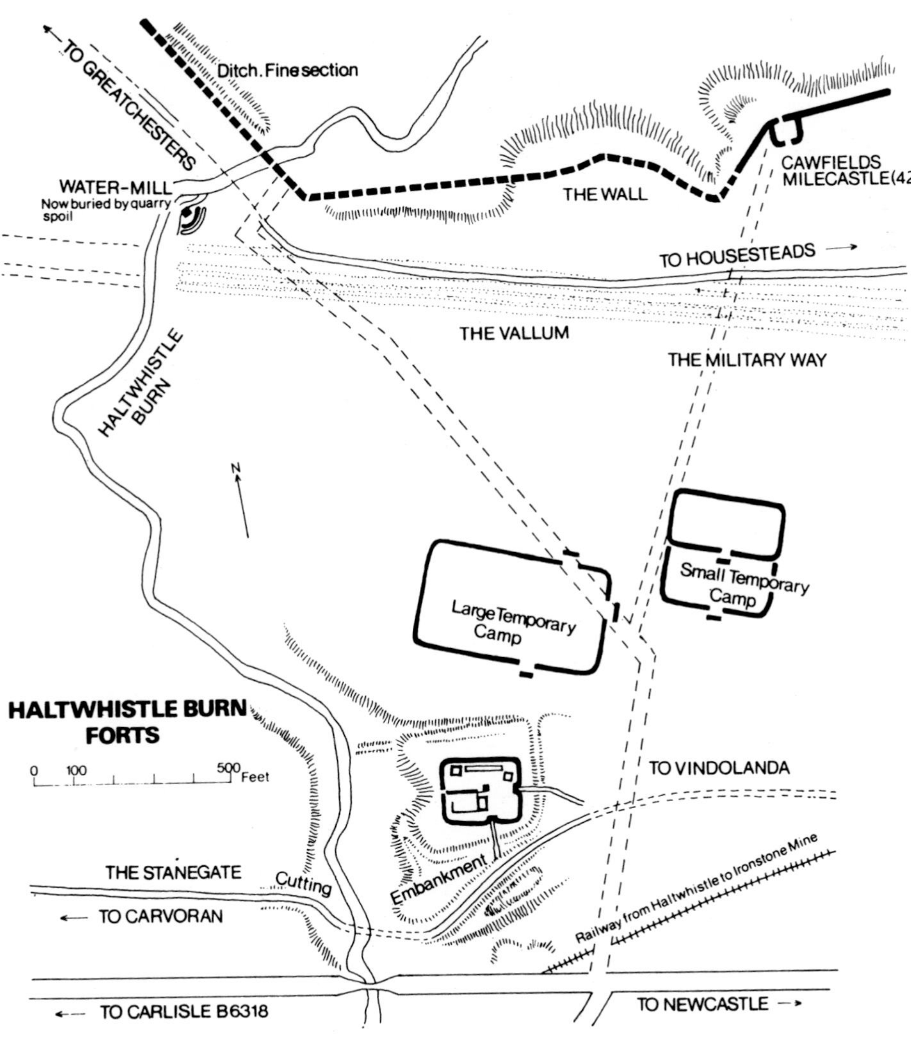


*Opposite. Roman officers hunting the Wild Boar*

The fort was built in the early days of Hadrian and was probably an addition to the series of Stanegate forts already built. It was later carefully demolished, probably at the time when the forts were moved forward to the line of the Wall.

Near the fort are a remarkable group of temporary camps. Two are shown on our plan. There is one 500 yards west and two to the north of the Wall. Four lie on the line of the Stanegate about two miles to the west and a very large one at Fell End. A medium sized camp lies south of the main road. All can be seen on the Ordnance Survey Map of Hadrian's Wall. They were probably used by the soldiers building the Wall.

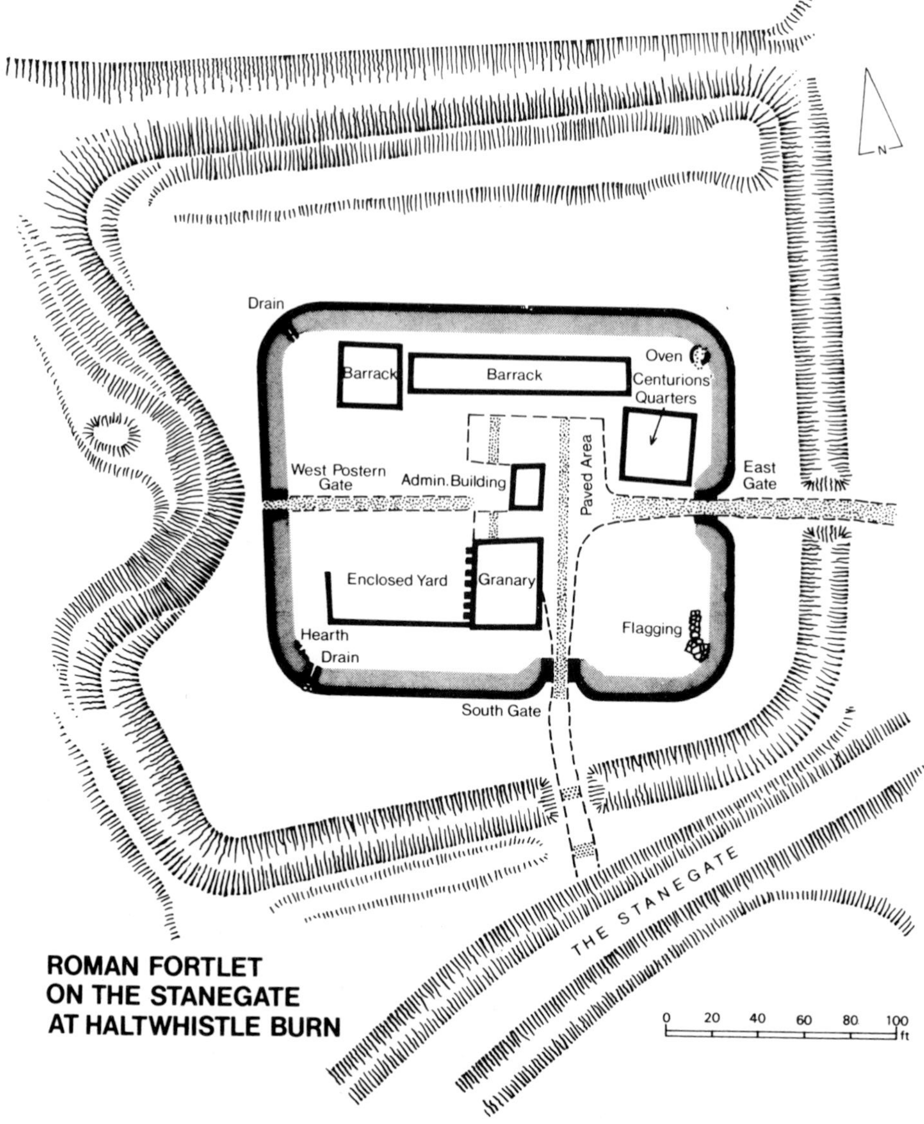


The Roman water-mill shown on our plans has been destroyed by the spoil from Cawfields Quarry. Its large millstones can be seen in Chesters Museum.

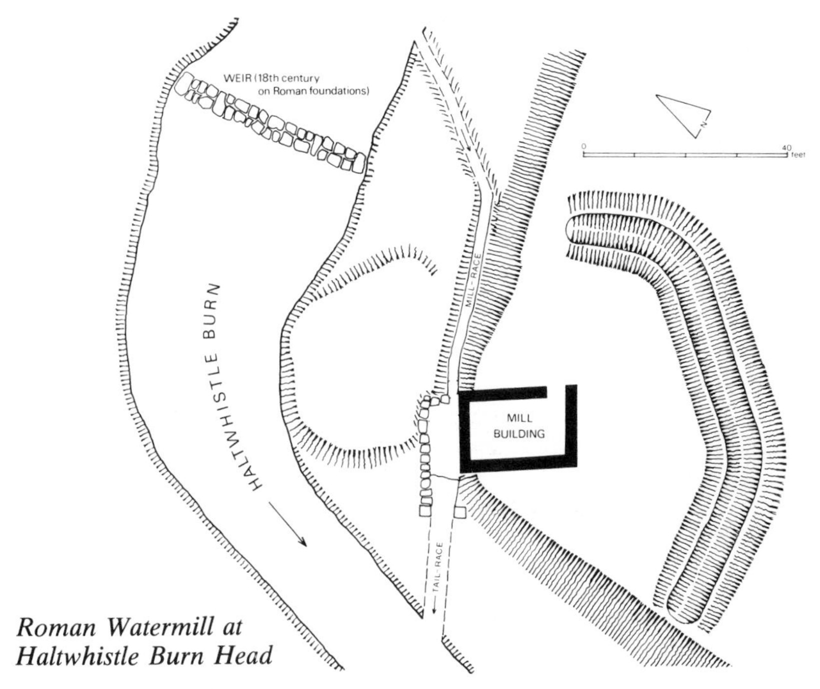


*Roman Watermill at Haltwhistle Burn Head*

*Roman Water Mill*

Greatchesters Fort

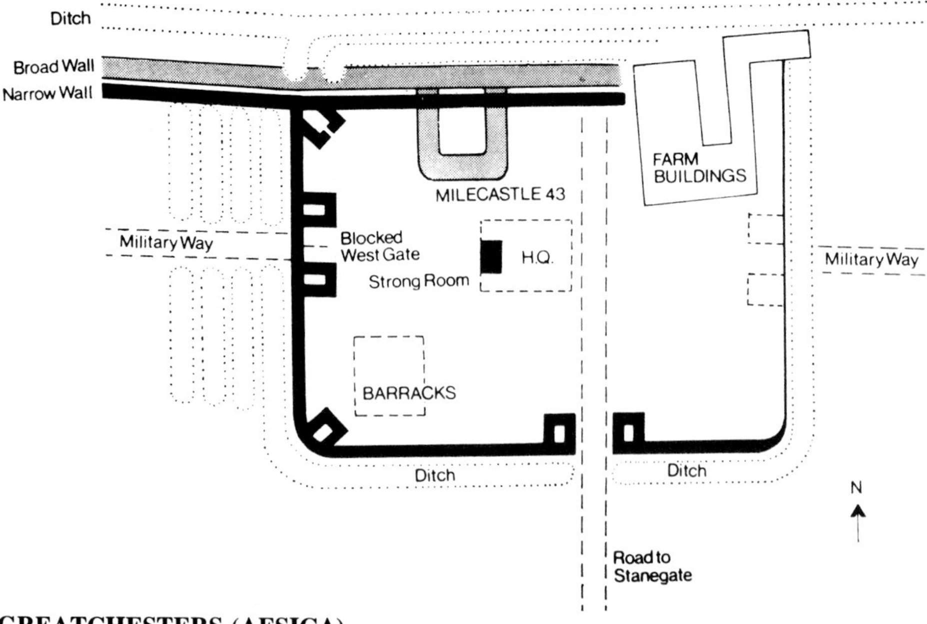


## GREATCHESTERS (AESICA)

The fort of Greatchesters is six miles west of Housesteads. The first printed account was by Robert Smith, in 1708, who wrote:

*At a place called the Chesters, two miles East of Caer-Vorran, are the Ruins of another square City, much about the compass of the above-mentioned Caer-Vorran where are likewise abundance of old House-steads, and tracks of houses, to be descerned, as there are likewise on the South side Vallum of it.*

The fort lies south of the Wall and is small of only three acres. Its purpose was to guard the Caw Gap (the Caw Burn being the name given to Haltwhistle Burn at this point). It is approached by the farm road which leaves the Newcastle - Carlisle road just west of Haltwhistle Burn. The fort is completely behind the Wall and longer from east to west. Farm buildings occupy the east corner of the fort but the farmhouse is outside. The second century garrisons were successively the Sixth Cohort of Nervians and the Sixth Cohort of Raetians. The third century garrison was the Second Cohort of Astures with a detachment of *Raeti Gaesati.*

> *MARIDI*

*Centuria Maridii*

*Size, 1 foot 3 ½ inches by 3 ¾ inches*

*Building stone found east of Aesica*

The *vexillatio gaesatorum Raetorum* was of Swiss Celtic origin. "These vexillations or detachments from regular auxiliary units were generally small bodies of men used to reinforce existing garrisons or were based at forts and spent the greater part of their service patrolling the country beyond the frontier.

"One may picture these troops wearing their native tunics, trousers and boots, generally bareheaded or wearing simple caps and carrying shields, spears or javelins and perhaps a knife or sword. The detachment described as *gaesatorum Raetorum* were armed with the large Celtic javelin called a *gaesum,* a broad, barbed weapon with a slender neck and long socker". Rusell Robinson.

In 1724 a visitor reported the fort-wall as still standing to a height of nearly 13 feet. All the west wall can still be traced, including the gateway. Originally a double portal is was altered several times, narrowed and finally closed. The south wall and ditch are almost complete. The west tower of the south gate provided a hoard of jewellery including the famous *Aesica Fibula.* It is a Celtic-Romano gilt bronze brooch of the late second century. It has been described: "Of its kind it is probably the most fantastically beautiful creation that has come down to us from antiquity".

The Aesica Hoard, found in 1894, comprised two brooches, three finger-rings, a necklace and a bracelet.

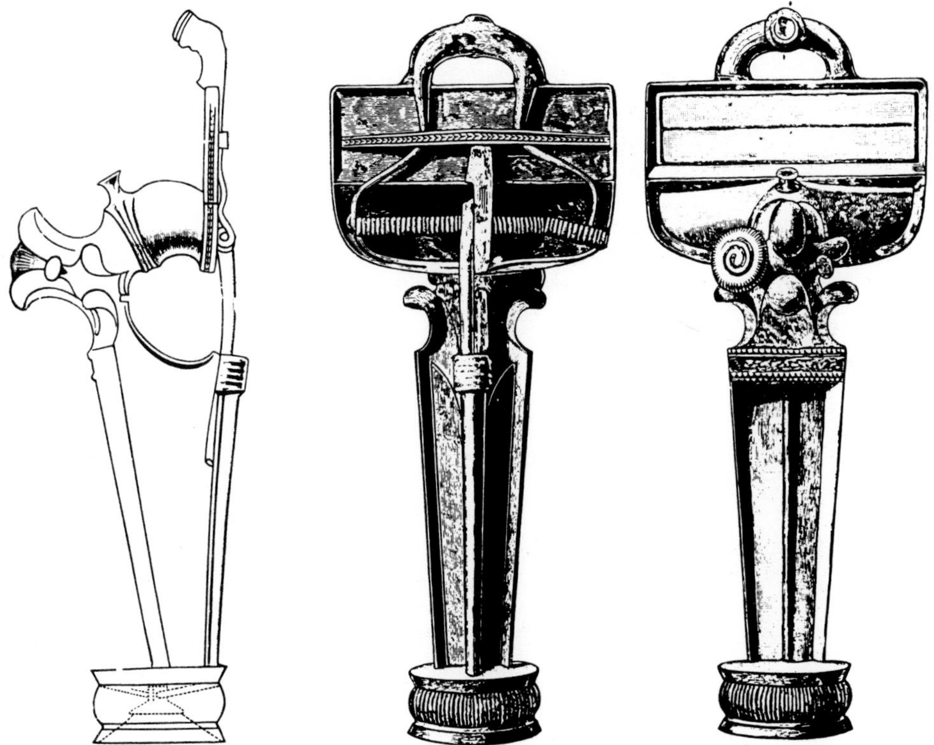

*Side, back and front views of Silver Brooch from Great Chesters*

The owner was probably one of the garrison and the hoard may have been buried in 296 A.D. when Allectus gathered troops to oppose Constantius Chlorus.

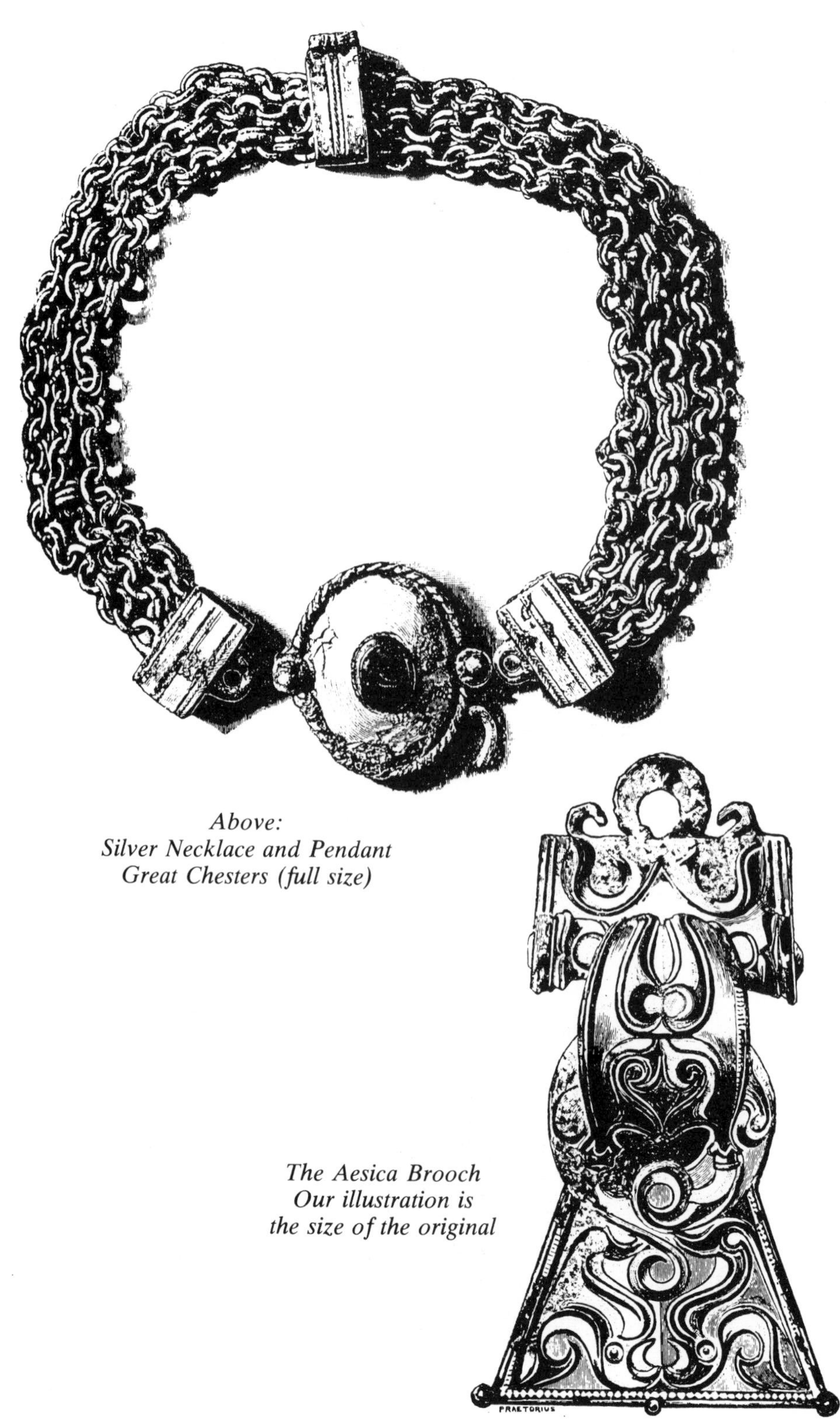


*Above:*
*Silver Necklace and Pendant*
*Great Chesters (full size)*

*The Aesica Brooch*
*Our illustration is*
*the size of the original*

The north west angle of the fort is of great interest. Here the north wall broad foundation can be traced and on it was Milecastle 43 with its gateway through the Wall. This was all planned before the fort was built. Then a decision was taken to bring the fort on to the line of the Wall. First four ditches were built on the west side. When the time came to complete the Wall, which was to be narrow, it couldn't be built on the broad wall foundations because the milecastle obstructed this work. So the narrow wall was built a little south of the broad wall foundations slightly covering the north side of the four ditches. The milecastle would then be demolished later.

The headquarters building was excavated in 1893 and its vaulted underground strong room can still be seen. A barrack block was also uncovered. The east gateway — the main entrance to the fort — cannot now be traced, neither can the east wall. A building inscription of Hadrian was found at this gateway.

Size, 3 feet 7½ inches by 2 feet 8 inches

IMP CAES TRAI(A)N HADRIA
NO AVG P P

Imperatori Caesari Trajano Hadriano Augusto patri patriae

The lettering is placed at the bottom so that it can be easily read when placed high up on the gate.

*Vaulted underground room*

Little is known of the internal buildings. A granary to the north of the Headquarters provided the following fine inscription which records its rebuilding under Severus Alexander in 225 A.D.

IMP. CAES. M. AVR. SEVE
RVS ALEXANDER PI(VS) F(ELIX)
AVG. HORREVM VETV-
STATE CONLABSVM M(ILITES)
COH. II. ASTVRVM S(EVERIANAE)
A(LEXANDRIANAE)[1]
A SOLO RESTITVERVNT

The Emperor Caesar Marcus Aurelius
Severus Alexander pious happy[2]
august. This granary through age
dilapidated the soldiers of the
second cohort of Asturians styled the
Severian Alexandrian
from the ground restored

Size, 4 feet 1 inch by 3 feet 4 inches.

*Inscription found in 1767 at Aesica*

The Military Way entered the fort by the east gate and left by the west. A branch road from the Stanegate (now the farm road) comes in by the south gate.

The *vicus* lay to the south and east of the fort and 100 yards south of the fort and east of the farm road was the bath house.

Size, 2 feet by 8 inches

VIC·TO·RI·AE · AVG COH · VI
NERVI·O·RVM · CVI PRAEEST · G ·
IVL · BAR·BA·RVS PRAE·FEC · V · S · L · M

Victoriae Augustae cohors sexta
Nerviorum cui praeest Gaius
Julius Babarus praefectus votum solvit libens merito

Statue-base.
Excavated at
Walltown Mill
Gaius Julius Barbarus
commanded the Sixth Cohort of
the Nervians at Aesica some
time in the second century

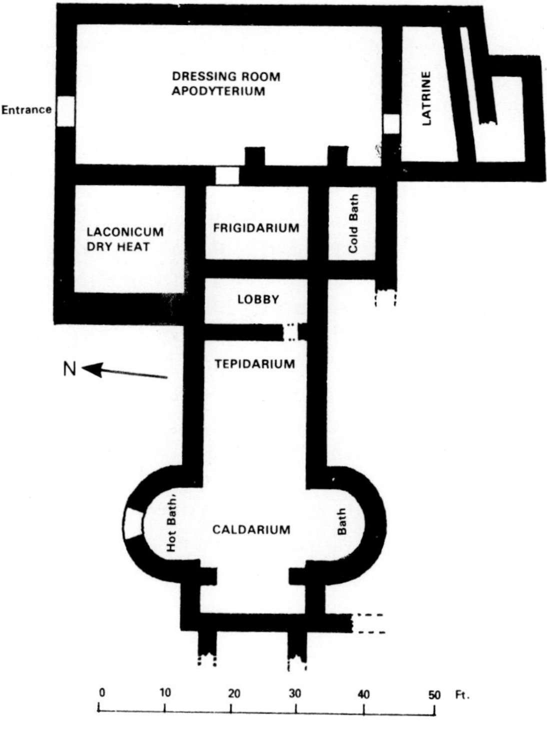


*Bath-house at Aesica*

Several civilian tombstones have been found in the *vicus*. We reproduce two of them. The first is to a girl called Pervica by her parents. The second is to Aurelia Caula who lived 15 years and 4 months and was erected by her sister.

Size, 5 feet 4 inches
by 2 feet 4 inches

The tombstone to Pervica reads:— "The spirits of the departed (and) his daughter Pervica". In view of the girl's name this unknown soldier was probably of Celtic origin. The SALVTE in the 19th century rendering here shown is incorrect. The first line should be DIS M.

There was one inscription at Greatchesters (now lost) which is of great importance. It is the tombstone of Aelius Mercurialis *(D. M. Ael. Merculiari cornicul. Vacia soror fecit).* He was a *cornicularius* (adjutant) probably of the second cohort of Asturians and the monument was set up by his sister. This is the only evidence found on the Wall of the system of local recruiting which was common in the third century. Their home would be in the *vicus* nearby. Probably their father had settled here after his discharge from the army and his son had followed in his footsteps. The *cornicularius* was a clerk or secretary and Mercurialis is the only one recorded on the Wall.

*Sculpture from Housesteads of an auxiliary soldier*

This is a valuable sculpture since it exhibits to us the accoutrements of a soldier belonging to an auxiliary cohort. His head dress is difficult to define. It has been described as a "galea with a plume of feathers", or a "mural crown". The lower part of his tunic is defended by scale armour.

Dr. John Lingard (1771-1851) writing in 1807 was the first to notice the remarkable aqueduct to be found here. He mentioned that the "water for the station was brought by a winding aqueduct still visible from the head of Haltwhistle Burn. It winds five miles". The aqueduct is actually six miles long but because it was necessary to wind in order to keep the water flow the direct line is just a little over two miles. Only one bridge was necessary and although it has now gone its site is called *Banks Bridge* today. The aqueduct is marked on the Ordnance Survey. Aqueducts are recorded in inscriptions from Chesters, South Shields and Chester-le-Street, and aqueduct channels have been identified at Lanchester and Bowes.

A short distance to the west of Greatchesters is a fine stretch of the Wall on Cockmount Hill.

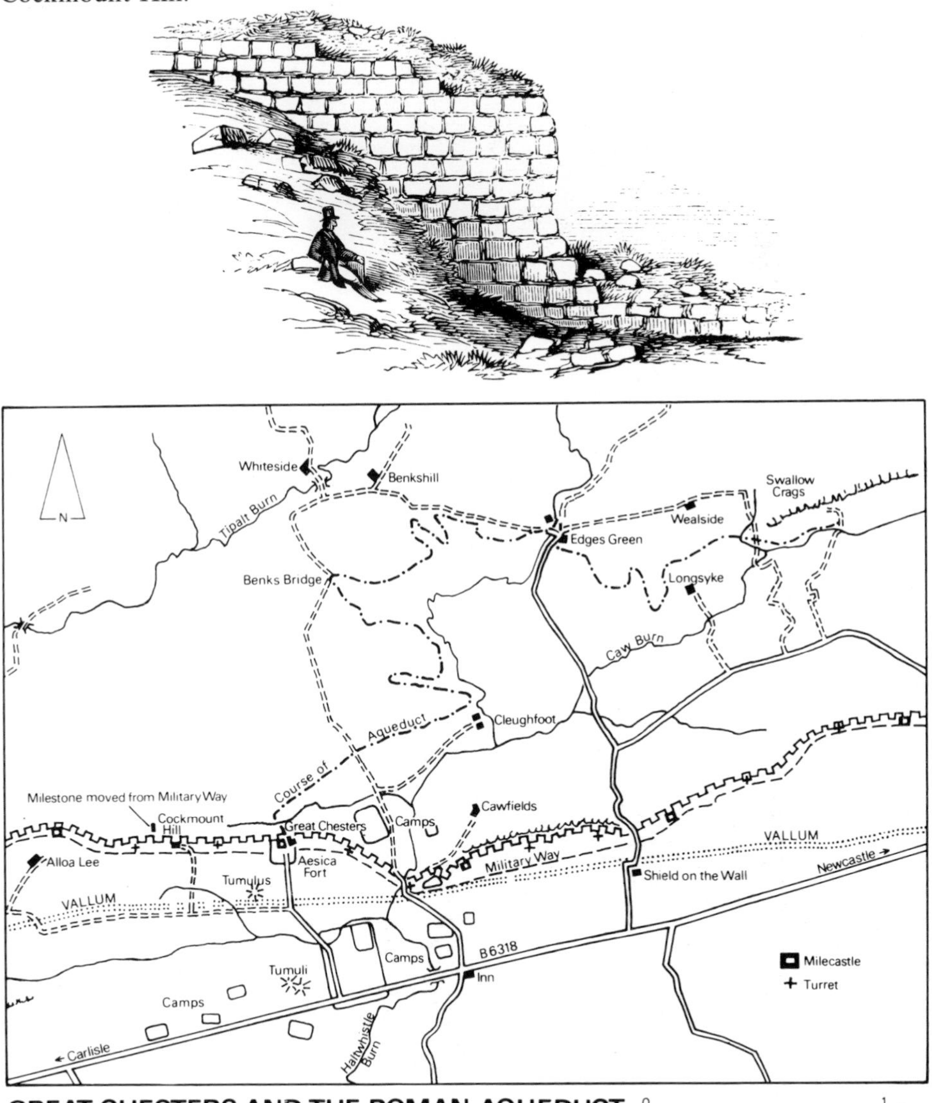


*Plan of Aqueduct.*

*Cockmount Hill.* *Lithograph from Bruce's Roman Wall, 1867.*

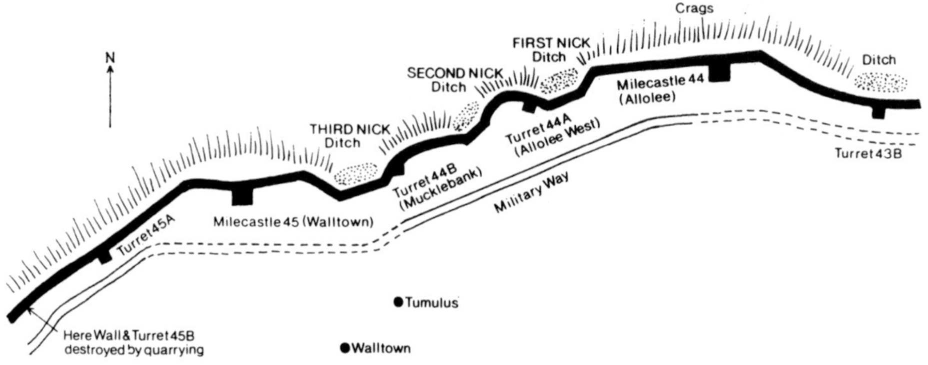


*The Roman Wall on the Nicks of Thirlwall*

## GREATCHESTERS TO CARVORAN

Between Greatchesters and Carvoran large sections of the Roman Wall can be seen, with its ditch where needed. There are also considerable stretches of the Vallum. Near Greatchesters one section is of great interest. There are ten complete crossings in succession with causeways across the ditch and gaps in both the north and south mounds. The causeways were built several years after the ditch was originally dug. This was proved from an examination of the vegetable matter in the ditch during the 1939 excavations.

Shortly after leaving Aesica the Wall slowly ascends the crags. It is the Narrow Wall, but runs behind the broad foundation, parallel with it for almost a mile. Perhaps at this point the engineers responsible considered the broad foundation as too shallow and built a new one for the Narrow Wall. Over this same stretch the Military Way is very clear. The long-axis Milecastle 44 (Allolee) can now only be traced by its earthworks. Beyond come several gaps in the crops called the Nine Nicks of Thirlwall.

*The Nine Nicks of Thirlwall*

*A Roman Surveyor*

Road building was part of the work of the Roman army, and the legions, with their skilled staff, must have been responsible for the earliest Roman roads in Britain. The routes were worked out by experienced surveyors — *agrimensores* or *gromatici* (so called from their surveying instrument the *groma* as shown above).

The Roman roads in the north form a complete network and, although they carried some civilian traffic, they were essentially military. They were a remarkable achievement and, even though local material was normally used, they show how hard working Roman soldiers were.

They were usually built in a straight line and only made detours to avoid difficult geographical features.

*Hunting Hares (based on a Roman mosaic)*

*Roman Boxer*

At the first three nicks the ditch reappears for a while, the section at Walltown being fairly long. Behind the Wall here is a spring surrounded by masonry called "King Arthur's Well". Tradition, quite erroneously, says that here Paulinus baptized King Egbert. Here among the rocks can be seen patches of chives said to have been planted by the Romans. Camden tells us: "There continueth a settled persuasion among a great part of the people thereabout, and the same received by tradition, that the Roman soldiers of the marches did plant everywhere in old time for their use certaine medicinable hearbs, for as to cure wounds; whence is it that some empirick practitioners of chirurgery in Scotland, flock hither every year in the beginning of summer, to gather such simples and wound-herbes; the vertue whereof they highly commend as found by long experience, and to be of singular efficacy".

The farmhouse of Walltown lies a short distance to the south. The village vanished long ago.

The tower here in 1542 belonged to John Ridley, the brother of the martyr, but only mounds in the field denote its site. The present farmhouse was built with stones from the tower. Hodgson said he saw in an old part of the house a lintel with the initials T.M.A. and the date 1713.

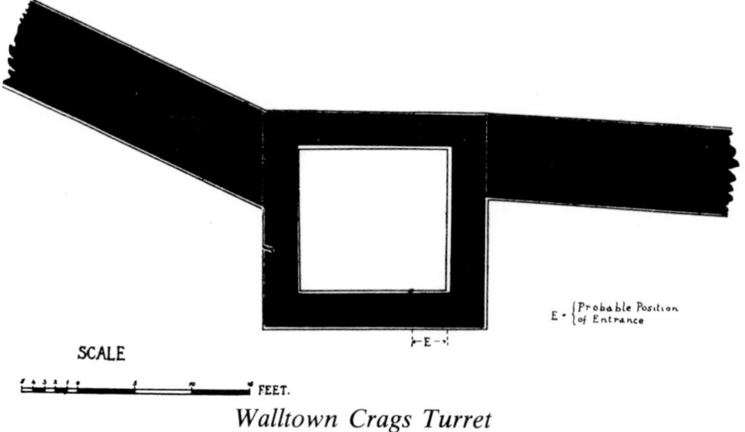


*Walltown Crags Turret*

East of Walltown a British camp stands on a small hill. The long-axis Milecastle 45 has been robbed of its stone but can be traced. It commands an extensive view. Turret 45a is 18 feet square and has a peculiar alignment with the Wall as the plan shows. This turret was standing before the Wall and it has been suggested it was used as a signalling tower for the Stanegate fort system. However, excavations carried out in 1959 showed it to have been built along with the Wall although a little earlier. Perhaps it was built early as an observation post, while the Wall was under construction. Turret 45b has disappeared into the huge Greenhead Quarry.

*Opposite. The Roman Wall near Carvoran*

Before its destruction in 1883, an engraving by C. J. Spence, here reproduced, was published, reminding us of the magnificent section of the Wall which was so wantonly destroyed.

West of the quarry the line of the Wall is visible but its stones have gone. The Vallum makes a detour here to avoid Carvoran which unlike the Wall forts lies to the south of it.

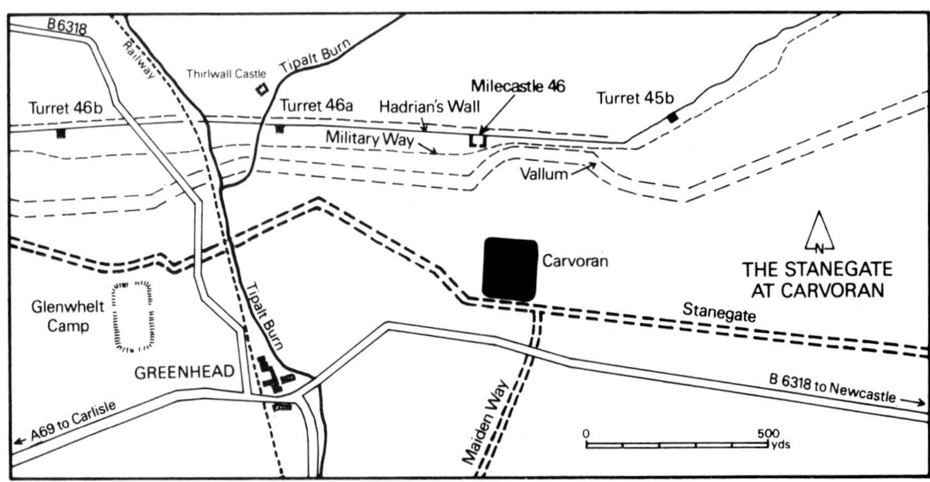


*Map of the Stanegate at Carvoran*

## CARVORAN

Carvoran was situated on the Stanegate at its junction with the Maiden Way from the south. It is the MAGNA of the *Notitia* where the Second Cohort of the Dalmatians was stationed. The tombstone illustrated below confirms this.

DEO SANC
VETERI
IVL PASTOR
IMAG C(O) H II
DELMA V S L M

Deo sancto
Veteri
Julius Pastor
imaginifer cohortis secundae
Delmatarum votum solvit libens merito

Size, 1 foot 2 inches by 9 inches

In Hadrian's time the garrison was the First Cohort of Hamian archers who came from Syria. Their commander Flavius Secundus set up an altar to Lucius Aelius Caesar, the adopted son of Hadrian who became Caesar in A.D. 136 and died during the life of the Emperor in A.D. 138.

FORTVNAE AVG(VSTAE)
PRO SALVTE L(VCII) AELI(I)
CAESARIS EX VISV
T(ITVS) FLA(VIVS) SECVNDVS
PRAEF. COH(ORTIS) I. HAM
IORVM SAGITTAR(IORVM)
V. S. L. M.

To Fortune the august,
for the safety of Lucius Aelius
Caesar, according to a vision,
Titus Flavius Secundus,
prefect of the first cohort of Hamian archers,
erected this altar in discharge of a vow, &c.

The same garrison, under Calpurnius Agricola, set up an altar in A.D. 162, their commander being the prefect Licinius Clemens.

*Roman soldier learning fencing from a veteran*

*Opposite. Preparing for a temporary camp*

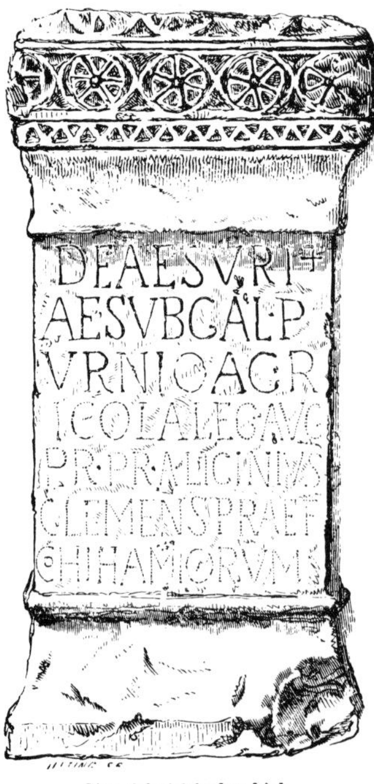

Size, 2 feet 9 inches high.

DEAE SVRI
AE SVB CALP
VRNIO AGR
ICOLA LEG AVG
PR PR A LICINIVS
CLEMENS PRAEF
COH I HAMIORVM

Deae Syri-
ae sub Calp-
urnio Agr-
icola legato Augustii
propraetore Aulus Licinius
Clemens praefectus
Cohortis primae Hamiorum
Size, 2 feet 9 inches high

Finally an inscription to the Emperor Constantine shows the fort was occupied in the first half of the 4th century.

IMP(ERATORI) CAES(ARI)
FLAV(IO) VAL(ERIO)
CONSTANTINO
PIO NOB(ILISSIMO)
CAESARI

To the Emperor Caesar
Flavius Valerius
Constantinus
the pious and most noble
Caesar

The fort stands to the south both of the Vallum and Wall, having probably been erected before them to command the valley of the Tipalt and guard the road junction although no remains of a pre-Hadrianic fort have been discovered. The fort measures 440 by 360 feet containing an area of three and a half acres. The north-west angle-tower is visible but little is known of the internal buildings which have not yet been excavated.

All the antiquarian writers from Camden onwards describe the remains of Carvoran as considerable. Robert Smith in 1708 wrote:

*Caer-Vorran above-mentioned has been a square Roman city, with a deep Vallum or Trench round it, one hundred and twenty yards one way, and one hundred and sixty or one hundred and seventy the other. Great Ruins of old Houseteeds are very visible, with the tracks of streets; and without the South side Trench, are likewise several long streets, and foundations of houses.*

The following is Stukeley's description:

*"A little upon the south side of the Wall was a great Roman city and Castle. We traversed the stately ruins: it stood upon a piece of high ground, about four hundred feet square; had a wall and ditch; vestiges of houses and buildings all over, within and without. We observed the Madan-Way coming over the fells from the south, where it passes by a work or labyrinth, called Julian's bower. We saw too the Roman road passing eastward along the Wall. The country hereabouts is a wild moory bog; and the Wall itself climbs all along the crag, and is set upon the southern edge of it; the steepness of the cliff northwards performing the part of a foss." Iter Boreale.*

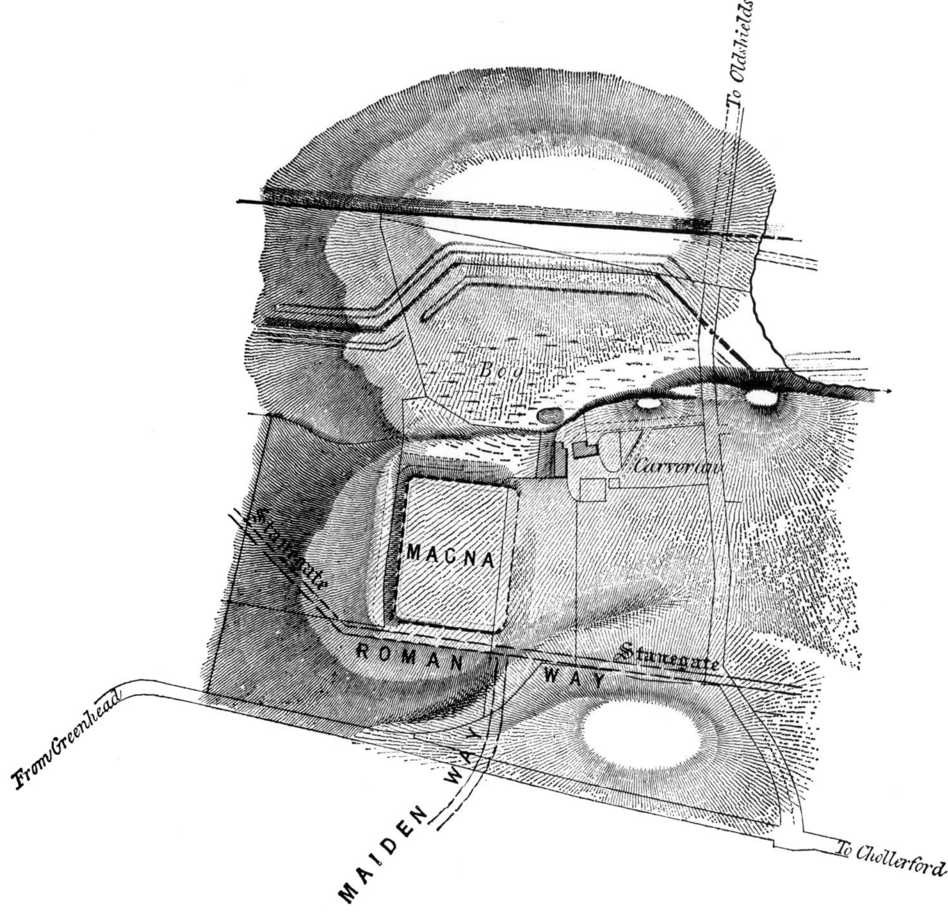


There have been casual discoveries made in the civilian settlement, the cemetery and the bath house. The most remarkable inscription is the metrical dedication to the Virgin of the Zodiac, a Syrian goddess.

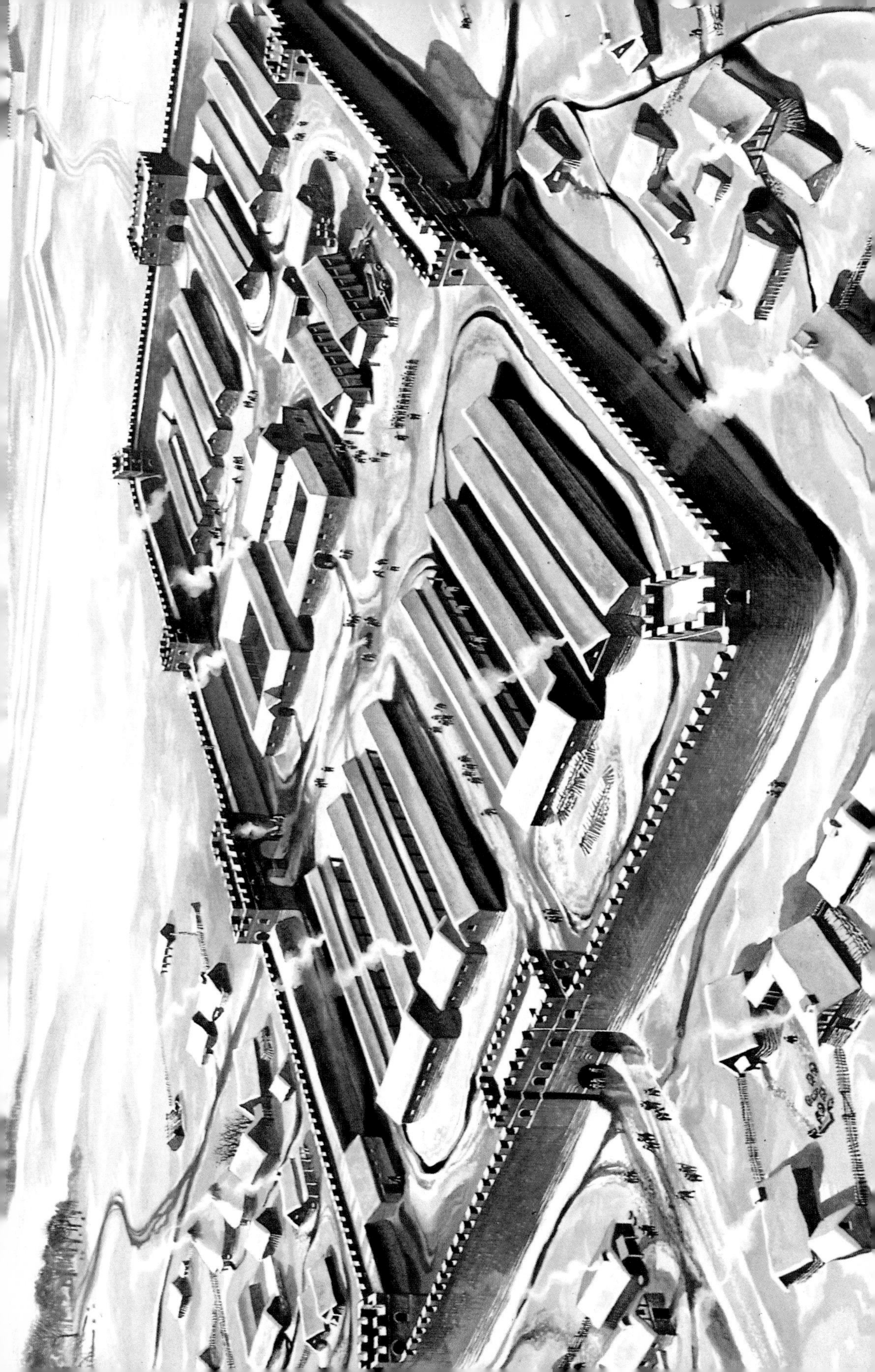

Size, 3 ft. 4 in. by 2 ft. 2 in.

IMMINET · LEONI · VIRGO · CAELES
TI · SITV · SPICIFERA · IVSTI · IN
VENTRIX · VRBIVM · CONDITRIX ·
EX QVIS MVNERIBVS · NOSSE CON
TIGIT DEOS ERGO EADEM MATER DIVVM
PAX · VIRTVS · CERES DEA SYRIA
LANCE VITAM ET IVRA PENSITANS
IN CAELO VISVM SYRIA SIDVS EDI
DIT LIBYAE COLENDVM INDE
CVNCTI DIDICIMVS
ITA INTELLEXIT NVMINE INDVCTVS
TVO MARCVS CAECILIVS DO
NATIANVS · MILITANS TRIBVNVS
IN PRAEFECTO DONO PRINCIPIS

*Metrical Dedication to the Virgin of the Zodiac.*

This well-preserved memorial in translation reads:—

*The Virgin in her heavenly place rides upon the Lion; bearer of corn, inventor of law, founder of cities; by whose gifts it comes that we know the gods, and therefore she is the Divine Mother, Peace, Virtue Ceres, the Syrian Goddess, weighing life and laws in her balance. Syria has sent the constellation which we see in the heavens to Libya to be worshipped; thence have we all learned. Thus has understood, led by thy godhead, Marcus Caecilius Donatianus, serving as tribune in the office of prefect by the Emperor's gift.*

The poem is in honour of Julia Domna the Syrian wife of the Emperor Septimus Severus. Probably the inscription was associated with a statue showing Julia Domna with a wreath of ears of corn, riding on a lion and holding a balance. The Mother Goddess was worshipped in the south and east of the Empire under various names - Ceres, Venus, Cybele etc.

But the most important discovery was made in 1915. A postman, delivering to the neighbouring farmhouse, noticed what appeared to be an old bucket sticking out of the ground. On picking it up he found it was a Roman dry-measure, or *modius*, of bronze in perfect condition. This remarkable object is now one of the treasures of the Chesters Museum. It bears an inscription in perfect lettering saying that it holds seventeen and a half *sextarii* (16.8 pints) and names the Emperor Domitian in whose reign it was made; his name has been officially erased following his condemnation by the Senate. The measure really holds twenty pints and it has been suggested this was a means of cheating the natives who were compelled to deliver a certain tribute of corn. However, a gauge lower than the rim may be missing since there are rivet holes which might hold it.

*Opposite. Carvoran Fort in winter*

Ronald Embleton

*Collecting tribute at Carvoran.*

## THE STANEGATE

Travelling between Newcastle (*Pons Aelius*) and Carlisle (*Luguvallium*) in the second or third centuries soldiers and government officials would have taken the Military Way which ran close behind the Wall north of the Vallum. However before the time of Hadrian lateral communications had to be along what we now call the Stanegate.

The Stanegate is the Roman road which ran from Corbridge to Carlisle. The name means *stone road,* a name given in the Middle Ages to distinguish it from the normal unpaved trackways. When the Romans advanced for the conquest of North Britain they drove roads north, on the west of the Pennines to Carlisle and on the east to Corbridge. As soon as Corbridge became the base for Agricola's advance into Scotland it became essential to link it with Carlisle across the Tyne-Solway gap.

After crossing the Tyne by a bridge Dere Street entered the base camp of Corstopitum and ran as far as the main east-west street. (Note that the present excavated area of Corstopitum is only a small part of the base). It joined the main east-west street about 100 yards west of the west granary. The Stanegate left the Roman base by this road. From the junction it ran 200 yards west towards the Cor burn. At the point where the stream was reached the crossing was rather difficult so the Stanegate turned south and crossed 100 yards downstream at a more convenient place. Remains of a bridge abutment have survived at the spot. On the west bank 80 yards south the Stanegate turned abruptly west for Carlisle. Here the Roman road provided the foundation for the later medieval road called the Carelgate (or Carlisle Road). From medieval Corbridge the Carelgate followed the north bank of the Tyne crossing the Cor burn by a ford. The Carelgate was replaced by two roads, Wade's Military Road (1751-2) and a new road south of the river between Corbridge and Hexham in 1752. The Carelgate had by then "become so ruinous that it was almost impossible for coaches, waggons, and other carriages, and dangerous for persons travelling on horseback".

Where it left the base of Corstopitum the Stanegate was 22 feet wide with covered stone gutters and a foundation of six inch cobbles and ten inches of gravel above. The width of Roman roads and their surfaces too, varied greatly, although 20-23 feet was normal for main roads. The materials used varied in accordance with availability. Gravel was the material preferred for surfacing.

East from Corbridge it has been conjectured the Stanegate may have run to Newcastle and Wallsend but it can only be traced a short distance beyond the main road through Corstopitum. The Roman fort discovered from aerial photography at Washingwells near Whickham (Co. Durham) and still undug may be connected with a Roman road between Corbridge and South Shields.

To the west the Stanegate can be traced for about a mile beneath the later Carelgate. After crossing the Cor burn traces of buildings have been uncovered along the road followed by a large cemetery in which is an important mausoleum, then came a military bathhouse belonging to a very early and large camp at the modern Red House. Beyond here the Stanegate cannot be traced for four miles till we reach a point on the west bank of the North Tyne near the village of Wall. Here just beyond Homer's Lane (which is the road from Warden to Walwick Grange) half a mile south of Walwick Grange near an old ruined wayside cross the Stanegate has been traced. Near this spot there must have been a Roman bridge to take the road across from Corbridge. The road runs west, skirting the northern slope of Warden Hill, to the village of Fourstones. But before reaching Fourstones a Roman road forks off to the right to Walwick Grange and Chesters. Less than a mile south of Chesters Fort a section is visible. The Stanegate passes Fourstones on the north side. At South View, where a branch road leads north to Frankham Farm it joins the modern road which passes through Newbrough and follows it as far west as Barcombe.

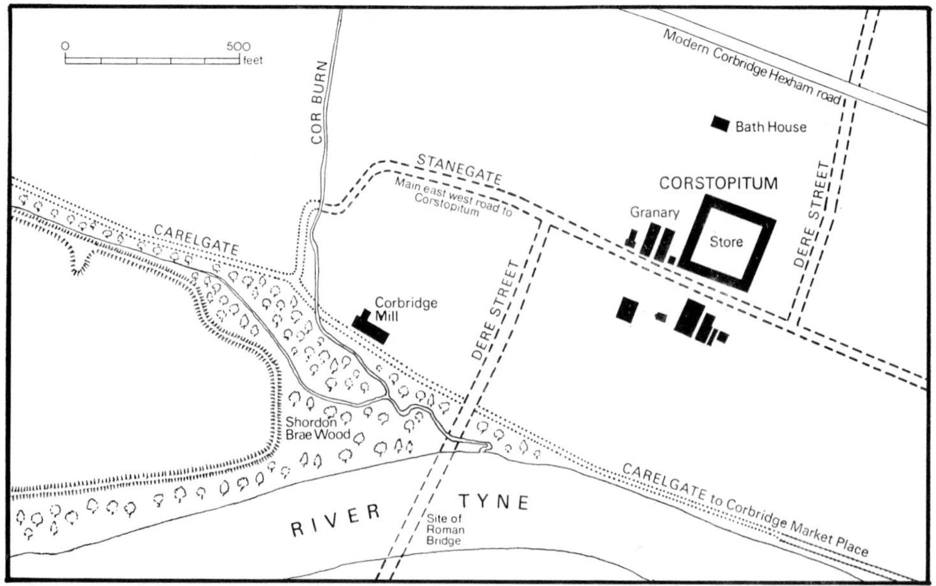


Newbrough lies seven miles from Corbridge and about six from Vindolanda just at the point where one would expect a Stanegate fort. In 1930 in Newbrough churchyard a small fort was discovered but the coins and pottery found were all of fourth century date, which poses a problem, since the Stanegate forts predated the Wall. Perhaps Newbrough was re-occupied at a later date and the early fort has as yet not been traced.

At Crindon Hill Farm, two and a half miles from Newbrough, a branch road leaves the Stanegate for Housesteads. It has been suggested there would have been a fortlet or signal station at this site. Almost three miles beyond Crindon Hill at Crindledykes seven milestones (two of them incomplete) were discovered in 1885 (A.A.2.XI). The earliest to Emperor Severus Alexander (A.D. 223) records the distance of 14 miles as measured from Corbridge. It is here reproduced.

Then comes Probus (A.D. 276-82), Maximinus Caesar (A.D. 305-9), Constantinus Caesar (A.D. 306-7) and Constantinus Augustus, Constantine the Great (A.D. 307-337) which is also shown.

Why so many milestones were found at one spot is probably because the milestones were renewed after each emporer ascended the throne.

Before reaching Vindolanda we see the large, dark hill of Barcombe to the south of the road. Here was a Roman signal-station linking Chesterholm with points east and west.

North east of the Longstone on a shoulder of the hill which commands a view of Vindolanda and the Wall to the north is a British fortification with a rampart still visible and in its north west corner is this Roman signal-station. It stands in a rectangular or circular enclosure with a turf built rampart, an outer ditch and a possible causeway. Although no trace of the wooden structure has survived, Flavian pottery has been found.

Upon approaching the steep sided Bradley burn the modern road bears south but the Stanegate continues straight on to cross the stream at Chesterholm. The road is clearly visible crossing the fields here. However there is some confusion because as can be seen on the O.S. Roman Wall map there is a second almost parallel road. The north-

IMP CA[ES]
SEVER [ALEX]
PIO [FEL. AVG. P. M.]
COS PP CVR
L[E]G AVG. [PR. PR.]
MP XIIII

Imperatori Caesari
Severo [Alexandro]
Pio [felici Augusto pontifici maximo]
consuli, patri patriae, curante
legato Augusti propraetore
millia passuum quatuordecim.

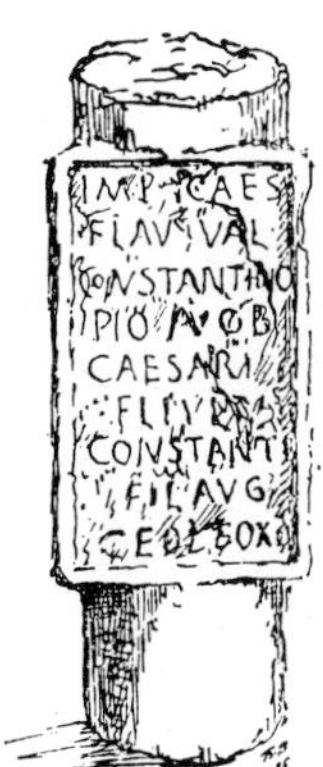

IMP CAES
FLAV VAL
CONSTANTINO
PIO AVG ET (?)
CAESARI
FL IVL
CONSTANTI
FIL AVG
· · E · LLO ·

Imperatori Caesari
Flavio Valerio
Constantino
pio Augusto et
Caesari
Flavio Julio
Constanti
filio Augusti
. . . .

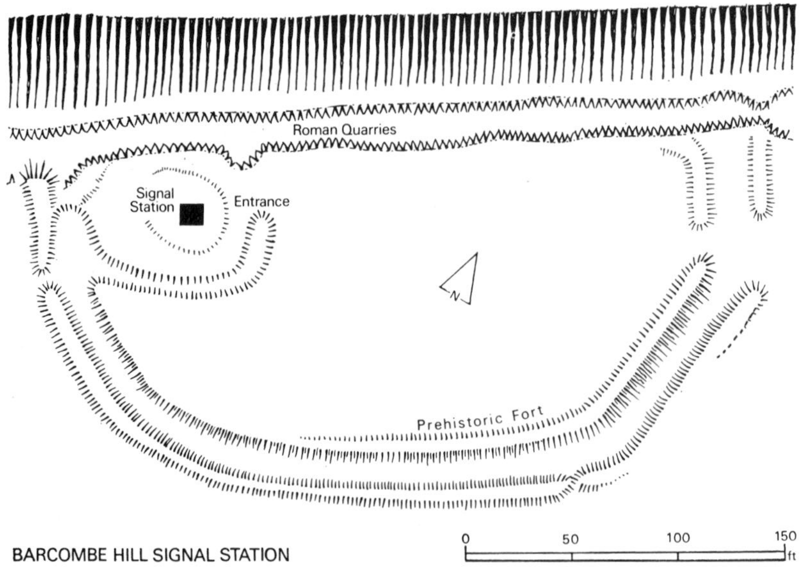


BARCOMBE HILL SIGNAL STATION

ern one is the Stanegate. The date of the southern one is uncertain, and probably not Roman. At the stream a fine cylindrical milestone can be seen, uninscribed, but standing in its original position. The base of another can be seen 1,700 yards to the west.

Beyond the milestone the Stanegate climbs the bank by a deeply sunken road, passable by car with difficulty, and then drives straight ahead passing the car park of Vindolanda. Half a mile brings us to Causeway House north of which was one of the cemeteries of Vindolanda. Here was found the tombstone of Ingenuus who lived 24 years, 4 months and 7 days.

Beyond the milestone base the road to Once Brewed crosses the Stanegate but the Roman road becomes the farm road to Seatside which stands inside a Roman marching camp. Although no longer visible the O.S. shows two more camps to the north and two small ones to the east. From Seatside the course of the road lies across rough ground where traces can often be seen. It crosses the Military Road at the point where a minor road leads to Shield-on-the-Wall. Passing the *Mare and Foal* standing stones it continues parallel to the modern road to the Haltwhistle burn forts. On the way it passes a huge marching camp whose south side, 600 yards long, can still be traced near Milestone House.

Passing south of the forts at Haltwhistle burn the Stanegate can be clearly seen for a mile. Where a branch road leads off to the fort of Aesica, a large camp can be traced with a smaller and later one in its north east corner. This part of the frontier has a remarkable series of such camps which were probably used as temporary quarters for the soldiers who built the Wall. One such camp can be seen south of Peastell Crags with the Stanegate passing straight through it. Midway between this camp and Carvoran a Roman milestone was found in 1932 in a culvert on the Military Road. It clearly came from the Stanegate. It is dedicated to the Emperor Aurelian who was emperor from 270 to 275 (A.A. 4.10). It is now 2 feet 3 inches high by one foot wide but has clearly been trimmed down. On Fell End the Stanegate turns slightly north. As it descends to Carvoran the road was lined by a cemetery on its north side. At Carvoran the Stanegate is joined by the Maiden Way coming from Whitley Castle to the south.

To cross the Tipalt burn with its steep banks the Stanegate makes a series of sharp bends and then runs straight towards Birdoswald for just over a mile, passing on the way three temporary camps to the south. The first, called Glenwhelt Leazes is an earth-

*Milestone dedicated to Emperor Aurelian.*

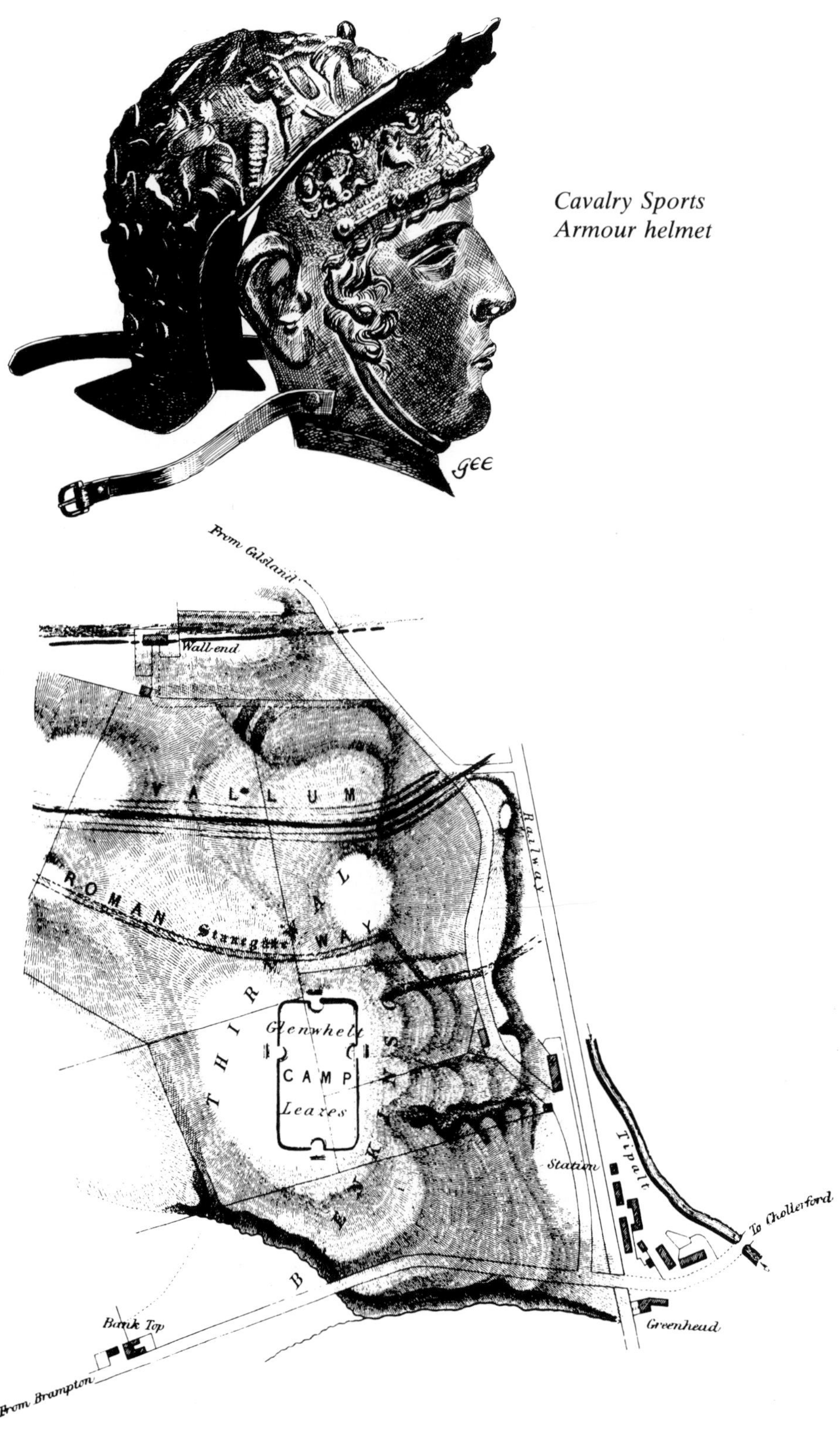


*Cavalry Sports Armour helmet*

*Above:*
*Mains Rigg*
*Signal Station*

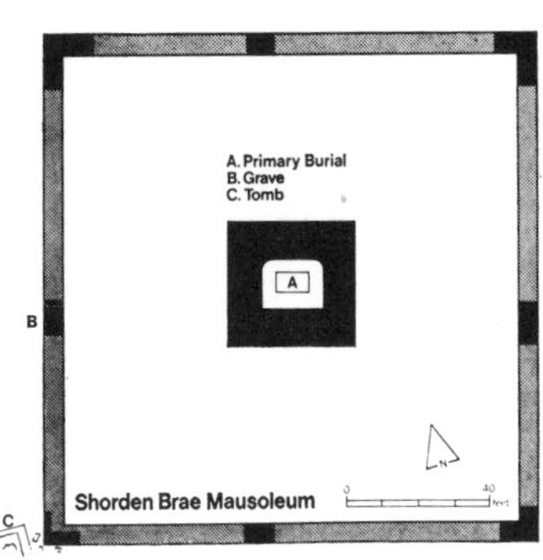

*Building a Roman road*

*Corstopitum. Reconstruction of Central area*

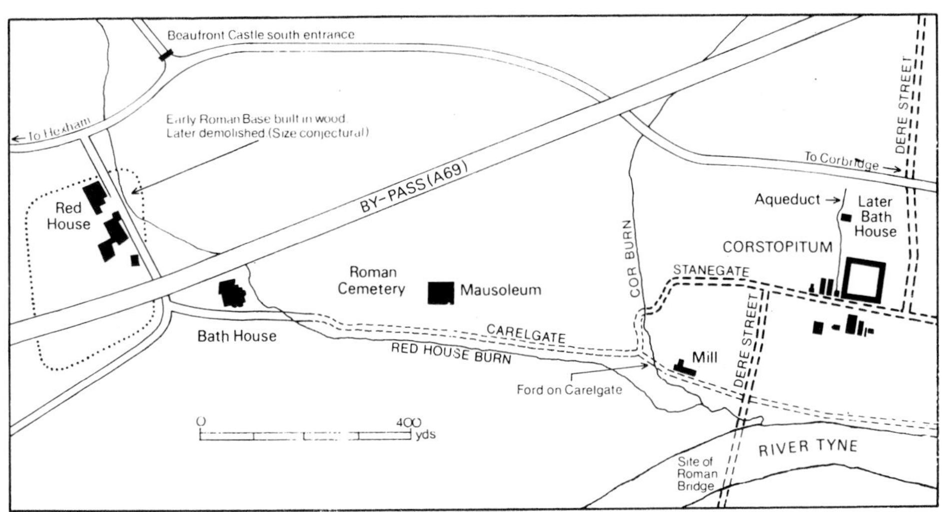

work only, covering almost three acres. Each of the four gates "had a straight traverse in front together with that peculiar semi-circular inflexure of the rampart opposite the gateway, so frequently noticed in camps on the line of Watling Street" (MacLaughlan). The second and smaller camp on Chapelrigg has similar gate defences. These are the only two camps on the Wall defended in this way. The third camp at Crooks has the conventional traverses. As it approaches the Tipalt burn and Milecastle 48 the Stanegate swings south passing Throp fort which was excavated in 1910. The rampart was of turf on a stone foundation with gateways of timber. It was occupied during the period of Wall building and later in the 4th century. The internal buildings were probably of wood. From the fortlet at Throp the Stanegate runs directly south west to the fort of Nether Denton. Midway it passes just north of Mains Rigg signal-tower. This was built to connect the two forts which were invisible from one another. The signal-tower was square with three feet stone walls surrounded by a ditch crossed by an undug causeway. The entrance appears to have been on the second floor, by an outside wooden ladder or staircase (see page 201).

The fort at Nether Denton was a cohort fort of three acres with a turf rampart. Two periods of occupation have been found. The next Stanegate fort is found one mile east of Brampton, at Old Church. It is about 400 feet square with a single ditch and a rampart of turf. The headquarters building, granary, workshop and barracks were all built partly in stone.

Although the Stanegate has been traced from here to Irthington the section to Carlisle is obscure. West of Carlisle the Stanegate probably ran as far as Kirkbride where we can assume it ended.

Kirkbride lies four miles due south of Bowness overlooking the river Wampool on an inlet of the Solway Firth. Recent excavations have uncovered a fort of about five acres with rampart and ditch and fragmentary internal wooden structures.

## CORBRIDGE (CORSTOPITUM)

The Roman site at Corbridge lies half a mile west of the village. It was originally a fort which flourished during the Roman occupation of Scotland and then a supply base. Later it became in the 3rd and 4th centuries an arsenal with a large civilian settlement around it.

The original fort was probably built during the governorship of Julius Agricola (78-84 A.D.) who conquered the north of England and the southern part of Scotland. Remnants of this Roman fort, with its earth rampart, have been discovered. It was probably garrisoned by a cavalry regiment from Gaul called the *Ala Petriana.* A tombstone in Hexham Church shows a standard-bearer of this unit. It probably came from a cemetery at Corbridge. When Hadrian built the Roman Wall in 122 A.D. the Corbridge fort seems to have been replaced by the one at Halton.

In 139 A.D. the fort at Corbridge was rebuilt in preparation for the invasion of Scotland, its position on Dere Street making it tactically important. But its period of greatest importance came after the withdrawal from Scotland, when Corstopitum became an ordnance depot for the whole eastern part of the frontier. It fulfilled this function until the Romans finally abandoned the north of England.

## CORBRIDGE MAUSOLEUM

Roman law srictly ordered that a city's cemeteries should be outside its wall or built-up area, and to be easily accessible they were normally placed alongside roads.

West of Corbridge and on the north side of the Stanegate at Shorden Brae was a large Roman cemetery. Here in 1950 a large mausoleum was found, unique in the northern frontier region. The mausoleum measures 32 by 34 feet with a large enclosing wall forming a precinct 134 feet square. The wall was 5 feet 6 inches thick. It was built in the second century but was demolished for its stones in the fourth. The central mausoleum appears to have been a tower like monument covering an underground burial shaft. Carved stone lions adorned the enclosure walls. Two were found in the excavating and although badly worn they clearly showed a lion crouching over a stag. The famous *Corbridge Lion* was clearly from the same source. It was reconditioned as a fountain group and cut to insert a leaden water pipe and then placed in the mansio where it was eventually found. The lion and its prey was often associated with death in Roman times.

The precinct would have had an entrance, possibly an imposing structure, but since all the dressed stones were removed in the 4th century and only the massive foundations are left we cannot now trace the entrance.

The four corners of the precinct wall were obviously the spots where the lion sculptures were mounted on ornamental pedestals.

We do not know who was commemorated by this magnificent monument. Could it have been a "millionaire" merchant of Corbridge, a powerful local official, a leading army officer, or a war memorial to a body of men killed in a major battle? All is conjecture.

*Mausoleum at Corbridge*

Roman bridge at Corbridge.

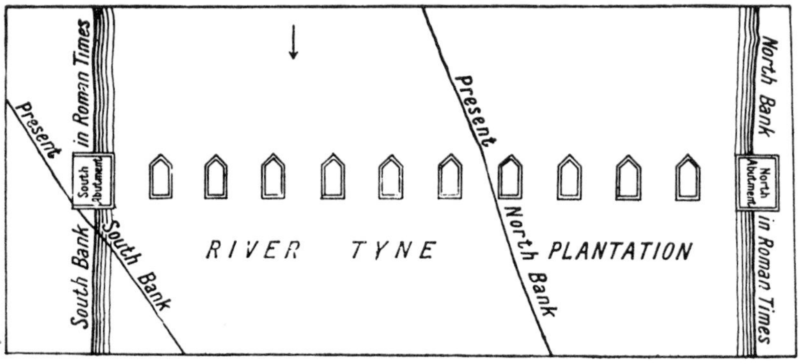

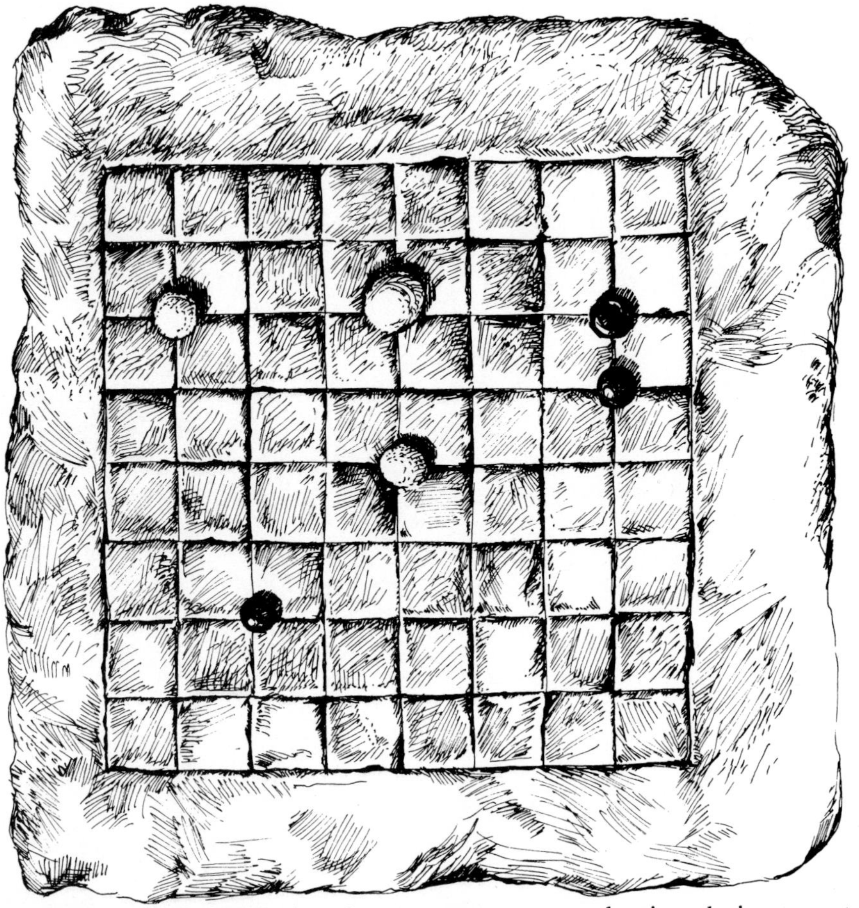

The soldiers on the Wall played many games to pass the time during monotonous periods off duty. One game was the *ludus latrunculorum* (a *latro* was a mercenary soldier), the ancestor of the present-day game of draughts. At Corbridge a collection of glass game pieces — *latrones* — was found, as well as several boards. The pieces seem to have moved like rooks in chess and the aim was to capture the enemy pieces by trapping one between two of your own.

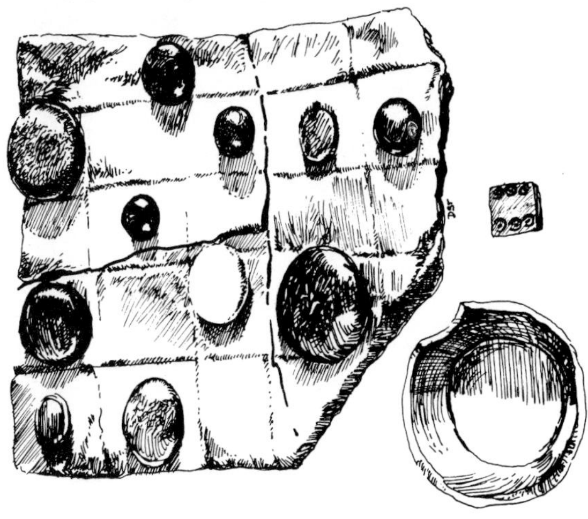

*Stone Gaming Board with counters, dice and dice box found at Vindolanda.*

The civilian settlement at Corbridge was very important. Here lived many wealthy merchants, as well as craftsmen such as smiths, potters and leather workers whose tools may be seen in the Museum. Besides catering for the needs of the troops the large civilian community was also engaged in trade with the natives to the north of the Wall. Corbridge was also the centre of a rich agricultural area and nearby mines of coal, lead and iron were exploited.

The fort was probably occupied until a few years after 400 A.D. What became of the civilian population we do not know for certain, but within a century and a half the village of Corbridge was in existence.

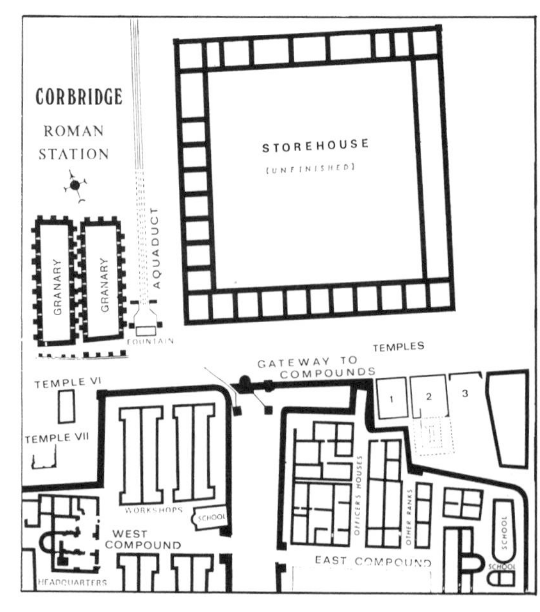


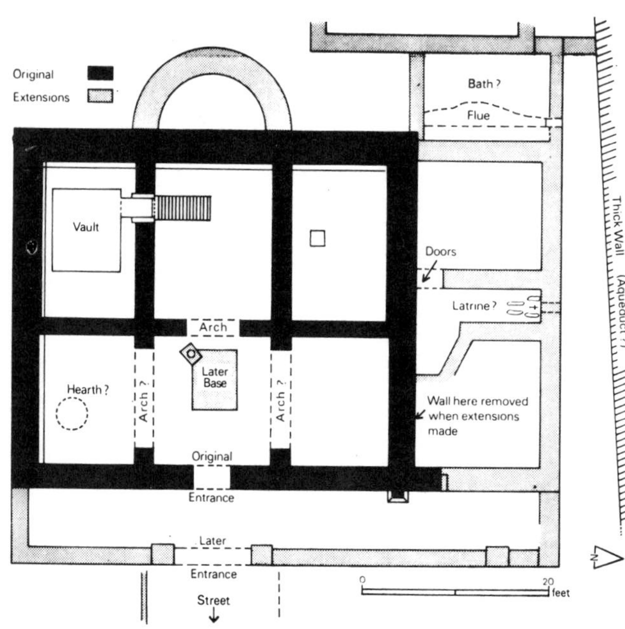


Plan of *Principia*, Corbridge.

Excavations at the Roman site were started in 1906, and a wealth of material illustrating Roman life in northern Britain has been found. The Museum exhibits many of these discoveries while the remains of numerous buildings can be seen on the site which is under the control of the Department of the Environment.

The headquarters building, the remains of which can be seen in the west compound, was a fine impressive stone building. It is not strictly in accordance with the usual headquarters buildings found in the wall forts,

*The chapel of the impressive headquarters building in the west compound. A flight of steps led down to a sunken strong-room once covered by a barred vault.*

but here it belonged only to a legionary detachment not a full auxiliary corps. The building was altered at various times. Our reconstruction shows it in the third century.

The vestibule, ante-chapel and shrine with the clerestory above were supported on large stone pillars, the one before the shrine being the largest. In the Saxon tower of the church at Corbridge we can see such an arch today. Probably it came from this headquarters building. The vestibule was probably divided off from the side aisles by screens.

The shrine could be seen from the outside. Here was the entrance to the strong room where the regiment's money, records and valuables were stored. On a raised bench (or *suggestus*) were placed the statue of the Emperor, the regimental standards, native offerings and an altar to the Emperor's Discipline. The front of the bench had five panels depicting the life of Hercules. The central panel has survived and shows Hercules and the Hydra. The coils encircle the left arm of Hercules and Athens stands on the right offering advice. Much of the building and probably all the statues were brightly coloured.

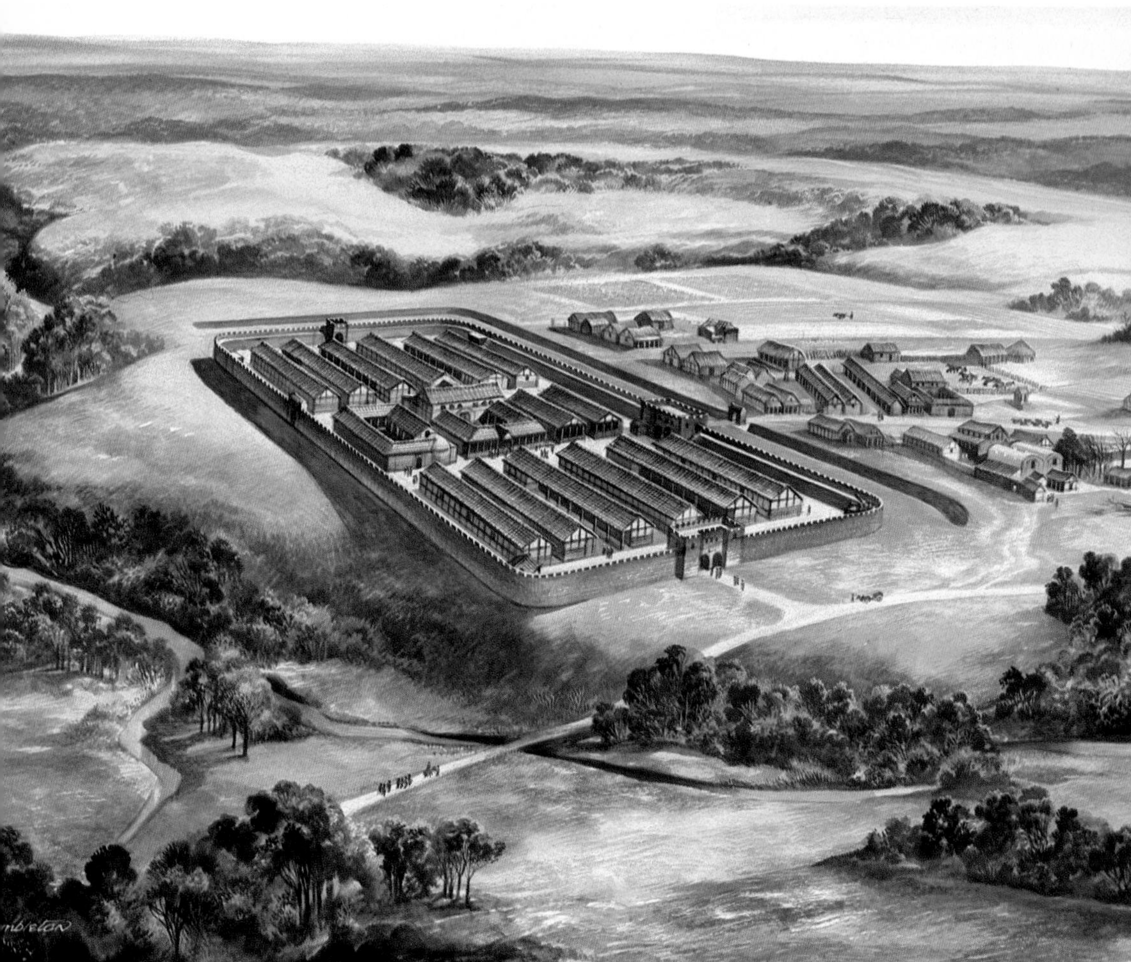

*Aerial view of Vindolanda Fort and civilian settlement.*

*Opposite. The "Mansio" at Vindolanda*

*FROM CORBRIDGE*

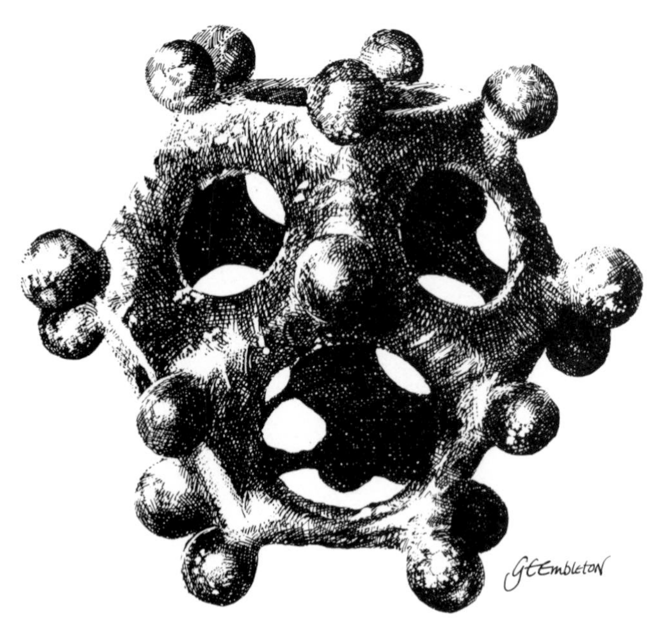


*DODECAHEDRON*
*Derived from the Greek word meaning twelve. Its use is unknown. Casting such an object in metal shows great technical skill. This is one of very few complete specimens still in existence.*

*UNQUENTARIEM*
*The glass contained oil and scent which was used instead of soap in Roman times.*

## VINDOLANDA

Before the Wall was built Vindolanda was an important part of the northern defences of Roman Britain, and after Corbridge and Carlisle was the largest military centre.

It was one of the original forts on the Stanegate, built on a plateau which except on one side is protected by nature. There were at least six forts here, four of wood and two of stone. The remains we see today are of the last fort built a little before 300 A.D. It had four gates of which the north and west were the most important. The remains in the centre of the fort are those of the headquarters building. The fort covers an area of three and a half acres.

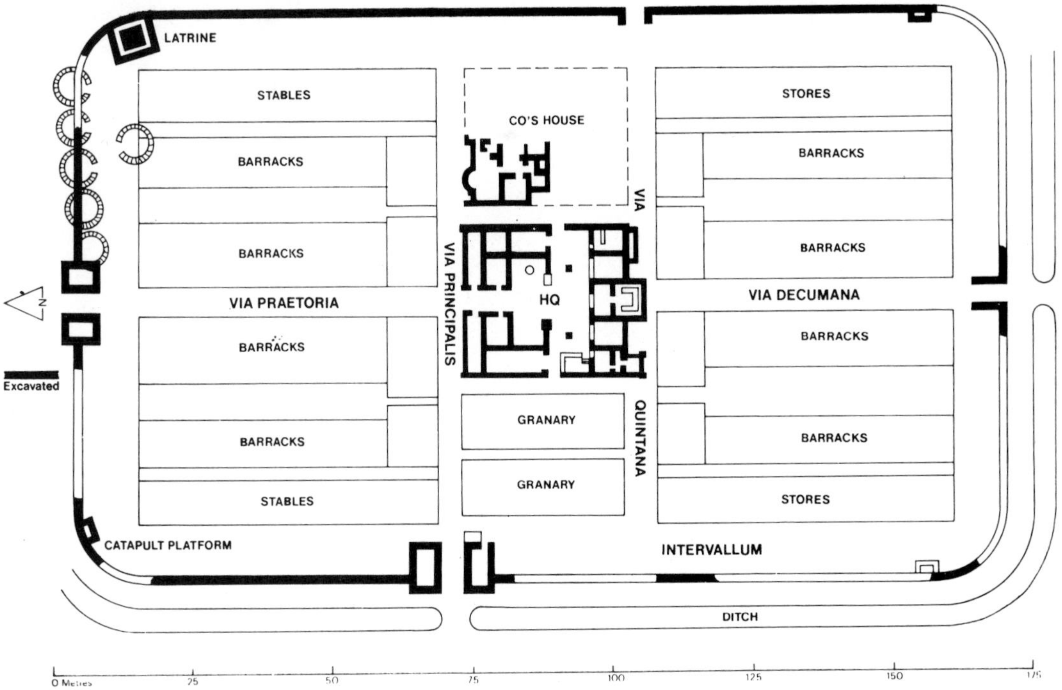

LATRINE
STABLES
BARRACKS
BARRACKS
VIA PRAETORIA
BARRACKS
BARRACKS
STABLES
CATAPULT PLATFORM
Excavated
N
CO'S HOUSE
VIA PRINCIPALIS
HQ
VIA
QUINTANA
GRANARY
GRANARY
STORES
BARRACKS
BARRACKS
VIA DECUMANA
BARRACKS
BARRACKS
STORES
INTERVALLUM
DITCH

Vindolanda, the Roman fort and civilian settlement, lies behind the Roman Wall. In recent years important archaeological discoveries have been made here including the unique writing tablets and a vast collection of leather. In the old house of Chesterholm is the largest Roman museum in the north and near the civilian settlement a full scale reconstruction of sections of the wall can be seen.

Sculptured stone, now in Chesters Museum, with signs of the Zodiac.
Found in the walls of a cottage near Vindolanda.

*Above. Roman troops approaching Vindolanda*

*Bronze Brooch with double-headed snake motif found at Vindolanda*

*Opposite. In the tannery at Vindolanda*

In the 2nd century the garrison was probably the 3rd cohort of Nervii. In the 3rd century it was the 4th cohort of Gauls (Notitia). A fine altar found in the Commanding Officer's house was dedicated by the prefects of the 4th cohort of Gauls to the Genius of the Praetorium and is shown here.

But one of the best altars at Chesterholm, erected by Quintus Petronius, was found in the praetorium. It is here illustrated.

I O M
CETERISQUE
DIIS IMMORT
ET GEN PRAETOR
Q PETRONIVS
Q F FAB VRBICVS
PRAEF COH IIII
GALLORVM
. . . . .
EX ITALIA
DOMO BRIXIA
VOTVM SOLVIT
PRO SE
AC SVIS

Jovi optimo maximo
ceterisque
diis immortalibus
et genio prætorii
Quintus Petronius
Quinti filius Fabia [tribu] Urbicus
præfectus cohortis quartæ
Gallorum
. . . . .
ex Italia
domo Brixia
votum solvit
pro se
ac suis.

Roman milestone near Vindolanda.

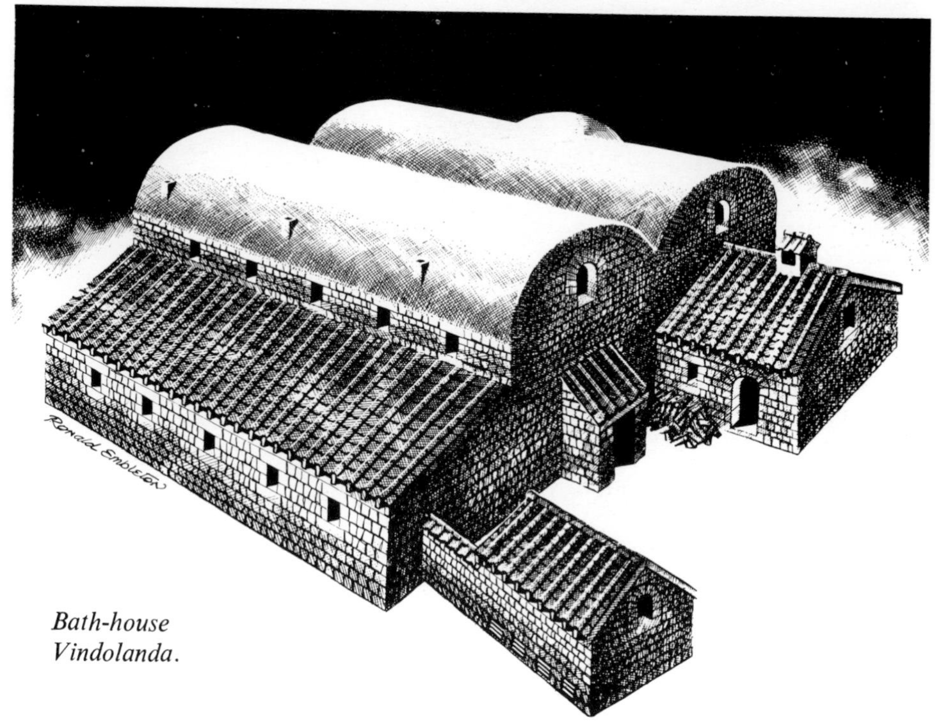


Bath-house
Vindolanda.

A tombstone was found re-used in the wall near the East Gate. It had originally been placed over the grave of Cornelius Victor, a member of the governor's bodyguard.

(See page 219).

The most important altar was found 120 yards west of the fort. It was set up by the *vicani Vindolandesses*. The lettering is very uneven but can be read on the opposite page.

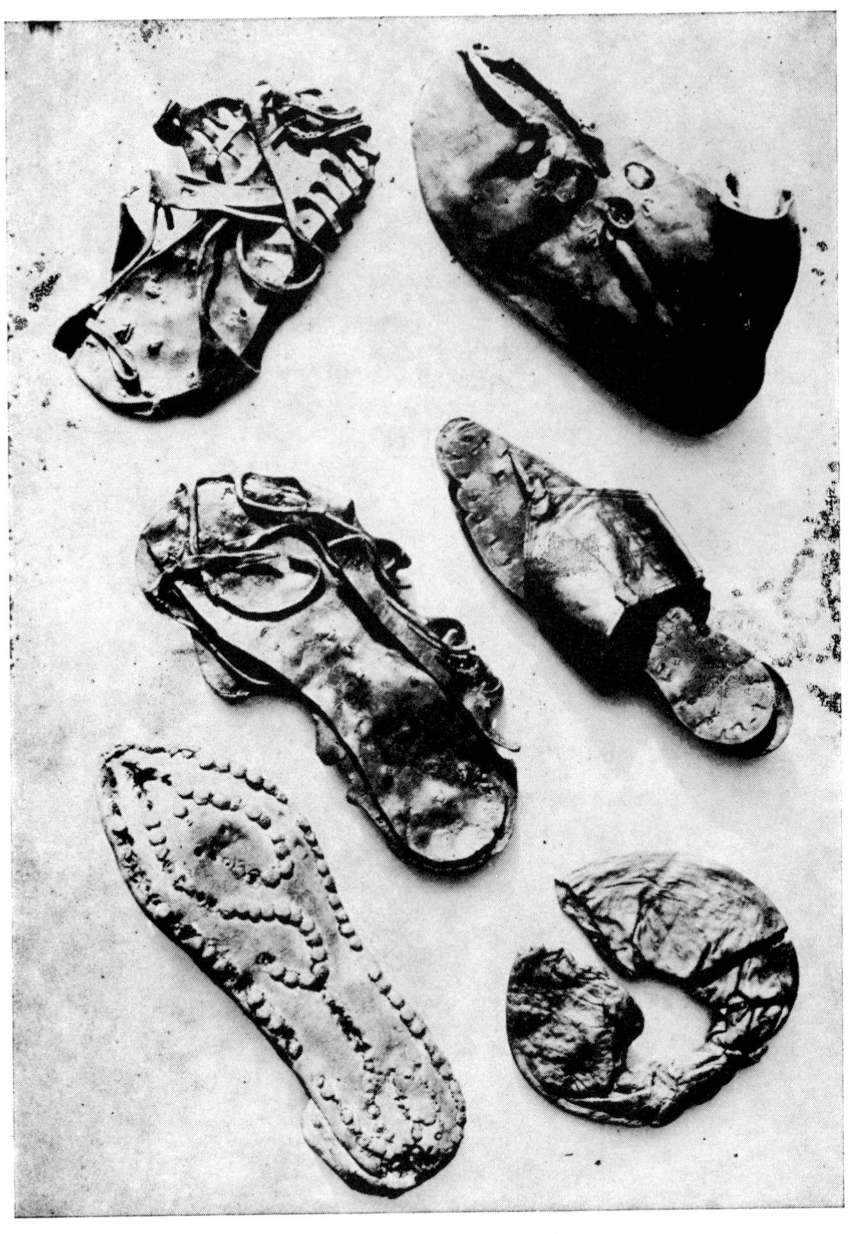

*Footwear from Vindolanda.*

*Tombstone of Cornelius Victor, a member of the governor's bodyguard.*

This is the first epigraph recording the name of any fort on the Wall (apart from Amboglanna on the Rudge Cup). The altar was dedicated to Vulcan for the safety of the Imperial House by the men of the *vicus* of Vindolanda. The people here obviously had a corporate existence. The name is often translated as 'white enclosed land', but why the name white should be used is a mystery.

| | |
|---|---|
| PRO · DOM/ | *Pro domu* |
| DIVINΛ · ET · NV | *divina et nu-* |
| MINIBVS : AVG | *minibus Aug-* |
| VSTOR\M · VOL | *ustorum, Volc-* |
| ΛNO SΛCR \M | *ano sacrum* |
| VICΛNI VINDOL | *vicani Vindol-* |
| ΛNDESSES · CV | *andesses, cu[ram* |
| ΛGENTE · · OI · · · | *agente . . . . .* |
| V S L M | *V(otum) S(olvit)* |
| | *L(ibens) M(erito)* |

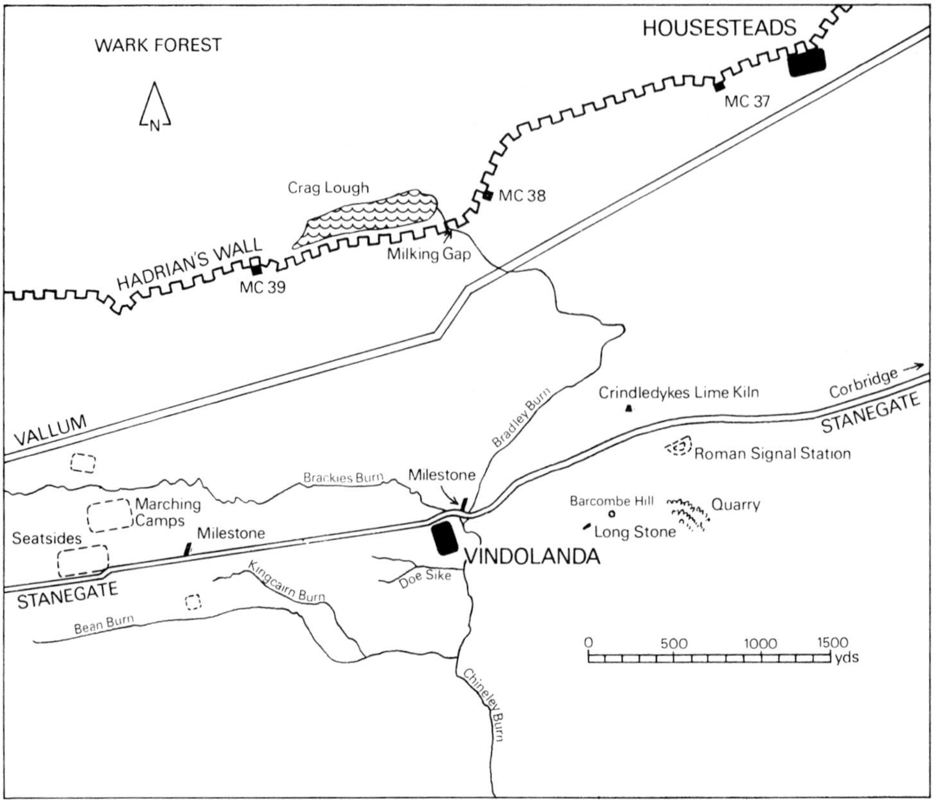

An interesting altar, probably from Vindolanda was found in the graveyard of Bellingham chapel. It was set up by the *Curia* or council of the Textoverdi, apparently a local tribe.

The second line is difficult to interpret but is now though to be the name of a local goddess *Sattada*. The generally accepted text today is DEA SAIIADAE CURIA TEX TOVERDORUM V.S.L.M.

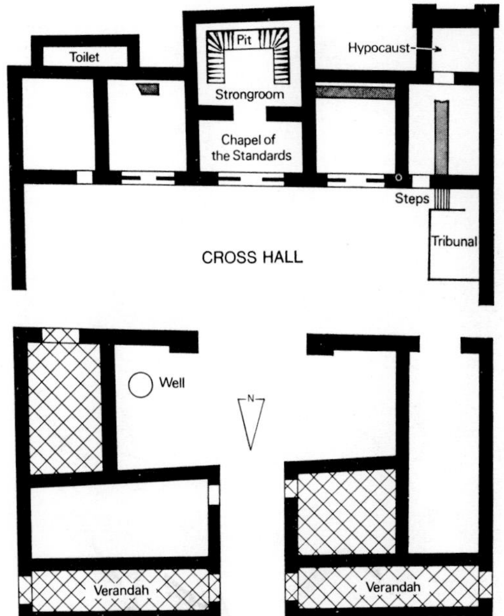

HEADQUARTERS BUILDING AT VINDOLANDA

However it is the civilian settlement which is of such great significance. It was built on land which is almost waterlogged and the dampness has helped to preserve the remarkable series of finds which have been made. There were two stone built settlements. The first was erected about 163 A.D. and abandoned in the middle of the third century. A few decades later another settlement of inferior quality was built which lasted until the end of the fourth century.

Of the buildings to be seen at the settlement three are of interest:—

1. The Military Bath-house which is well preserved.
2. The *Mansio* or inn for travellers. It was of great importance since Vindolanda was on the Roman road called the Stanegate.
3. The corridor house, the largest building yet discovered.

In the waterlogged ground, which was ideal for the preservation of articles left there, a fantastic collection of writing tablets has been found which are slowly being translated and providing important historical information. For Britain an unique collection of textiles has been discovered along with vast quantities of leather. These can be seen in the large, well equipped museum.

*Headquarters at Vindolanda.*

*Worship before a meal in a small house at Vindolanda*

*Roman hairstyle*

*Roman hairstyles*

*Interior of a Roman middle-class house*
*There were probably such houses at Corbridge*

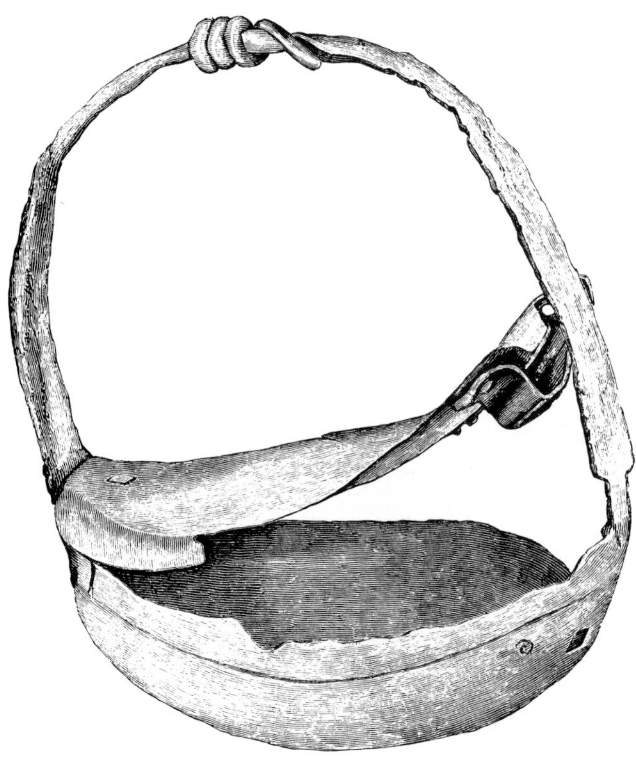

*Bronze purse found at Barcombe*

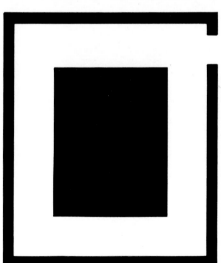

*Plan of latrine*

**Latrine in the *Mansio* at Vindolanda**

This was a dry latrine possibly with buckets under the seats. It could have accommodated two on each side. It was difficult to draw the interior of such a small latrine so the artist has omitted the seats on one side.

*Bronze Military Standard found at Vindolanda showing a horse with his leg on the head of a snake*

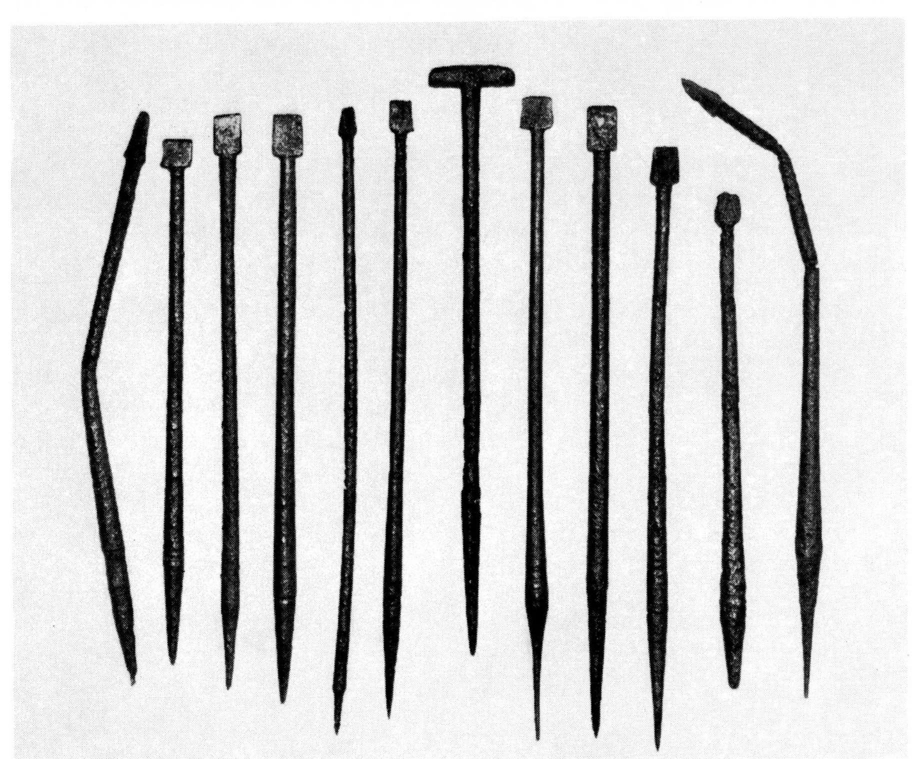

*Iron stylus pens used for writing on wax*

*Writing Tablets from Vindolanda*

*Writing a letter at Vindolanda*

*Opposite. A Roman kitchen, reconstructed at Vindolanda*

*Photograph by P. Graham.*

*Phallic Symbol on Barcombe. Photo: P. Y. Graham*

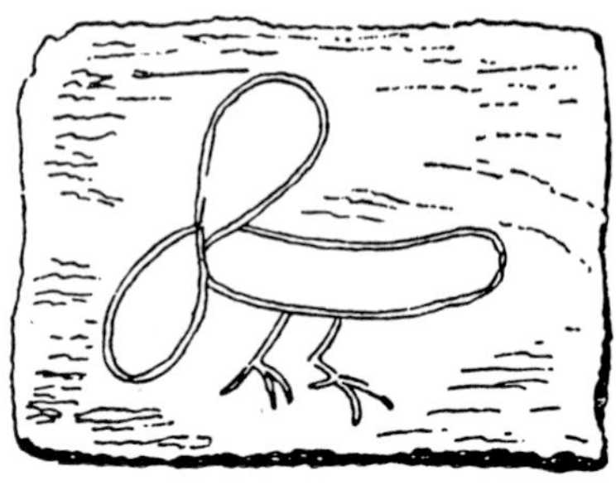

**PHALLIC SYMBOLS**

Phallic symbols represented fertility and good fortune, and therefore were potent against the evil eye. They were regularly placed on military buildings. There are several at Chesters including a magnificent one on the northward water-face of the abutment of Chesters Roman bridge. The wall of the guardhouse at one of the entrance gateways of Housesteads fort once had a stone slab as shown here. The crude phallus has the legs of a fowl.

**ROMAN QUARRYING**

Several inscriptions show the army was involved in extracting stone for building the Wall. Wedge holes have been found at Barcombe Hill, overlooking Vindolanda and at Limestone Corner on Hadrian's Wall. Natural cracks in the rocks were used and bung holes at about one foot intervals were made. Into these wooden wedges were inserted. The wedges were then soaked in water and as they expanded they split the rock. The quarries were often worked in winter when ice performed the same function.

Iron wedges were also available. The stones would be trimmed on site to reduce the weight for transport. When Vindolanda was being built the stones were quarried at Barcombe and rolled down the steep hill which took them more than halfway to the fort without any effort.

At Barcombe can be seen one of the finest phallic symbols found on the northern frontier. Its main significance is religious not sexual. It was a symbol of good luck.

In 1837 a small bronze "arm"-purse was found in the quarry at Barcombe (a similar one was found at Birdoswald), carefully placed beneath stone chippings. It contained three imperial gold coins wrapped up in a piece of leather resembling kid, and sixty silver coins. Of the silver denarii, 17 coins of Trajan and 4 of Hadrian are almost unworn by circulation. This indicates the coins were lost early in Hadrian's reign and after that the quarry was unworked until their discovery in 1835 when the quarry was reopened for the building of the Newcastle-Carlisle Railway.

How they came there is a mystery. No quarryman would hide and then forget such a valuable collection of coins. Perhaps they were stolen and then hidden, or the soldier to whom they belonged may have been killed by an accident at work.

These bronze purses (length about 4 inches) are always called "arm"-purses because they were supposed to be worn on the wrist. Once you see one the idea is clearly ridiculous. It would need a small child with a "skinny" wrist to wear such a small and uncomfortable object. The only suggestion I can make is that they were worn on the belt.

The money was carried in the oval container and the handle was formed by bending round the two long strips of metal that were left attached to it for this purpose, and twisting them round each other. The cover had edges to fit tightly to the cavity. At one end was a spring fastening and at the other a strong spring catch.

## WILLOWFORD BRIDGE TO BIRDOSWALD

Just before reaching Birdoswald from the east the river Irthing has to be crossed. Here are the remains of Willowford Bridge which is reconstructed on page 249. During the centuries that have passed the river has changed its course so that the bridge is now entirely on the east bank. The west bank in Roman times would probably not be as steep as today. The remains of the Roman Bridge are extremely complicated since there were probably three bridges on the site. The first bridge abutment was built of large blocks of stone guarded by a small turret where the Broad Wall ended. The Wall was 10 feet wide but was not completed to this measurement. At the second offset the width was reduced to 6½ feet. The first alteration led to the destruction of the turret and the Wall being extended to the west. A new but larger turret was erected a few feet east of the original turret. The extended Wall ran over the old abutment and ended at two narrow sluices which probably served a mill. In the second and final reconstruction the bridge was enlarged to carry the Military Way (previously only a footpath), part of the old mill race was filled in but replaced by a larger one, and the abutment also increased in size. The only surviving pier is 34 feet long by 7 feet wide. Two other water piers were traced in 1940.

The visitor in Roman times must have been impressed at this point on the Wall by the magnificent stone bridge dominated by the powerfully fortified camp of Camboglanna with a large cavalry garrison in its early days and later an infantry garrison drawn from eastern Europe. It would be a busy spot with much traffic, with regular traffic passing north to the outpost fort of *Fanum Cocidii.*

On the cliff summit west of the Irthing the Wall is still standing to a height of seven courses. At the Irthing the Broad Wall ended and the Turf Wall began. When the Turf Wall was replaced in stone the Narrow Wall took its place. In a few yards we come to Milecastle 49 measuring 75 feet from north to south and 65

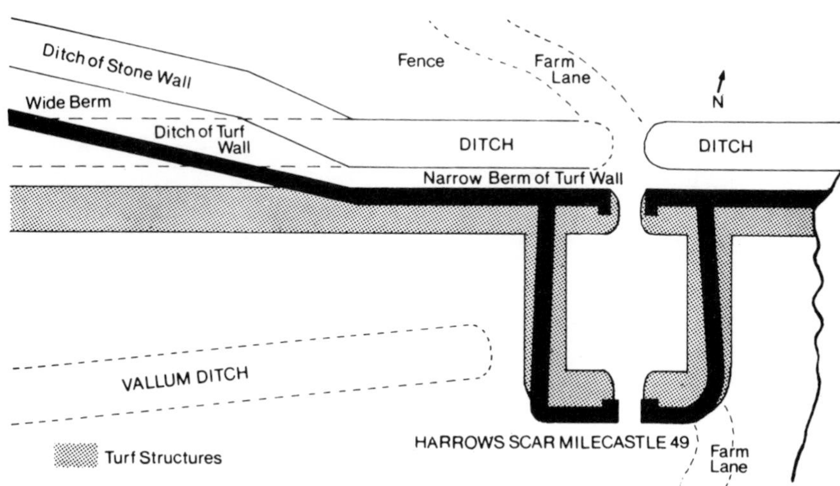


feet east to west. The excavation carried out in 1953 revealed the turf turret beneath the stone one. The Vallum ditch as shown on the plan ends shortly before the milecastle wall and did not continue down the cliff to the river.

From Harrows Scar almost to Birdoswald a fine section of the Wall has been preserved, standing ten courses high in many places. This section is noteworthy because of the large number of drainage channels which occur almost every 20 feet. This was probably necessary because the land to the south was very marshy.

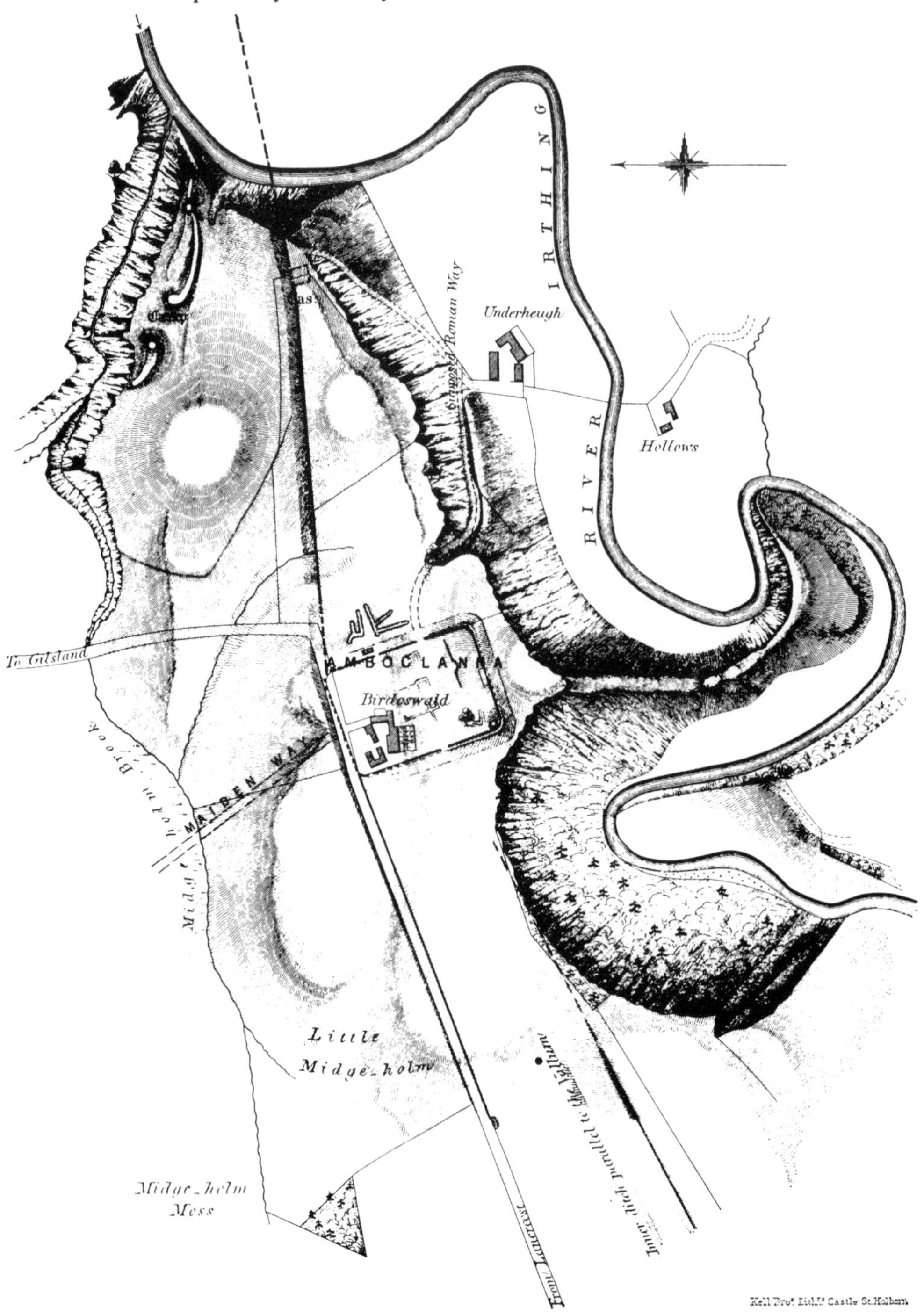

The section is also unique because the centurial stones, a mason's mark, and phallic symbols are found here in their original position. Nowhere else can such stones be found in situ, and there are eight in all. The parade ground of the fort lay to the south of this Wall section. From here have come over 20 parade ground dedications, a remarkable collection.

Parade grounds were probably attached to most Roman forts, but their exact locations can in most cases only be guessed at. The finest example is that of Hardknott Fort in the Lake District.

**BIRDOSWALD (CAMBOGLANNA)**

Birdoswald is first mentioned by Reginald Bainbrigg in 1599.

*Frome Lanercost I followed the wall all ruinated, till I came to Burdoswald, wiche doth seame to have been some great towne by the great ruynes thereof, the inhabitants did shew me the plaice wher the churche stode, the inscriptions ther are either worne out by the tract of tyme, or by clownishe and rude inhabitants defaced. I found this inscription in a stone at Thomas Tweddaile's house, at Burdoswald.*

This stone was a dedication by a tribune of *Cohort I Aelia Dacorum Tetricianorum* here reproduced.

I O M
COH I AEL DAC
TETRICIA . . .
. . . C P POMPO
NIVS DESIG
NA . . . .

Jovi optimo maxim
cohors primae AElia Dac
Tetriciana
cui praeest Pompo-
nius Desig-
natus

Size, 3 feet by 1 foot 1 inch

Horsley's description is very detailed:

*The foundations of the houses within this fort are very visible. I measured the thickness of their walls, and found them to be about twenty eight inches, and the distance, or breadth of the passage, between the rows of houses or barracks to be no more than thirty two inches. The ramparts about the fort are in the third degree, and the ditch in the second, excepting on the north side, where it is not so much. The foundation of the west rampart is distinct, and measured about five foot. There are regular entrances visible on the north and south sides, opposite one to another, as also faint appearances of entries on the east and west. In the northern part of the station there seems to be the remains of a temple. The turrets in the south rampart on each side of the gate are still very visible; and over-against the entry are the ruins of the praetorium, on which a house or two stand at present.*

*Decumana Gateway, Camboglanna. Inside View. John Storey*

The first excavations were carried out in 1850 by Henry Norman, the owner, in collaboration with Henry Glasford Potter, a Newcastle surgeon, whose report was illustrated by the fine lithographs of John Storey here shown. Serious excavations didn't begin till 1896 and ended in 1950 but the internal buildings have never been properly investigated. If fully uncovered the fort would probably be of more interest than either Chesters or Housesteads. It lies 3¼ miles from Carvoran and

7½ miles from Castlesteads. It stands in a prominent position with the Irthing Gorge on the south and the marsh of Midgeholm Moss to the north. Its main function was to guard the Irthing Bridge at Willowford. It measures 580 feet by 400 feet covering almost 5½ acres. The generally accepted Roman name is *Camboglanna* (Notitia — *Amboglanna,* Rudge Cup — *Camboglans,* the Amiens Skillet — *Camboglas).* The garrison is by no means clear. The fort was designed for a cavalry regiment but in the 2nd century was garrisoned by a milliary cohort (perhaps the First Cohort of Tungrians recorded on a building inscription found near Hare Hill). Early in the 3rd century the First Cohort of Thracians is recorded. The 3rd and 4th century garrison was the Hadrian's Own First Cohort of Dacians who are recorded in many inscriptions of which we reproduce a building stone from the East Gate (219 A.D.), See page 240.

*Ground plan of the Decumana Gate with restoration. An early example of reconstruction by John Storey, 1850.*

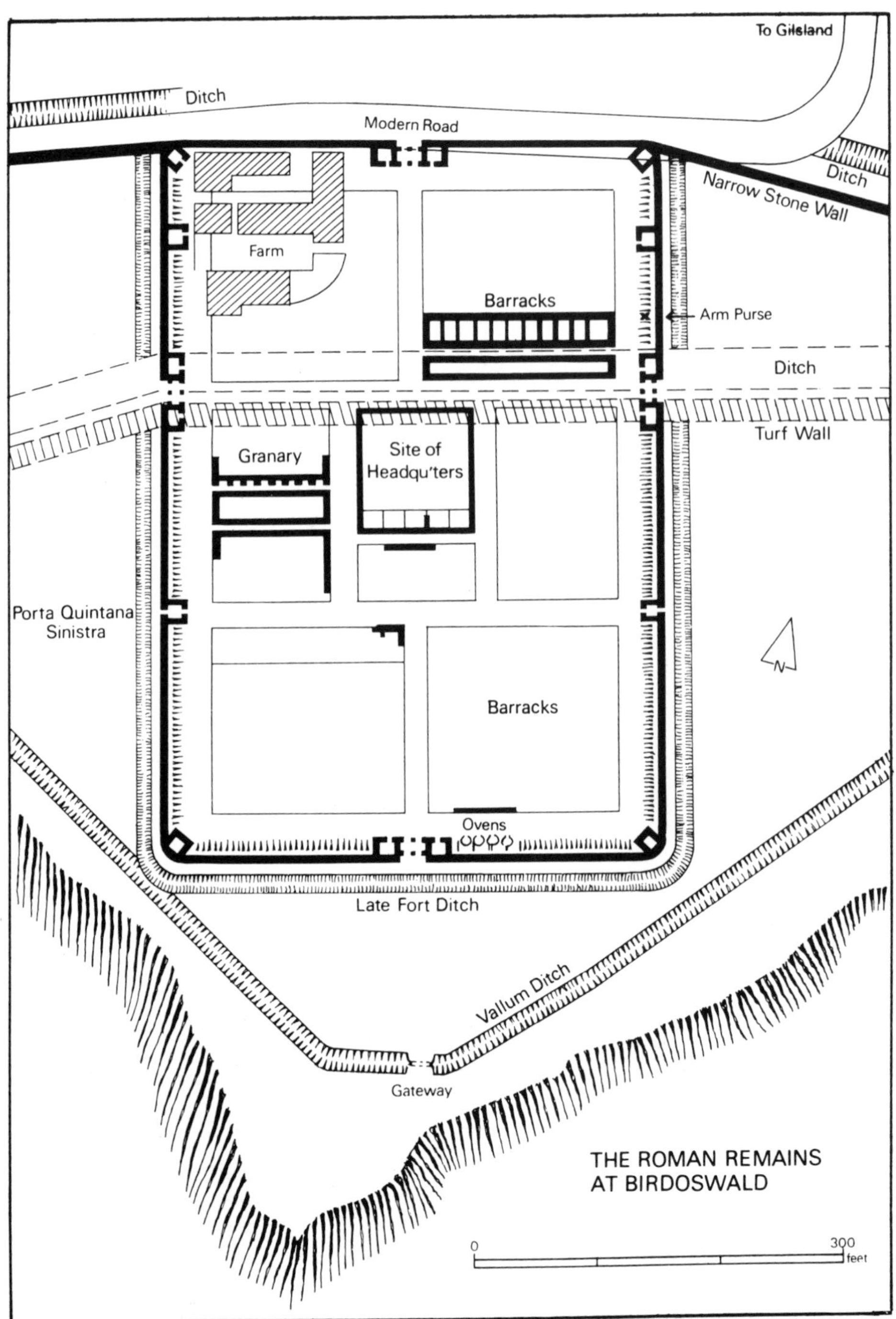


When the Romans first came to Birdoswald they found a native promontory-fort with a palisade and a pair of ditches almost on the site where they built their fort. The first Roman building was a rectangular signal station within the settlement ramparts. In A.D. 122 the Turf Wall was built with turret 49a at Birdoswald. But before long a cavalry fort was built on the site. Its date was early in the reign of Hadrian as can be proved by a collection of Roman coins and a purse lost by one of the builders but found in 1949. The coins help us to date the building work. Cavalry forts always had three gates projecting beyond the Wall so that the cavalry could be deployed quickly. So at Birdoswald they demolished a section of the Turf Wall and where the Turf Wall joined the new fort they built the east and west gates. The plan illustrates this.

*These two illustrations show the original turf wall of the fort and the later wall of stone.*

Size, 3 feet 1 inch by 2 feet 2 inches.

| | |
|---|---|
| SVB MODIO IV-<br>LIO LEG AVG PR ·<br>PR COH I AEL DAC ·<br>CVI PRAEEST M<br>CL MENANDER<br>TRIB | Sub Modio Ju-<br>lio Legato Augusti Pro-<br>praetore cohors primae AElia Dacorum<br>cui praeest Marcus<br>Claudius Menander<br>tribunus |

The cavalry who occupied this fort are unknown. But they cannot have been there long because as soon as the fort was completed a decision to replace the Turf Wall with the Narrow Stone Wall was taken. The Stone Wall was to be built on the line of the Turf Wall. But at this point a decision must have been taken to change the fort to one for infantry. This meant that when approaching the fort the Stone Wall had to turn north to meet the east and west angles instead of the east and west gates. Then about A.D. 128 the Vallum was built, but without a north mound because of the lack of space and two or three years later is was filled in for reasons unknown to us.

Little of Hadrian's original fort is left since Birdoswald underwent major reconstruction in later centuries. The rebuilding carried out when Diocletian and Maximian were joint emperors is recorded in the following building inscription which tells us how the First Cohort of Dacians "restored the commandant's house *(praetorium),* which had fallen into ruin, and the headquarters building *(principia),* and the bath-house *(balneum),* under the charge of centurion Flavius Martinus".

The defences of Birdoswald are well preserved but little can be seen of the internal buildings. The North Gate lies under the modern road. On entering the fort by the farm track, the east side of the drive is formed by the north-west angle of the fort, 12 courses high. A small section of the Narrow Wall abutting the fort here is not bonded because it was rebuilt in the 4th century. The north-west angle tower with its two ovens and blocked-up doorway is well preserved. Passing an interval tower we find the main west gateway is covered by a shrubbery and then come to a stretch of the west wall preserved for half its length. The west postern *(porta quintana sinistra)* was blocked at some date but wheel ruts can still be seen in the threshold. The south west angle of the fort shows two successive periods of rebuilding, probably at the end of the 2nd and 3rd centuries after a disaster had damaged the fort.

All the south wall, including the main gateway, stands several courses high. The south gate was cleared in 1851 and found to have twin portals and guard chambers. The east portal was blocked soon after it was built and the other portal was blocked towards the end of the Roman occupation. The guard chambers contain ovens and are entered from the fort, not from the gate passageways.

Almost the whole of the eastern Wall is standing about 10 courses high, but no traces of the postern *(porta quintana dextra)* can be seen. Between the postern and the main east gateway the Wall was rebuilt in the late 4th century. The east gate was a double portal gateway and the northern impost is standing to its full height. Both gates had two pivot-stones showing the road was relaid. Originally the guard chambers did not open onto the portal but the gateways were rebuilt and altered on several occasions. Near the south portal the Turf Wall can be seen. Since part of the east gate was built over the Wall ditch, it was given extra strong foundations to counteract subsidence. So effective were these measures that subsidence has taken place on the part where there was no ditch and consequently lighter foundations were provided.

Size, 3 feet 7 inches by 1 foot 7 inches

In the interior traces of barracks, the commandant's house (where the statue of Fortuna was dug up), the headquarters building and granaries have been found, but the fort buildings await thorough excavation.

Birdoswald has been suggested as the site of the battle in which King Arthur, the legendary Celtic hero, was killed. The *Annals of Wales* tell us (c. 511 A.D.) there was a "fight at Camlann in which Arthur and Medraut were killed".

Philologists believe that *Camlann* could be derived from "Camboglanna" and means a "curved bank" referring to the River Irthing which passed Birdoswald. (We must however note that recent research has suggested "Banna" as the Roman name for Birdoswald, which makes "Camboglanna" the name for Castlesteads and the river Cambeck which flowed past the site may preserve part of the early name).

## THE MAIDEN WAY AND GILLALEES BEACON

From Birdoswald to Bewcastle ran a Roman road to which the Rev. John Maughan, rector of Bewcastle, gave the name of *The Maiden Way*. Sections of it can still be seen today. A little over half way to Bewcastle the road crosses the "Gillalees Beacon". At Robin Hood's Butt (Little Beacon Tower) is "a small cairn-like object" thus described by Bruce (R.W. 2nd Edition):

*It is encumbered with rubbish, but, if cleared, would probably exhibit walls six or seven feet high. It is eighteen feet square, the walls are three feet thick; it stands on the west side of the Way, and has an entrance on the north; the masonry is undoubtedly Roman. As this tower, locally known as the Little Beacon, is planted on the southern side of the summit, the view northwards from it is very limited; not so that to the south, the whole country from Sewingshields to the Solway is spread as a map before the spectator; signals might easily be exchanged by the watchman in it with the soldiers at Housesteads, Birdoswald, Stanwix, Carlisle, Wigton or Bowness.*

In the next edition Bruce included a rather amusing lithograph of the cairn, here shown.

When excavated it was found to be a square stone-built tower measuring 19 feet externally and 13 feet internally with walls standing 4 feet. There was no doorway at ground level (entrance would be on the second floor as at Mains Rigg). It was surrounded by a ditch with a causeway on its east side leading to the Maiden Way. Half a mile from Bewcastle an altar to Cocidius was found beside the road, erected by Annius Victor, a centurion of the 6th Legion (L.S. No. 735).

It has been suggested that the purpose of this signal station was to pass messages to the south without them being seen by the enemy to the north. This would mean that the fort at Bewcastle would be mainly used for collecting information about any possible enemy movements.

## BEWCASTLE FORT (FANUM COCIDII)

Bewcastle lies seven miles to the north of Birdoswald. Its name was probably *Fanum Cocidii* as in the Ravenna List. Its garrison is uncertain but under Hadrian was probably the First Cohort of Dacians, and in the 3rd century the First Nervian Cohort of Germans, 1,000 strong. The site is famous because here still stands an outstanding 8th century Anglian cross-shaft next door to a medieval tower. Three altars to Cocidus have been found here of which we show one.

SANCTO CO<br>CIDIO AVRVNC<br>FELICISSI<br>MVS TRIBVN<br>EX EVOCATO<br>V S L M

Sancto Co-<br>cidio Auruncius<br>Felicissi-<br>mus tribunus<br>ex evocato<br>votum solvit libens merito

Size, 1 ft. 10 in. by 1 ft. 1½ in.

And two silver plaques to the same god were dug up in the Headquarters building. The centre of the cult of this Romano-British deity seems to have been here, which explains the name of the fort which is the only one in the north with a religious name.

For distribution of altars to Cocidius see A.A. 1937.

Bewcastle fort occupies the whole plateau, an area of six acres, and unusual with Roman fortifications, is six-sided. The unusual shape arose from a desire to

use the whole plateau. The first fort was of turf and timber built in the time of Hadrian. Only the bath-house is known from this period. The fort as displayed today was built in the 3rd century. It was twice destroyed. The first time was in A.D. 296 when the Wall forts suffered the same fate. The second time was in A.D. 343 when Bewcastle alone was laid waste. It was finally abandoned on the orders of Count Theodosius after A.D. 367.

The map shows the fort's layout and the buildings which were uncovered in the limited excavations of 1937, 1954 and 1956.

The view from Bewcastle was not extensive but was probably the best site the Romans could find. Due to its isolation it would not be a popular posting even for troops used to the loneliness of garrison life on the Wall.

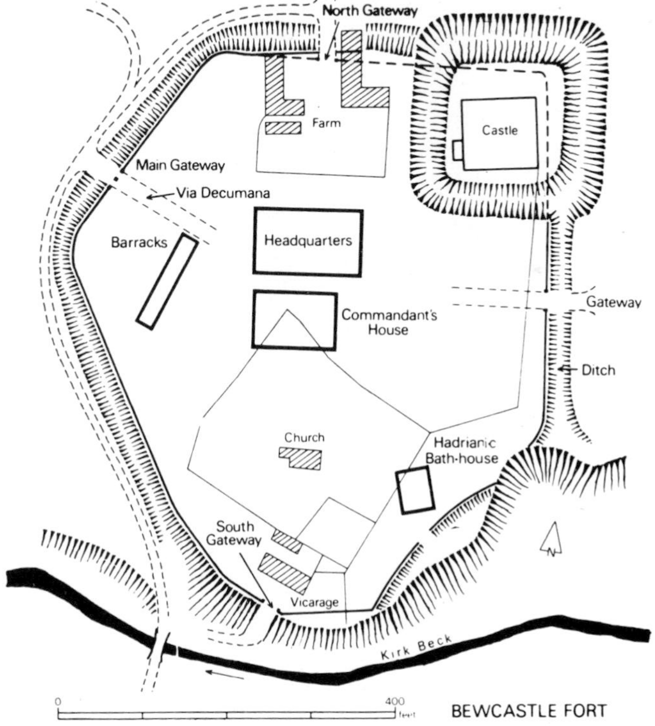

BEWCASTLE FORT

## BIRDOSWALD TO CASTLESTEADS

Westward of Birdoswald the Wall is in an unusually good state of preservation. For 500 yards beyond turret 49b a section of the Wall can be seen on the south side of the road. The Wall west of Birdoswald is the Narrow Wall. Large stretches of the Vallum can be seen for almost five miles. Half a mile uphill from the fort brings us to the site of Milecastle 50 which was excavated in 1911 and found to measure internally 76 feet north to south, and 60 feet east to west, built with the Narrow Wall. Turrets 50a and 50b were also uncovered in 1911. Here the Turf Wall ran south of the Stone Wall from Milecastle 49 to 51 and is visible over large sections. Excavations in this area have told us much about the Turf Wall. Both Walls have been proved to be the work of Hadrian. The Turf Wall did not run east of the Irthing but continued to Bowness. Turrest 49b and 50a of the Turf Wall were examined in 1934. They were found to be of stone. At the same time Milecastle 50 T.W. was excavated. It was a typical milecastle but with a turf rampart instead of stone, the gateways and internal buildings were of timber. Its life was short. The Vallum in this section was built later than the Turf Wall. It followed so close to it that the north mound was omitted in places and the south mound increased in size. A patrol trench was established between the ditch and the south mound.

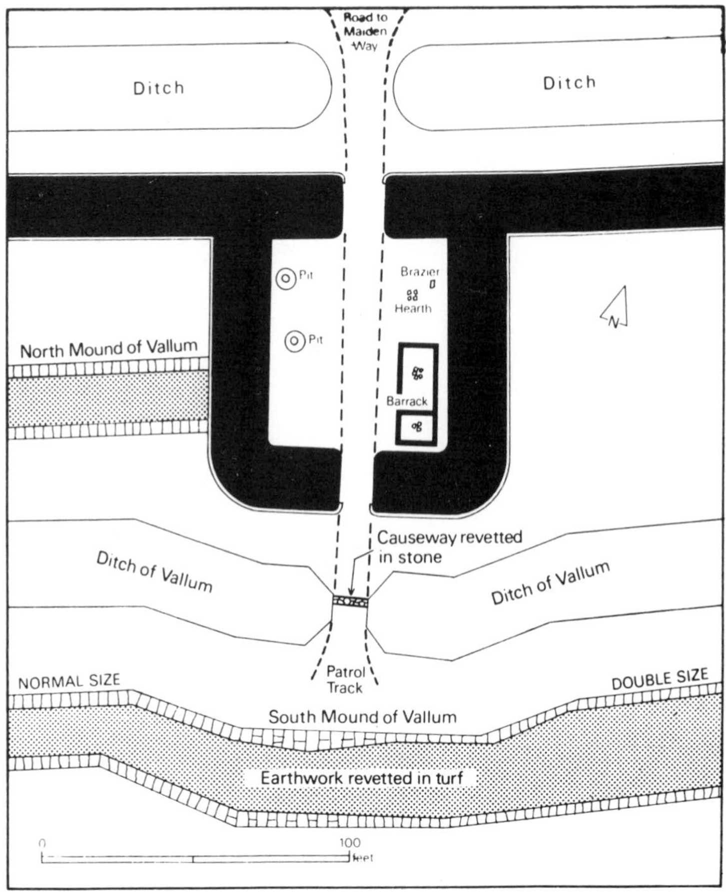


*Milecastle 50 T.W.*

Roman skillet *(patera)* cast in bronze

*Milecastle 50 T.W. Reconstruction*

## SIGNAL TOWER AT PIKE HILL

West of Birdoswald stood the interesting signal tower at Pike Hill.

The Signal Tower has an extensive view but is not part of the normal Wall system. Because of its unusual alignment the ditch, the Turf Wall and the Stone Wall have to make a peculiar diversion to accommodate it. The signal tower faces Gillalees watch-tower and Nether Denton for on its two east sides and Boothby fort and Netherby on its western sides. It was clearly a pivotal station in a system of long distance signalling.

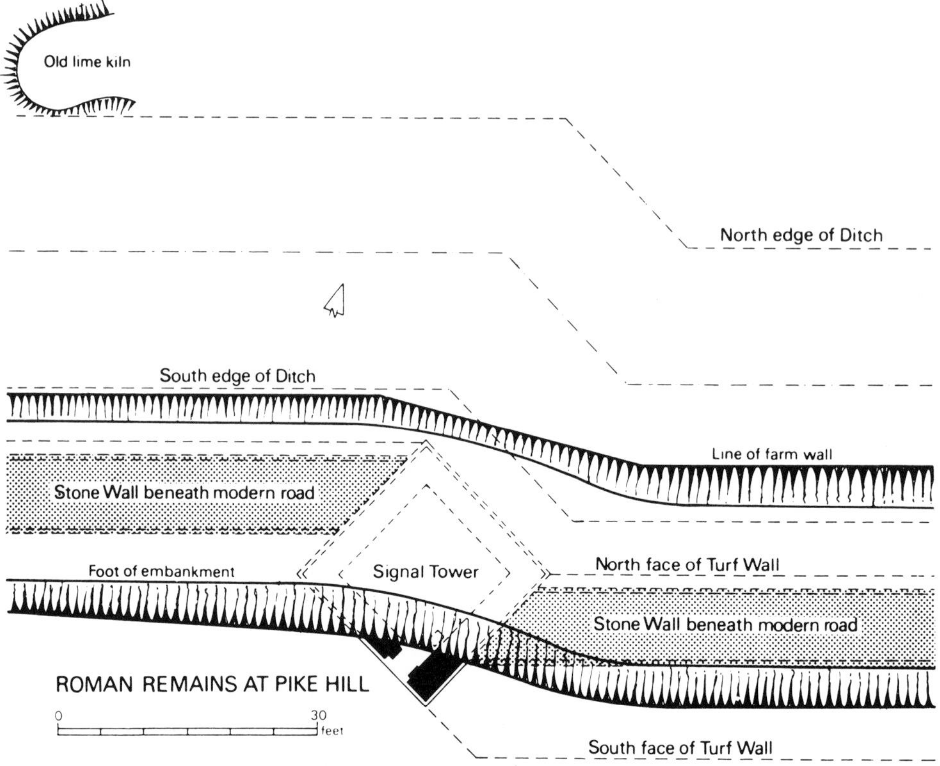


## WILLIAM HUTTON AT BIRDOSWALD — 1801

*"When I entered the house of Mr. Bowman, who is the proprietor, and occupier, of these once imperial premises, I was received with that coldness which indicates an unwelcome guest, bordering upon a dismission; for an ink-bottle and book are suspicious emblems. But, as information was the grand point in view, I could not, for trifles, give up my design; an expert angler will play with his fish till he can catch him.*

*"With patience, with my small stock of rhetoric, and, above all, the simplicity of my pursuit, which was a powerful argument, we became exceedingly friendly; so that the family were not only unwilling to let me go, but obliged me to promise a visit on my return. They gave me their best; they wished it better. I had been, it seems, taken for a person employed by Government to examine private property, for the advancement of taxation".*

Willowford Bridge

Scale, Half-an-Inch to the Foot

VEXIL(LATIO) LEG(IONIS) II AVG(VSTAE) OB (VIRTVTEM)? APP(ELLATAE)?
SVB AGRICOLA OPTIONE

A vexillation of the second legion styled the August on account of its bravery, under Agricola the optio (lieutenant) . . . .

APRO ET MAXIMO
CONSVLIBVS
OFFICINA MERCATI(I)

IVLI(I) N(VMERVS)?

Aper and Maximus
being consuls (A.D. 207)
The workshop (quarry) of Mercatius.

The band of Julius.

MERCATIVS FERMI

IVL. PECVLIARIS?
VEXILLATIO LEG. XX. V.V.?

Mercatius (the son of) Fermus

Julius Peculiaris?
a vexillation of the 20th
legion (styled) Valeria and Victorious

*The Written Rock of Gelt*

## WRITTEN ROCK OF GELT

From Willowford Bridge west the Wall was originally of turf due to the shortage of limestone. Lime was needed for grouting of the Wall as we use cement today. Quarries for red sandstone worked by the Romans can be seen west of Birdoswald. The most famous is on the rocky banks of the Gelt where Roman quarrymen have left their marks. This famous inscription is the *Written Rock of Gelt* here reproduced. Half a mile higher up the river on the opposite bank is Pigeon Crag where we find the names of men of the Sixth Legion.

*Pigeon Crag*

## CASTLESTEADS FORT (UXELLODUNUM)

This fort has had two other names. Horsley called it Cambeck Fort and Bruce (3rd edition) and MacLaughlan used the title Walton House Station. It stands on a tongue of land above the River Cambeck. On the north the ground is precipitous, to the south it slopes gently to the Irthing. The Rudge Cup and Amiens Skillet give the Roman name as *Uxellodunum,* the Notitia as *Axellodunum.* The earliest account of the site is by Reginald Bainbrigg (1601).

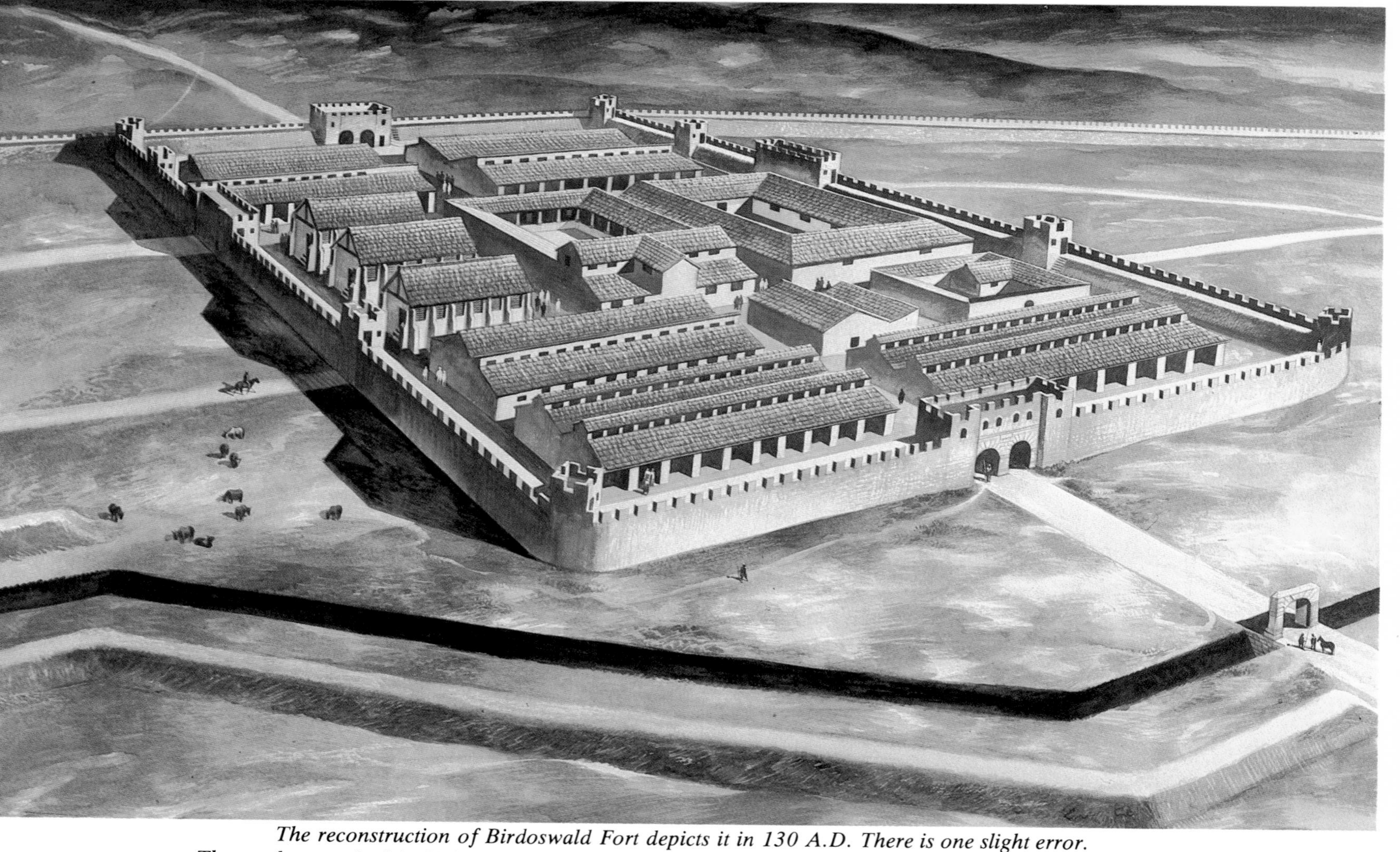

*The reconstruction of Birdoswald Fort depicts it in 130 A.D. There is one slight error. The north mound of the Vallum was never built due to lack of space because the land fell away so steeply*

*First century Legionaries with bullock cart*

FAVST(INO) ET RVF(C) CO(N)S(VLIBV)S. In the consulship of Faustinus and Rufus.

*Two Roman quarry inscriptions.*
*The first gives the names of two soldiers, SECURUS and JUSTUS*

*"was digged upp this last yeare by a country man, that buylded a square howse neare this place, he sunke deape into the ruynes of this castle, wher he found faire and strong walls of hewen stone, among the wiche I saw the rarest worke that ever I saw in my liff: it was included after the maner of a quadrangle within fower hewen walls, about some iiij ells brode, it stode upon manie little arches wiche was blacke with fire, upon thes arches stode a vaut, and upon that a faire leavell plaice finelie plastered. I told the gentlemen that was ther present, that is was hypocaustum Romanum . . .".*

He seems to be referring to the commandant's bath house within the fort. The square house he mentions is probably the one marked on MacLauchlan's map as "site of old Mansion". In 1791 the estate came into the hands of John Johnson who erected a mansion which he called Walton House (later changed to Castlesteads House, the name first used for the Roman fort by Camden). He later converted the station into a garden.

Hutchinson's Cumberland (published in 1794 but written before Walton House was built) has the following description:

*The whole fortress seems to have been a very sumptious and fine building. Most of the stones that are dug up are black, as if the whole place had been burnt; and what confirms me more in this opinion is, that in several places, as yet dug into, there are great numbers of iron nails, pieces of iron and brass, that are run into lumps, though now in a mouldering condition . . . There are several foundations of the houses yet standing distinctly in the fort, pretty high, but hard to be come at for the brushwood growing in them.*

*Several rooms were found, the floors of which, consisting of thick masses of strong cement, were supported upon pedestals. There were many other curious floors found among the ruins, and some coal ashes . . . There was also a cold bath found near the place, and not far from it something like a cistern, about five yards by one and a half, composed of thick slate stones, very large, and set edge-ways, curiously cemented so as to refuse passage to any liquid.*

*The altars (except the largest) were found within the fort, about eighteen inches below the surface of the upper soil, several little troughs were also found there, with their bottoms turned up; conduits were discovered in all directions, and channel stones, apparently made for carrying off day water.*

*Several coins were found, of one of the Constantines, of Maxentius, and others.*

The following statement probably relates to the platform of a ballista, or other engine, for projecting heavy missiles:—

*On the south side, without the walls of the fort, was a large platform of stones five feet below the surface, covering eleven yards in length and eight feet in breadth.*

*At some little distance from the fort the foundations of a building were found, and about it a quantity of ashes and some wheat, the grain entire but turned black. Here the largest altar was discovered; it is cracked, perhaps by the effect of fire . . . Ashes and burnt wheat have frequently been found.*

In 1934 the fort was partly excavated: the east, south and west walls were uncovered, the two side double gates and south-west angle tower, surrounded by a single ditch. The north wall had collapsed into the valley. Originally the fort was about 400 feet square covering an area of almost 4 acres. Traces were found of an earlier building on the site with an earth rampart and ditch but on a slightly different spot. Pottery from the end of Hadrian's reign was discovered. The garrisons in the second century were the First Cohort of Batavians and the Fourth Cohort of Gauls, and in the third century the Second Cohort of Tungrians, part mounted and 1,000 strong. The *Notitia* also mentions the First Cohort of Spaniards. The garrison was usually so large that it couldn't have been accommodated in such a small fort and part was probably stationed somewhere nearby.

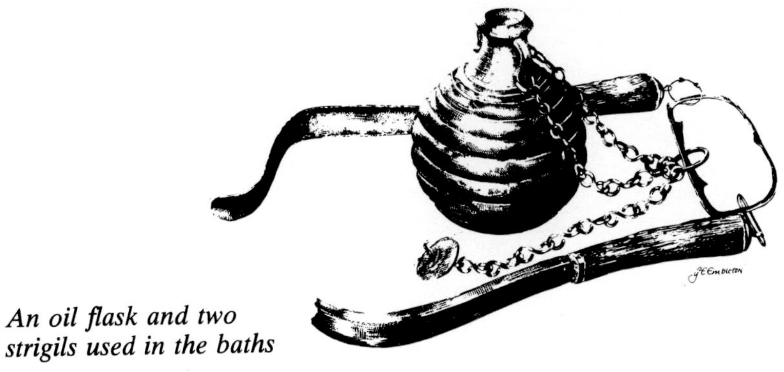

*An oil flask and two strigils used in the baths*

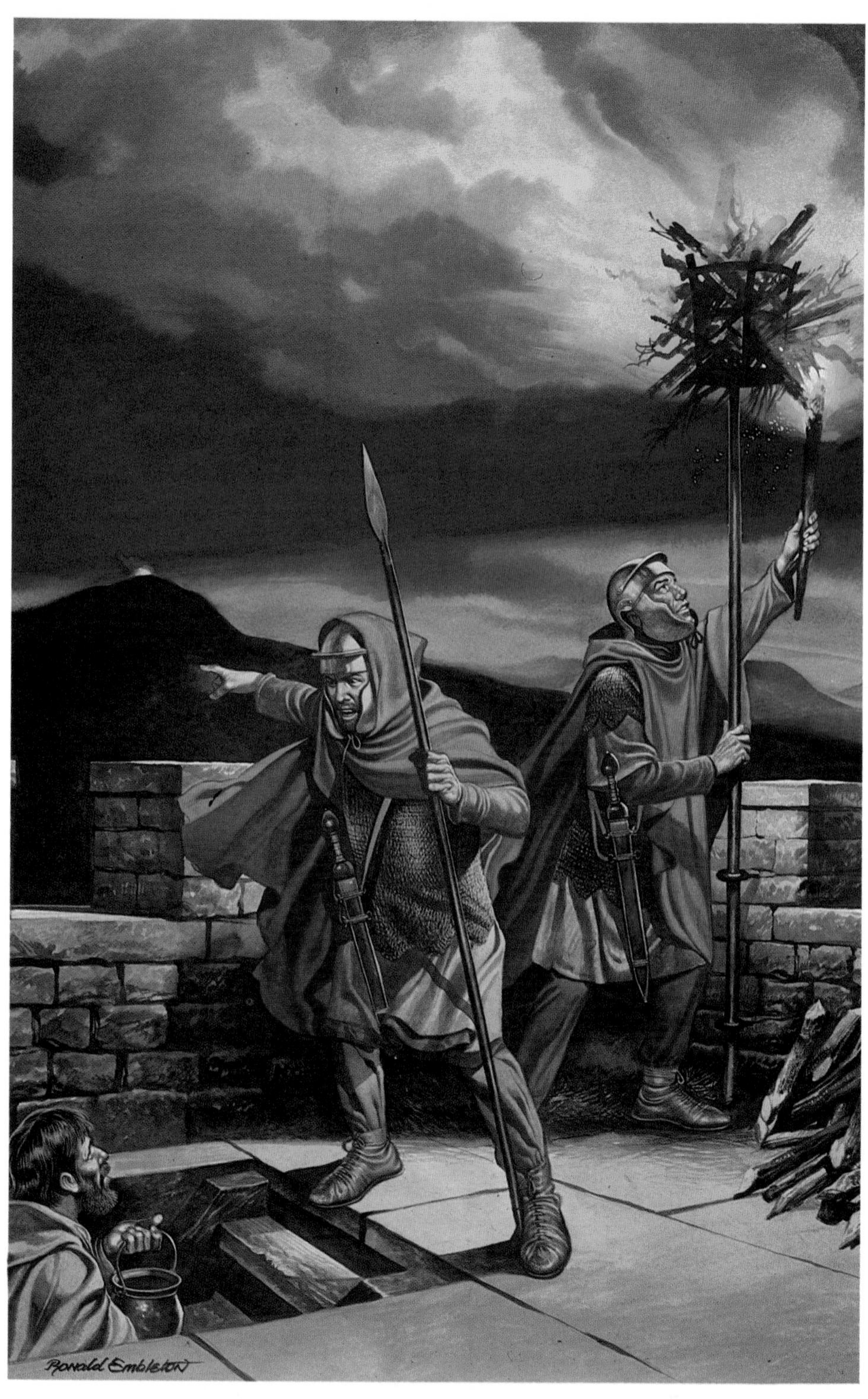


*Sounding the alarm at the Signal Tower at Pike Hill*

*Birdoswald from the East c.1850*

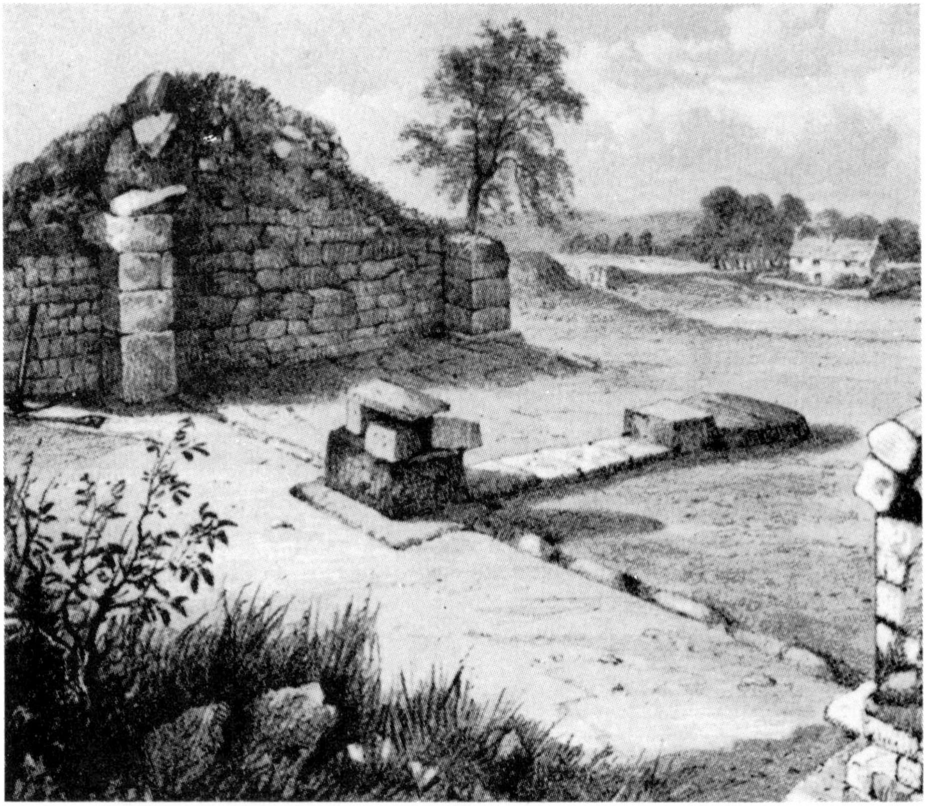

*Decumana Gateway, Camboglanna. Outside View. John Storey, 1850*

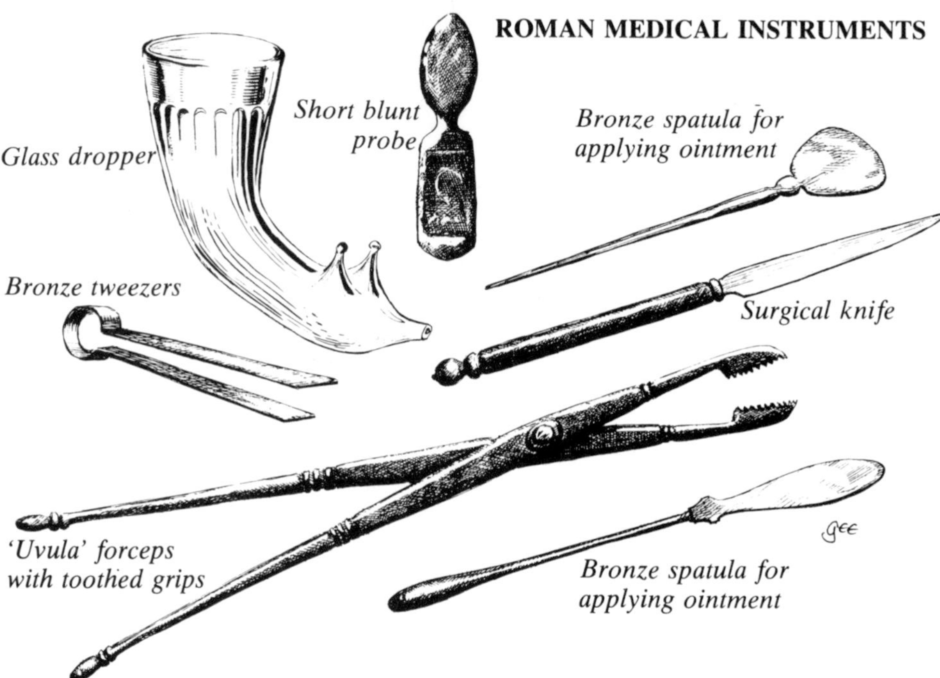

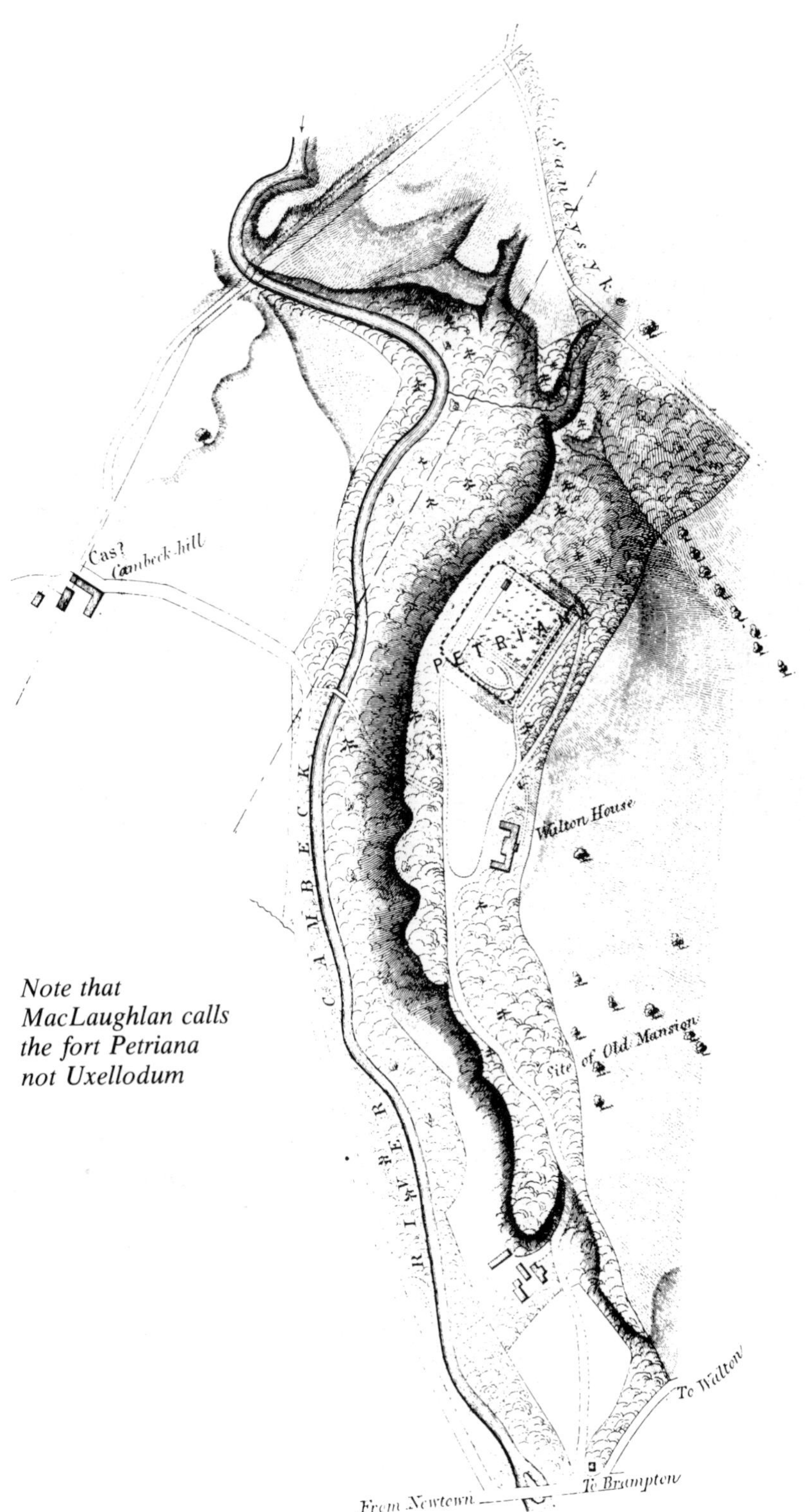


*Note that MacLaughlan calls the fort Petriana not Uxellodum*

Numerous inscriptions have been found, of which the best is the following:—

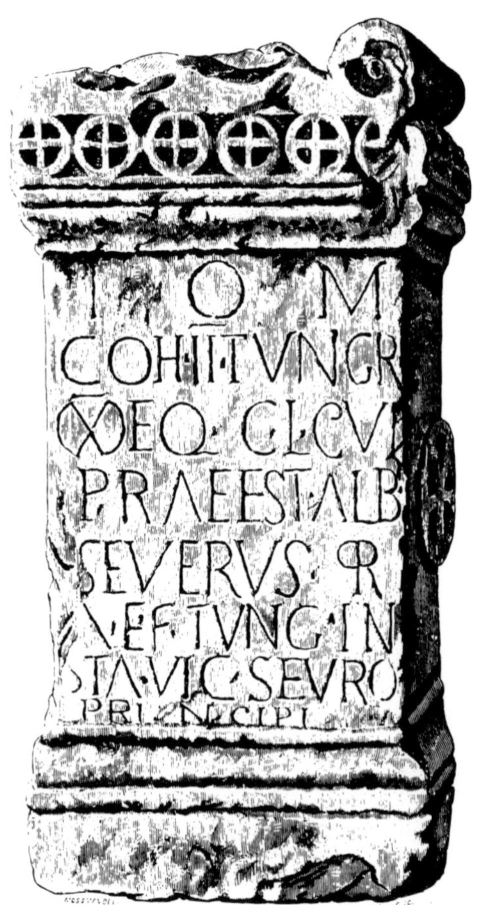


Size, 4 feet by 2 feet.

I(OVI) O(PTIMO) M(AXIMO)
COH(ORS) SECVNDA TVNGRO(ORVM)
M(ILLIARIA) EQ(VITATA) C(IVIVM)
L(ATINORVM) CVI
PRAEEST ALB(VS)
SEVERVS PR-
AEF(ECTVS) TVNG(RORVM) IN-
STA(NTE) VIC(TORE) SEV(E)RO
PRINCIPI

To Jupiter the best and greatest
the second cohort of Tungrians
a milliary cohort with a due proportion of cavalry citizens
of Latium
commanded by Albus
Severus pre-
fect of the Tungrians (ercted this)
under the superintendency of Victor Severus
princeps

The adornment of one side is Jove's Thunderbolt and on the other is the Wheel of Nemesis. Another interesting altar is to *Discipline* (c.210). The third line originally AVGGG, dedicated to the three emperors — Severus, Caracalla and Geta, but on the death of Severus and the murder of Geta, part was erased. Altars to Mithras, the Mothers, Maponus, Belatucadrus and the unknown Vanauns have been found but as yet no temple sites.

Castlesteads lies within the Vallum but not adjacent to the Wall, the only one in such a position. The Wall had already been built at the most convenient point for crossing the Cambeck (the bridge has not been found), then later the fort was built on the strongest spot. The way the Vallum deviates to pass the fort suggests it was laid out in relation to the first of the two forts on this site. The road from Castlesteads to the Stanegate has not yet been found. The Wall to the north of the fort was demolished when building Castlesteads House. The ditch however is still visible. Milecastle 57 can only be inferred since no remains have been found.

Size, 3 feet by 1 foot 9 inches

*Altar to Discipline*

*This alter by the "Hunters of Banna", now in Lanercost Priory, is probably from Birdoswald. This suggests the name of Birdoswald Fort was Banna and not Camboglanna*

Size, 2 feet 3 inches by 1 foot 6 inches

*Altar to Silvanus by the Hunters of Banna. (Birdoswald)*

*Romans taking prisoners*

*A study of two beggars in the Wall Country*

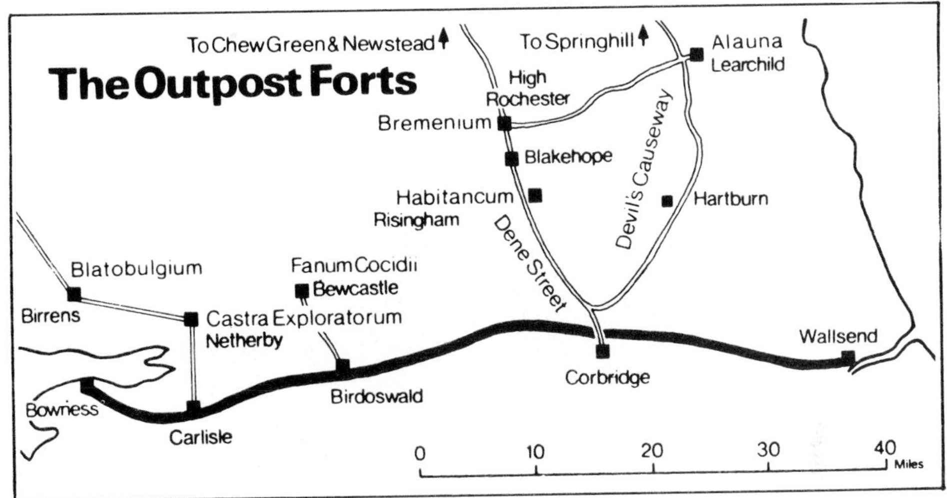


## THE OUTPOST FORTS

There were several major forts beyond the Wall and a number of fortlets and signal stations. Their importance varied as the Roman military strategy for defending the northern frontier changed during the centuries. Only occasionally were all occupied at the same time.

The first forts to be built in the early Flavian period (85-90) were High Rochester, Cappuck and Newstead, with Birrens a possibility. Under Hadrian three outpost forts at the western end of the Wall (Birrens, Netherby and Bewcastle) were established. It is unclear whether they indicated a threat from S.W. Scotland or were a protection for part of the Brigantian tribal territory which had been divided by the construction of the Wall. The forts on Dere Street seem to have been abandoned at this period.

With the Antonine occupation of Scotland, Risingham, Rochester and Newstead were reoccupied and rebuilt. When Scotland was abandoned the seven outpost forts were still in use controlling a large zone in advance of the Wall.

But by 180 Birrens, Newstead (and probably Cappuck) were abandoned, and a few years later Risingham (and probably High Rochester) suffered the same fate.

Under Severus, Netherby, Bewcastle, Risingham and High Rochester were rebuilt and strengthened, but Newstead and Birrens appear to have been abandoned. Under a new policy many of the military units defending the province were moved north to the outpost forts. All four forts were garrisoned by *Cohortes Milliariae Equitate,* mixed cavalry and infantry units one thousand strong. These auxiliary forces were powerful and versatile fighting units of which there were only five in Britain at this time. In addition Risingham, High Rochester and Netherby had additional detachments of scouts *(exploratores).*

With these large mobile forces carrying out widespread patrolling peace was maintained for several decades well into the fourth century. All the forts were reconstructed early in the century and Bewcastle and Risingham were rebuilt about 343. But twenty five years later the whole system ended and the forts were abandoned.

## NETHERBY

This outpost fort overlooks the River Esk and at one time was a port where silting up has been so extensive that today it is several miles from the sea. In the days of the Romans it was probably the lowest point at which the Romans could bridge the river. A road led north to Broomholm (where there was a fort rediscovered a few years ago) in Eskdale. The main road however was to the west to Birrens and then north to Scotland. To the south the road led to Stanwix.

Little is known of this fort since Netherby Castle is built on the site, preventing excavation. However the early antiquaries provide much valuable information. Leland describes it as a port as well as a fort — "Men alyve have sene Rynges and Staples yn the Walles, as yt had bene Stayes or Holdes for Shyppes". The area of the Roman encampment, though now scarcely discernible, was strongly marked in Camden's time. That antiquary speaks of "the little village of *Nether-By,* where are such strange and great ruins of an ancient city", and where "now dwelleth the

Size, 2 feet 10 inches by 2 feet 8 inches

IMP. CAES. M. AVRELIO
SEVERO ALEXANDRO PIO FEL. AVG.
PONT. MAXIMO TRI(I)B. POT. COS. P.P. COH. I AEL.
HISPANORVM (X) EQ. DEVOTA NVMINI
MAIESTATIQVE EIVS BASILICAM
EQVESTREM EXERCITATORIAM
IAMPRIDEM A SOLO COEPTAM
AEDIFICAVIT CONSVMMAVITQVE
SVB CVRA MARI(I) VALERIANI LEG.
AVG. PR. PR. INSTANTE M. AVRELIO
SALVIO TRIB. COH. IMP. D(OMINO) N(OSTRO)
SEVERO ALEXANDRO PIO FEL(ICE)
AVG(VSTO) CO(N)S(VLE)

To the Emperor Caesar Marcus Aurelius
Severus Alexander, pious, happy, august,
chief-priest, having the tribunitian power, consul, father of his country. The first cohort the AElian,
of Spaniards, a thousand strong, provided with horse,
devoted to his deity
and majesty, this basilica
for exercising horses,
long ago from the ground commenced,
built and completed,
by direction of Marius Valerianus imperial
legate and propraetor and under the inspection of Marcus Aurelius
Salvius, tribune of the cohort the emperor our lord
Severus Alexander, pious, happy,
august, being consul.

chiefe of the *Grayham's* family, very famous among the borderers for their martiale disposition". Stukeley's description (1725) is very valuable:—

*The foundations of the Roman castrum at Netherby appear round the house or present castle; it stood on an eminence near the river. Many antiquities are here dug up every day. The foundations of houses and streets are visible . . . A litter lower down has been some monumental edifice, or burial place, where they find many urns and sepulchral antiquities. — Iter Boreale, 58.*

His description of the countryside in his day is interesting:—

*The valley by the river is very good land, with some shadow of nature's beautiful face left; but everywhere else about us is the most melancholy, dreary view I ever beheld, and as the back-door of creation; here and there a castellated house by the river, whither at night the cattle are all driven for security from the borderers. As for the houses of the cottagers, they are mean beyond imagination; made of mud, and thatched with turf, without windows, only one storey; the people almost naked.*

Perhaps the Romans shared his views of the barren area when they were stationed there. The fort *vicus* lay to the north and west and in 1732 workmen, while digging near the house, found an external bath house whose plan was recorded. Flavian occupation of the site cannot be proved but an inscription of Hadrian and the 2nd Legion has been recorded. The garrison in the 2nd century was a quingenary cohort. The magnificent slab of 222 A.D., here reproduced, records the building of a cavalry drill-hall. It shows the garrison was the First Aelian Cohort of Spaniards, part-mounted and 1,000 strong *(Coh·I Aelia Hispanorum Milliaria).* This hall most probably stood in the middle of the fort, across the two principal streets, as did a similar one at Haltonchesters in the third century.

The original name of Netherby is unknown, (Eric Birley suggests BROCARA: Charles Daniels AXELODVNUM) but the *Antonine Intinerary* gives the 3rd century name as *Castra exploratorum* — "Fort of the Scouts".

The site in early days produced many important inscriptions and sculptures, some of which are shown here:—

D · M<br>TITVLLINIA<br>PVSSITTA ·<br>CIS · BAETA<br>VIXSIT ·<br>ANNOS · XXXV<br>MENSES VIII<br>DIES · XV ·

Diis manibus<br>Titullinia<br>Pussitta<br>civis Raeta<br>vixit<br>annos triginta quinque<br>menses octo<br>dies quindecim

To the spirits<br>of the departed;<br>Titullinia<br>Pussitta,<br>a Raetian lived<br>35 years,<br>8 months,<br>15 days . . . .

*Tombstone of Titullinia Pussitta, from Netherby*

*A Romana-British settlement*

*pposite. Roman soldiers in camp.*

*Cuculatti*

Size, 9 inches by 8 inches

*A fine sculpture, representing the Genius of the Camp. He wears the mural crown and holds in his right hand an offering to the Gods*

A number of altars to local deities have been found including Mogons Vitris, Mars Belatucadrus, and Cocidius. One of the most interest sculptures found at Netherby is that of the three *Genii Cuculatti.* This small relief shows three men standing erect wearing hooded cloaks *(cuculli),* and close fitting trousers, holding in their right hands an object, probably an egg, the symbol of fertility and immortality. Similar sculptures have been found at Housesteads and Carlisle. These little deities are found over a large area of the Roman Empire, but were probably Celtic in origin.

A typical Hadrianic bath-house was found in the *vicus* in 1732 and a plan made. In the cold room an altar to Fortuna was found dedicated by Marcus Aurelius Salvius, the same soldier responsible for rebuilding the Drill Hall (RIB 968).

In 1725 Stukeley and Roger Gale were on a visit to Netherby and Stukeley records: "We passed by a Roman fort upon the River Leven, where antiquities have been found. Westlinton on the River Lyne (the modern name for this river) midway between Stanwix and Netherby was probably the site of this fortlet but nothing definite has been found".

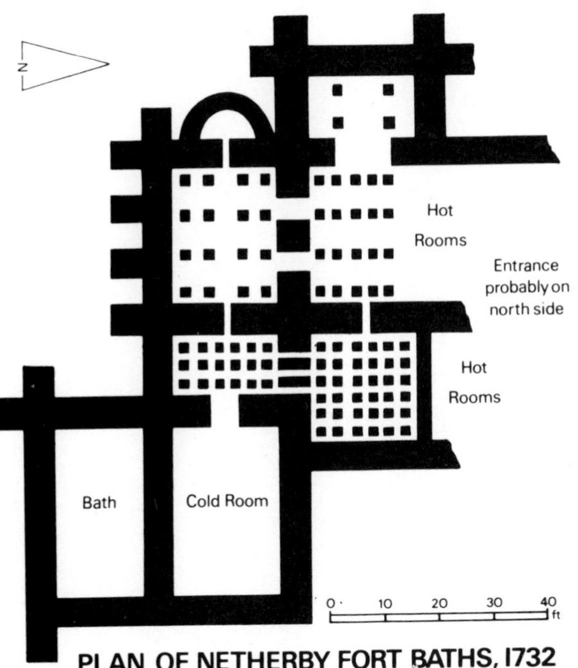


PLAN OF NETHERBY FORT BATHS, 1732

| | |
|---|---|
| DEAE SANCT | Deae sanct- |
| AE FORTVNAE | ae Fortunae |
| CONSERVATRICI | conservatrici |
| MARCVS AVREL | Marcus Aurelius |
| SALVIVS TRIBVN | Salvius tribun- |
| VS COH I AEL HI | us hortis AEliae Hi- |
| SPANORVM | spanorum |
| (X) EQ | milliariae equitatae |
| V S L M | votum solvit libens merito |

To the holy goddess Fortuna Conservatrix Marcus Aurelius Salvius, tribune of the first cohort of Spaniards, one thousand strong, part-mounted, willingly and deservedly fulfilled their vows

Size, 3 ft. 6 in. by 1 ft. 5 in.

*Romans burning a village as punishment*



*posite: 1st century Roman Legionaries with a 'Scorpion' Catapult and Balearic slingers*

## BIRRENS (Blatobulgium)

This outpost fort controlled the northern approaches to the Solway. The earliest fort was Flavian in date and very small, only 1.3 acres. It was replaced by a larger Hadrianic fort. An inscription, now lost, but quoted by Pennant, refers to the Twentieth Legion Victrix *(legio XX Vict(rix))* as the builders. The fort had a turf rampart with timber buildings and the central range in stone.

With the Antonine advance into Scotland the Hadrianic fort was demolished and replaced with a larger one in stone. The defences were provided by a turf rampart on a stone foundation with extensive ditches. On the north side six can still be seen. It is this fort which is still visible today. It was destroyed by fire (probably from enemy action), but was rebuilt in 158 A.D. under the governor Julius Verus as recorded in an inscription (RIB 2110).

When the Antonine occupation ended Birrens was still maintained as an outpost of Hadrian's Wall but was abandoned before the end of the second century. Near the fort was an "annexe" which could possibly be an earlier Agricolan fort. Before 158 the garrison was the *coh. I Nervia Germanorum Milliaria* as the following inscription (RIB 2097) records.

From 158 and onwards it was *coh. II Tungrorum Milliaria equitata C.L.* recorded on this altar to *Disciplina* (RIB 2092).

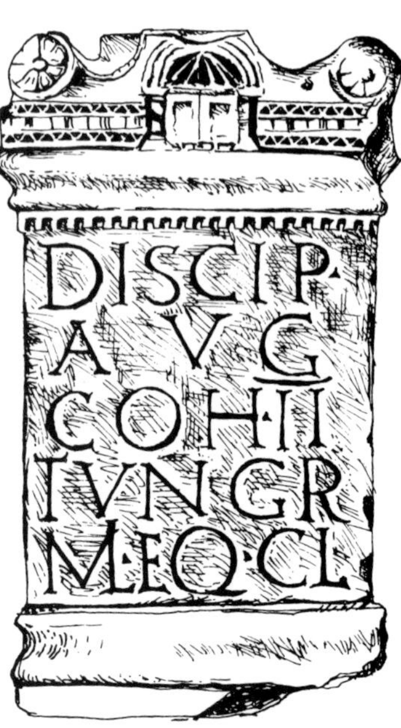


*Altar to Disciplina*

Dedications to *Disciplina* or *Discipulina* are rare in Britain. Two have come from Corbridge, one from Greatchesters, one from Chester, one from Castlesteads, one from Birrens, one from Bewcastle, and one from Bertha (near Perth), making eight in all. Altars to *Disciplina* were official and were erected in the aedes of the Headquarters Building which was the centre of the state religion. The altar from Birrens shows on its capital a front view of the *aedes* with its doors closed.

A detachment from the Second Cohort of Tungrians was serving in Raetia from 121 to 153 and there recruited some Germans. There are a number of altars from Birrens recording the local gods of these German recruits. The goddesses *Harimella, Ricagambeda* and *Virodecthis* are all mentioned.

At the end of the *Ravenna Cosmography* there occurs a list of tribal meeting places called *loca*. These are Maponi, Mixa, Panovius, Minox, Taba, Manavi, Segloes and Dannori. The *locus Maponi* has been identified with the *Clochmabenstane,* a large boulder which was once part of a megalithic monument on the coast south-west of Gretna. *Maponus* was a youthful Celtic god also found at Castlesteads and Corbridge. At these meeting places the local tribes met the Roman troops and officers responsible for maintaining peace and order.

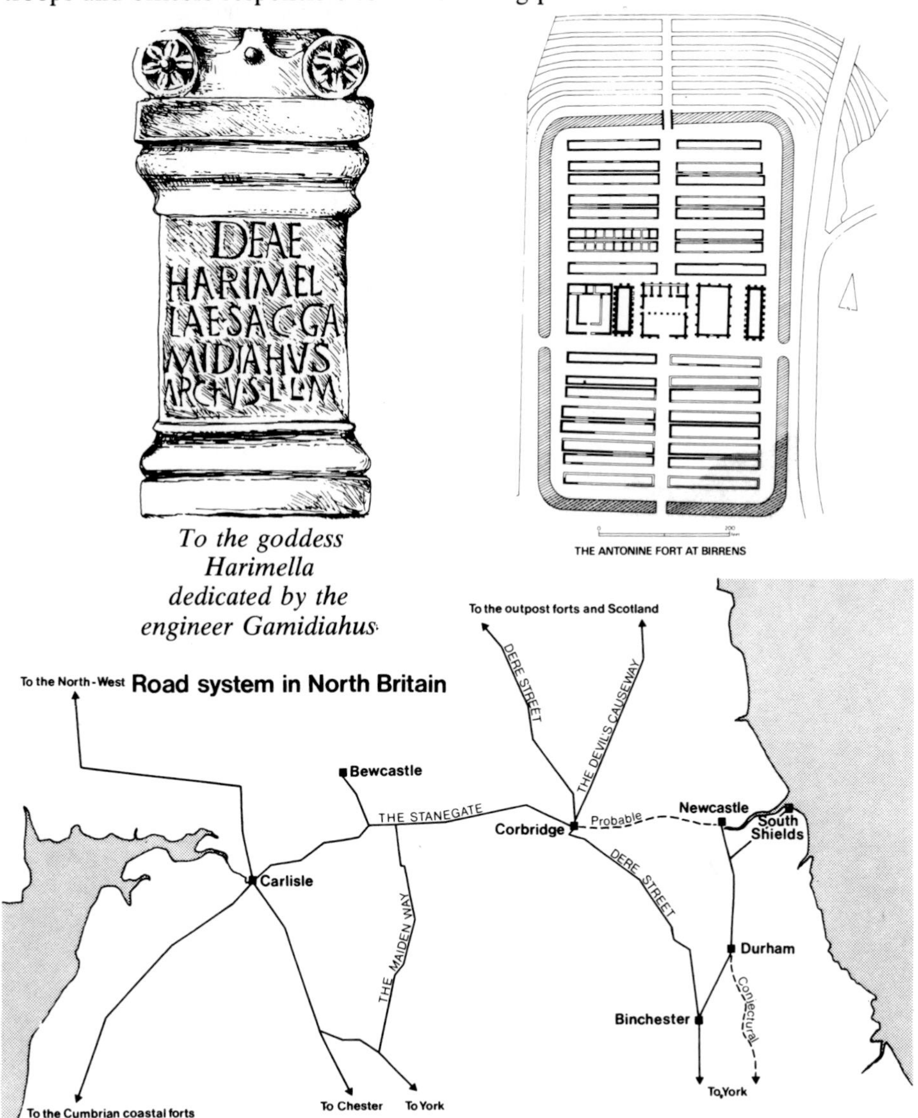


*To the goddess Harimella dedicated by the engineer Gamidiahus*

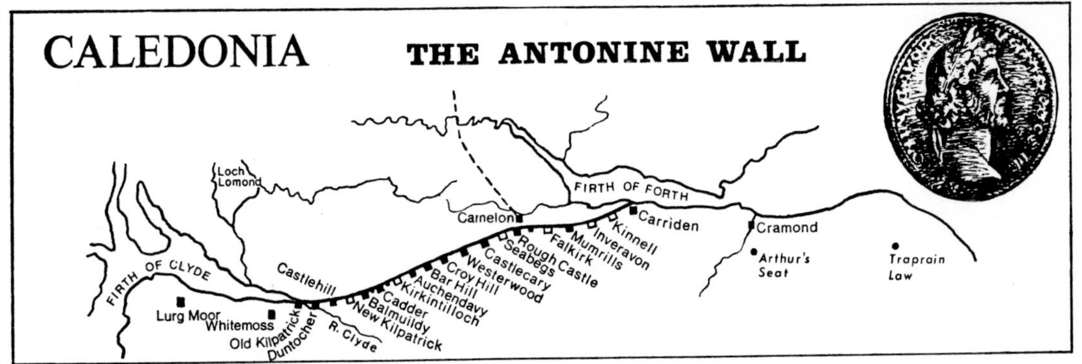


# THE ROMANS IN NORTH BRITAIN

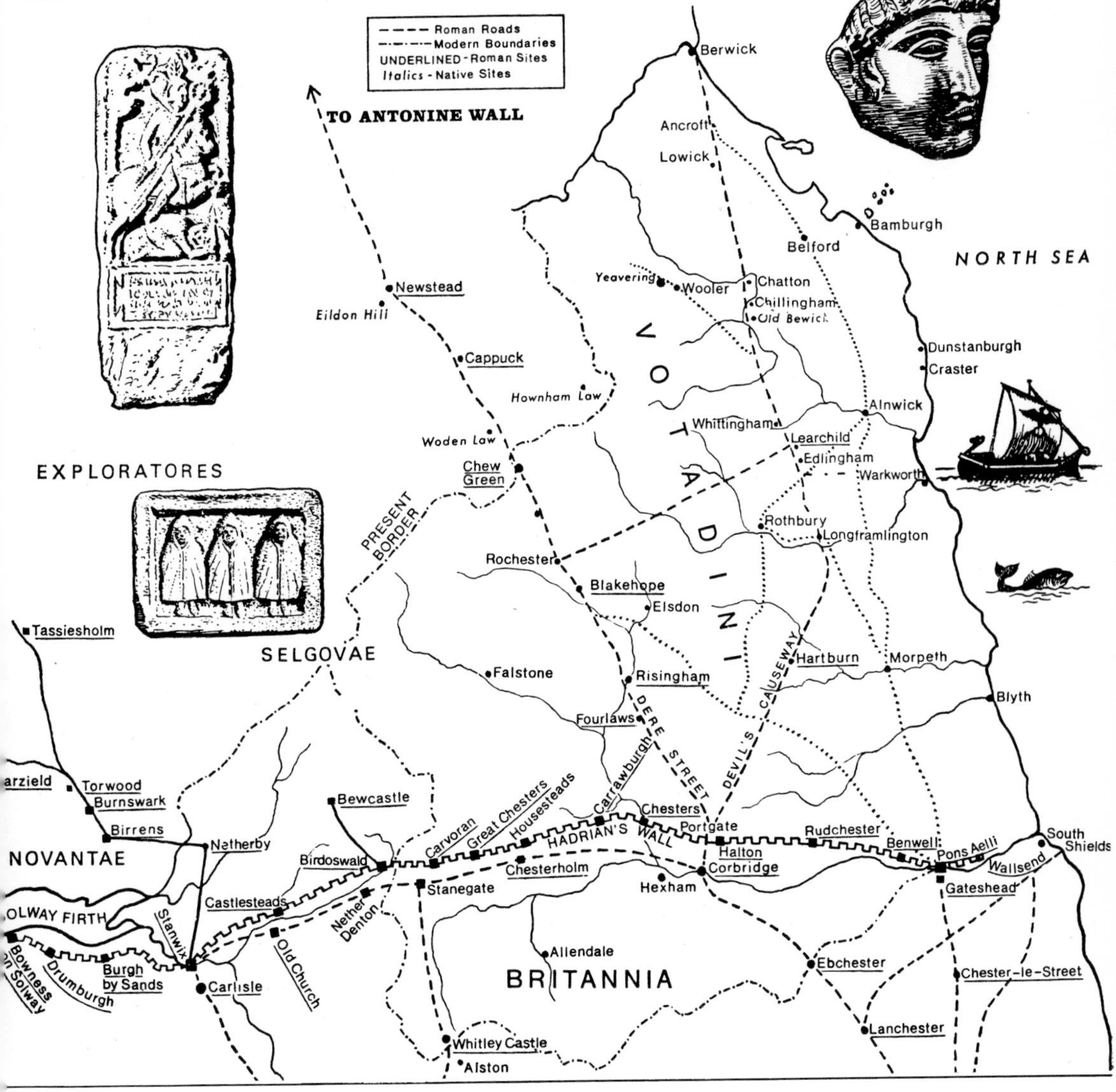

- - - - Roman Roads
-·-·- Modern Boundaries
UNDERLINED - Roman Sites
*Italics* - Native Sites

TO ANTONINE WALL
EXPLORATORES
Berwick
Ancroft
Lowick
Bamburgh
Belford
NORTH SEA
*Yeavering*
Wooler
Chatton
Chillingham
*Old Bewick*
Newstead
*Eildon Hill*
Cappuck
*Hownham Law*
Dunstanburgh
Craster
VOTADINI
Alnwick
Whittingham
Learchild
Edlingham
Warkworth
*Woden Law*
Chew Green
PRESENT BORDER
Rothbury
Longframlington
Rochester
Blakehope
Elsdon
Tassiesholm
SELGOVAE
Falstone
Risingham
Hartburn
Morpeth
Blyth
DEVIL'S CAUSEWAY
DERE STREET
Fourlaws
Carrawburgh
arzield
Torwood
Burnswark
Bewcastle
Birrens
Netherby
NOVANTAE
Birdoswald
Carvoran
Great Chesters
Housesteads
HADRIAN'S WALL
Chesters
Portgate
Rudchester
Benwell
Pons Aelli
South Shields
Wallsend
Halton
Corbridge
Chesterholm
Hexham
Gateshead
Castlesteads
Stanegate
Nether Denton
OLWAY FIRTH
Stanwix
Old Church
Allendale
Bowness on Solway
Drumburgh
Burgh by Sands
Carlisle
BRITANNIA
Ebchester
Chester-le-Street
Lanchester
Whitley Castle
Alston

*Opposite, Cavalry and Infantry of a Mixed Cohort, mid 2nd century, A.D.*

## RISINGHAM (Habitancum)

Shortly after the erection of Hadrian's Wall is was decided, in order to control the area north of the Wall, to re-occupy Dere Street. The operation was conducted by Quintus Lollius Urbicus in 139 A.D. It was then that Risingham was built. The garrison (the Fourth Cohort of Gauls, mounted) is commemorated on a remarkable sculptured slab now in the Library of Trinity College, Cambridge. The left panel shows Victory flying through space on a globe, while the right panel shows the war-god Mars in panoply. Near the top of the slab are two human heads, the one on the left a three-headed Janus. Beneath Victory is a stork striking fish, beneath Mars is a goose or cock.

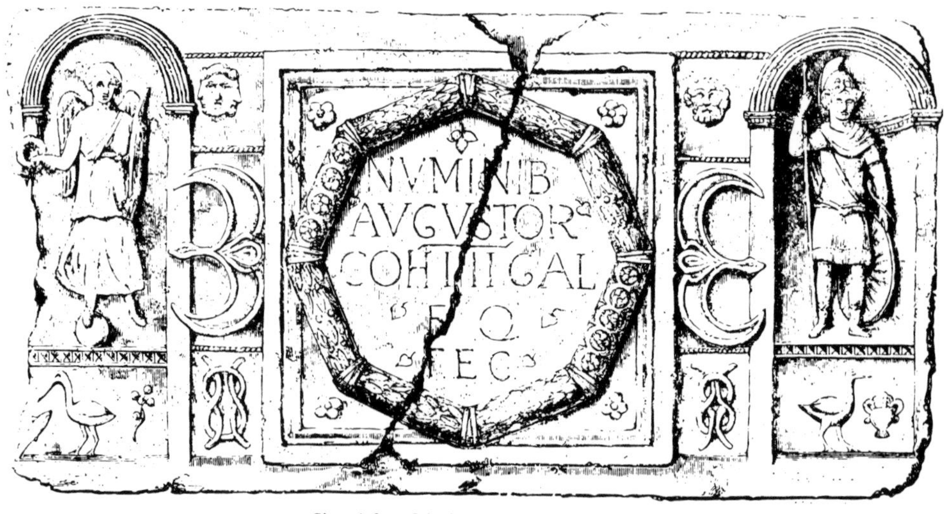


Size, 1 foot 8 inches by 2 feet 4 inches

| NVMINIB | Numinibus |
|---|---|
| AVGVSTOR | Augustorum |
| COH IIII GAL | cohors quarta Gallorum |
| EQ | equitata |
| FEC | feeit |

Risingham is eight miles south of High Rochester where Dere Street crosses the Rede. Although not mentioned in the *Antonine Itinerary* its Roman name is known to be *Habitanacum* from a later inscription. It occupies a site which was probably an island in a swamp on the edge of the Rede. The bridge across the Rede can still be traced by some tumbled stones.

At the end of the 2nd century when the Governor of Britain Albinus withdrew large numbers of troops to the Continent, *Habitancum* was either abandoned or destroyed which the entire northern defences collapsed. However, within a few years the Emperor Severus restored the wrecked forts and the Wall. A fine inscribed slab, dated 205-8 A.D., and here reproduced, comes from the south gate of *Habitancum.* It shows that the fort was completely rebuilt by the First Mounted Cohort of Vangiones, 1,000 strong. The fort measuring 400 by 450 feet over its ramparts was small in relation to the size of the garrison (standard size of a Hadrianic fort is 400 x 600 feet). However the third century garrison also included a *Numerus Exploratorum* or Unit of Scouts and a detachment of *Raeti Gaesati.* The *gaesati* were light footmen armed with the *gaesum,* a kind of spear. The entire garrison is mentioned in the fragments of an elaborate inscription.

Size, 5 feet 11 inches by 3 feet 7 inches

(To) . . . . Adiabenicus Maximus  
consul for the third time and Marcus Aurelius Antoninus pious  
consul for the second time august . . . . . .  
this gate with the walls through age di-  
lapidated by command of Alfenius Senecio an illustrious man  
of consular rank under the care of Oclatinius Adventus the procurator  
of our emperors the first cohort of Vangiones . . . .  
with AEmilius Salvianus its tribune  
from the ground restored

*Roman Gateway at Risingham (reconstruction)*

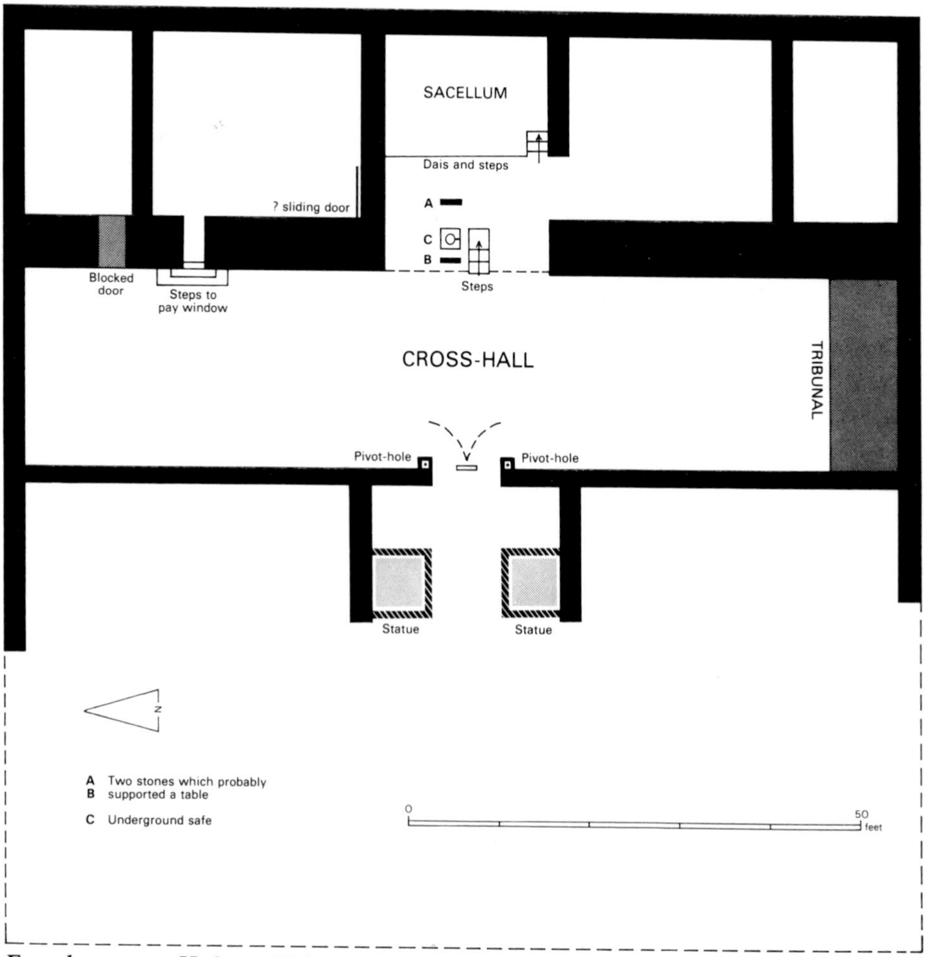

SACELLUM
Dais and steps
? sliding door
A
C
B
Blocked door
Steps to pay window
Steps
CROSS-HALL
TRIBUNAL
Pivot-hole
Pivot-hole
Statue
Statue
N

A Two stones which probably
B supported a table

C Underground safe

0 50 feet

*Fourth century H.Q. at Habitancum*

After a plan by Ian Richmond

*Formation of the Tortoise (Testudo)*

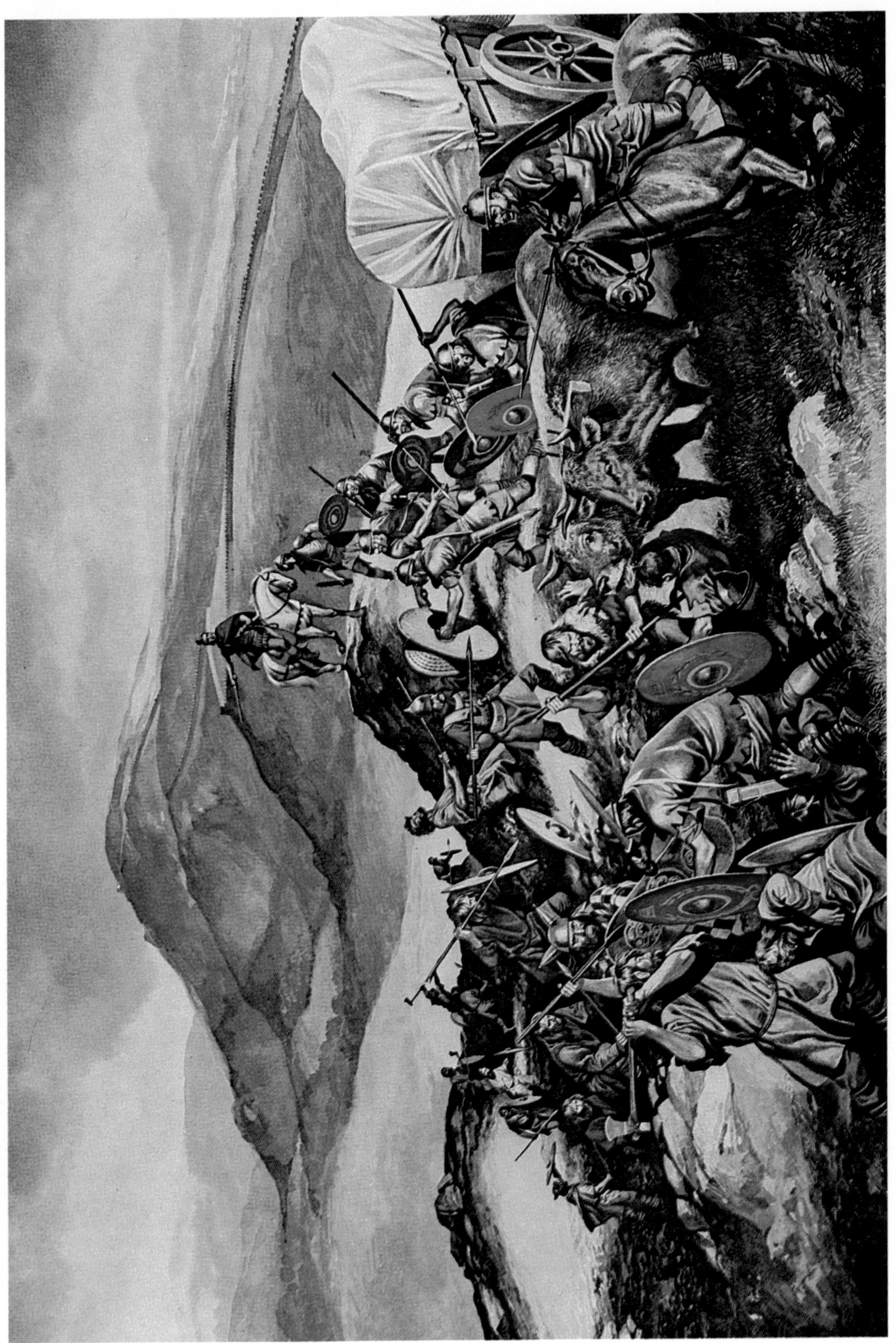

It is clear the garrison of Risingham was on regular patrol and some of the troops would be in temporary camps. The defences of *Habitancum* are very fine, partly because there was a supply of fine sandstone nearby, obtainable in large blocks. The south gate is of a type rare in Roman Britain at this date. The fort was apparently left in ruins when Count Theodosius restored the Wall in 368 A.D.

Camden, in his *Britannia,* 1607 edition, refers to Risingham as follows:—

"There is also another towne beneath of ancient memory, which *Rhead* watereth, or rather hath now well neare washed away; they call it at this day *Risingham,* which is in the ancient English and German language, *The Giants Habitation,* as *Risingberg* in Germany, *the Giants Hill.* Many shewes are there, and those right evident of antiquity. The inhabitants report that God Mogon defended and made good this place a great while against a certain *Soldan,* that is, *an Heathenish Prince.* Neither is this altogether a vaine tale. For that such a god was there honoured and worshipped is plainly proved by these two altar stones lately drawn out of the river there . . .".

One of these altars is here reproduced from Horsley.

The translation reads:— *"To the god Mogons of Cad . . . and to the spirit of our august Lord, Marcus Gavius (?) Secundinus, governor's staff officer, on completion of his first term of office at Habitancum, paid his vow willingly and deservedly for himself and his staff".*

(Horsley guessed that the word DEO should start the inscription. He was right because today the word can be traced with difficulty on the stone).

MOGONT CAD
ET·N·D·N AVG
M·G·SECVNDINVS
BF·COS·HABITA
NCI PRIMA STA
PRO SE ET SVIS POS

*Deo* Mogonti Cadenorum et
Numini Domini noſtri Auguſti
Marcus Gaius Secundinus beneficiarius c̃onſulis Habitanci
prima ſtatione pro ſe et ſuis poſuit

*Mogons* was a Germanic God associated with the Rhineland from which the Vangiones came.

The legend of Mogon has become attached to a remarkable sculpture called "Robin of Risingham". John Hodgson (1827) tells us that Parkhead Farm had become a mecca for visitors for here could be seen:—

*"the remains of the celebrated figure, called ROBIN OF RISINGHAM, which was cut in high relief upon a huge block of 'slidden' sandstone rock, on the brow of the hill, a few yards to the west of the modern Watling Street. The stone itself was five sided, six feet on the base, eight feet high, five feet on the two sides to the right of the middle of its front, seven feet on the uppermost side to the left, and four on the lower: its thickness six feet.*

*The figure itself was about four feet high; had a panel above it about 29 inches long, and 20 broad, as if intended for an inscription; and a square block or altar opposite the right knee, probably left for the same purpose. When West Woodburn-bridge was building, the masons had cut wedge holes in this stone to board and quarry it for ashlars; but Mr. Shanks, the proprietor of Park-head, pointing to the crag from which it had fallen said: 'No: this hill of rock is at your service; but no man shall destroy my images'. His son, however, has taken away the figure as far down as the girdle, by cutting the stone into gate-posts. This act of spoilage, it is said, was done to prevent the curious from trespassing over a few yards of barren land, and from enjoying the pleasure of visiting 'the man in stone', who for so many ages had been the talk and wonder of the neighbourhood.*

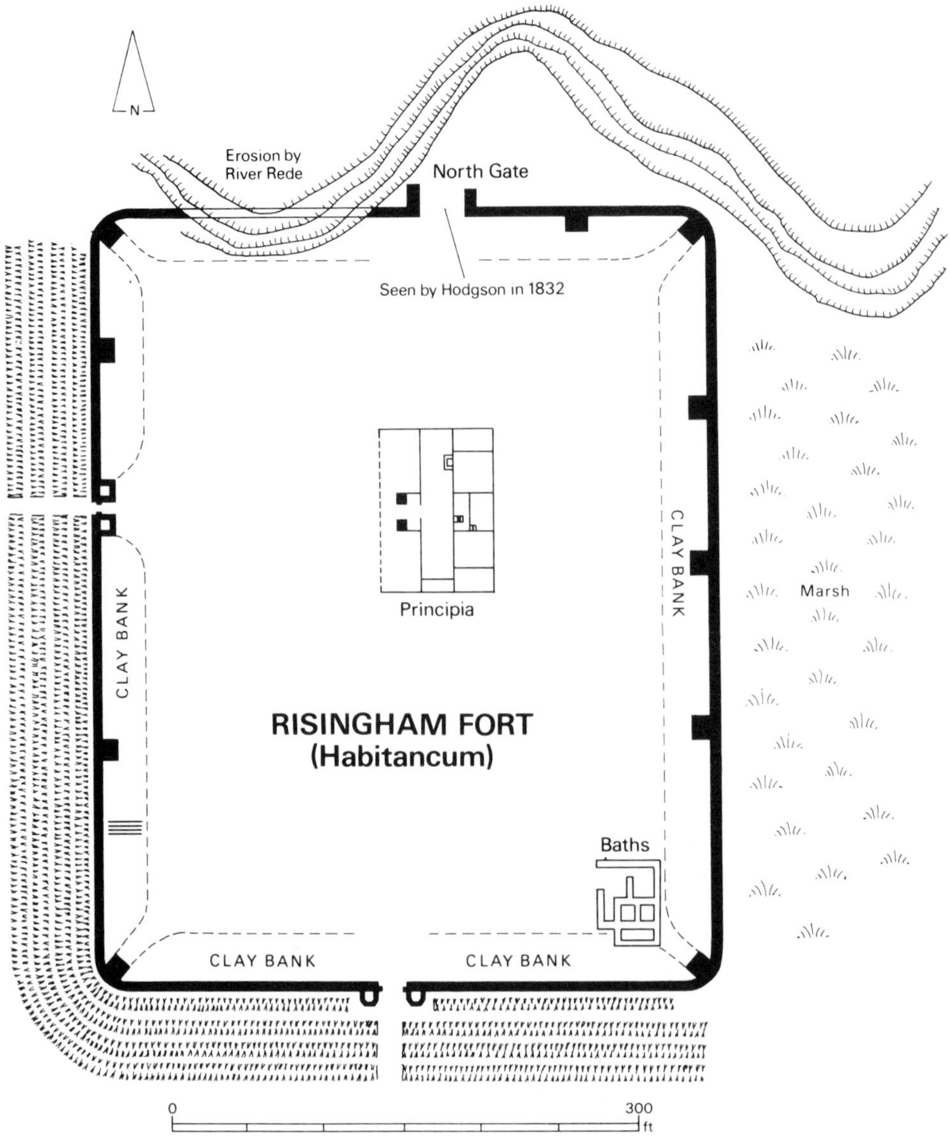

N

Erosion by River Rede

North Gate

Seen by Hodgson in 1832

Principia

CLAY BANK

CLAY BANK

Marsh

RISINGHAM FORT
(Habitancum)

Baths

CLAY BANK

CLAY BANK

0 300 ft

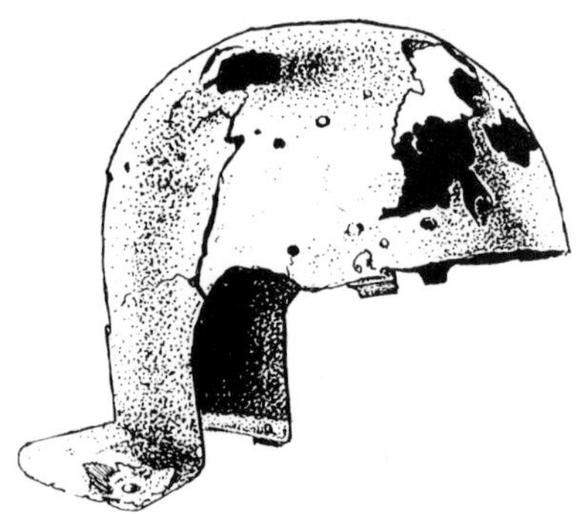

*Iron skull of a helmet from the fort at Newstead.*
*Museum of Antiquities, Edinburgh.*
*Late 1st century, A.D*

Sir Walter Scott mentions the carving in his poem "Rokeby".

"Some ancient sculptor's art has shown
An outlaw's image on the stone;
Unmatch'd in strength, a giant he,
With quivered back and kirtled knee,
Ask how he did, that hunter bold,
That tameless monarch of the wold,
And age and infancy will tell
By brother's treachery he fell".

He added a note that:—

One popular tradition is, that it represents a giant, whose brother resided at Woodburn, and he himself at Risingham. It adds, that they subsisted by hunting, and that one of them, finding the game become too scarce to support them, poisoned his companion, in whose memory the monument was engraved".

The sculpture almost certainly represents a god worshipped by the Romans. Rock carvings of this kind were often found near Roman quarries. They were living sculptures.

## RISINGHAM BROOCH

The following brooch was found at Risingham. It is Celtic in workmanship and similar brooches have been found elsewhere in the north of England. Celtic influence was strong in the north and the Celtic element continued to hold its own in this part of the Roman province long after the Roman occupation.

*Bronze brooch from Risingham.*
*Now in the Black Gate Museum.*

An interesting altar to Cocidius Silvanus was found near Risingham. The front part of the elaborately carved frieze upon the capital of the altar is here shown. It depicts Cocidius, a hunting dog, and stags in a forest. It has been suggested that Cocidius is really Robin of Risingham since the god on the frieze is very similar to the drawing of Robin.

*Altar to Cocidius*

Risingham has provided a very large collection of inscriptions. Although the plan of the internal bath-house is difficult to understand, five inscriptions have survived, two of which are remarkable altars to Fortuna.

The famous "Dream Altar" (RIB 1228) was found by the side of a spring on the east side of Dere Street where it is crossed by the road from Redesdale to Broomhope Mill.

Although the *vicus* area is not known, sixteen tombstones, mainly civilian, have been recovered.

Size, 3 feet by 1 foot 5 inches

Size, 2 feet 9 inches by 1 foot

SOMNIO PRAE
MONITVS
MILES HANC
PONERE IVS
SIT
ARAM QVAE
FABIO NVP
TA EST NVM
PHIS VENE
RANDIS

*The Dream Altar*

## BLAKEHOPE CAMP

Dere Street passed Risingham on the west side and from the south and west gateways branch roads probably joined it. Remains of a Roman bridge were found west of the fort which probably carried Dere Street (note that near here the Rede has changed its course several times). After passing the fort Dere Street takes a north east line until it joins the A68 about one mile north of West Woodburn. Four miles along the A68 brings us to Troughend. Another mile and a half we find to the west of the road the marching camp of Dargues. It measures some 330 yards by 220 yards but is not quite rectangular in shape, covering 15 acres, almost large enough to take a legion. Each side has a gateway with an internal traverse of bank and ditch for extra protection. Fourteen temporary or marching camps can be found along Dere Street in Redesdale, a collection matched only by those near Haltwhistle Burn on Hadrian's Wall. The number of gates in these camps vary. The front gate is the *porta praetoria,* so called because it led to the general's tent or *praetorium.* The two main side gates are the *portae principales dextra* and *sinistra* on the left and right sides of the *praetorium.* Very large camps also had minor side gates called the *portae quintanae dextra* and *sinistra.* The near gate, the *porta decumana,* is in the centre of its side opposite the *porta praetoria.* The gateways nearly always had an extra defence as a substitute for permanent doors. There were two methods, The more common is the traverse which is a rampart and ditch similar to the main defences placed in front of the gateway at a distance equal to the width of the gateway. The Roman name is *tutulus,* derived from the Roman priest's spiked hat. The second and less common method is the clavicle (the Roman word for *clavicula* — a hooked key or collar-bone). The clavicle is usually used internally and is a quarter extension of the rampart at the gateway. It is always on the right side and so exposes the attackers unshielded side. The Dargues camp has clavicles to defend the gates. Both types can be seen at Birdhope. A mile beyond Dargues is the Roman fort of Blakehope on the east of the road, with its ramparts and ditches clearly visible, overlooking the Rede. It was first described by MacLaughlan:

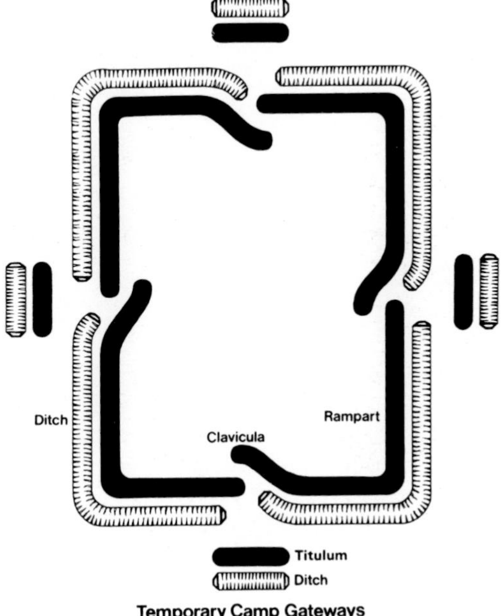

Temporary Camp Gateways

"It is on a rising ground where the turn-pike road makes a turn to the east to Elishaw Bridge. The place is called Brown Rigs, and the camp is on Blakehope Farm. The ramparts have been so utterly destroyed, and the ditch filled up, that it is with the greatest difficulty that the whole of the outline can be made out. It appears to have consisted of an interior area of about three acres; the sides being, as well as can be ascertained; about 130 and 110 yards respectively, and with probably four entrances, for the traces of three can be made out, and that in the west front retains faint traces of its traverse in front; but what was the height of the rampart, or the breadth of the ditch, it is impossible to conjecture, for the plough has been over it after it has been levelled".

In 1955 the camp was partly excavated and the rampart was found to be of turf and later burnt. Inside some pre-Hadrianic pottery was recovered. It is a cohort fort, single ditch, and with at least two gates with an annexe to the south. Air photography in 1955 revealed the larger camp, as shown on MacLaughlan's map, measuring 240 by 310 yards.

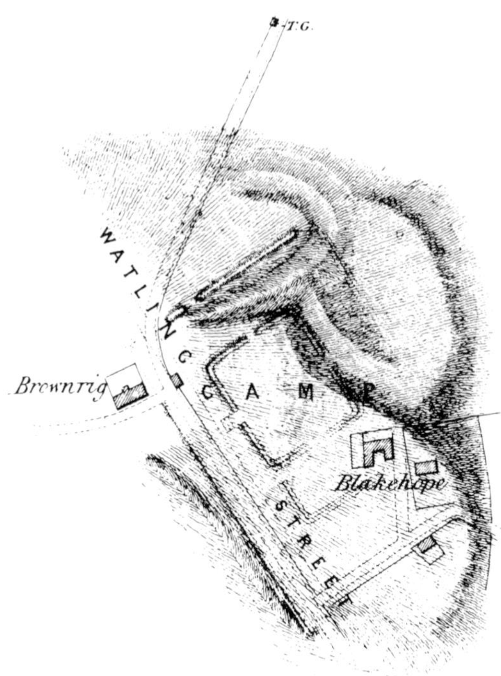


Blakehope fort was probably established to guard the bridge which carried Dere Street across the Rede nearby at Elishaw. Wallis wrote: "At Elishaw . . . the river crossed by Watling Street by a bridge of arches; some of the stones still to be seen with iron cramps in them and melted lead. Beyond the A68 joins the Otterburn-Newcastle road (A696), but Dere Street continues on the west of the modern road. It crosses the A68 at Blagrow and then makes straight for Rochester. At Blagrow is a large oblong marching camp measuring about 500 by 180 yards, able to accommodate a legion but later reduced to half size by a cross rampart and ditch. Three gates can be traced guarded by external traverses.

*Signal Tower*

## SIGNALLING ON DERE STREET

The method of signalling between Birdoswald and the outpost fort at Bewcastle is well known. On Dere Street some signal system would have been established. Between Bremenium and Habitancum signalling would have been difficult due to the rolling terrain. Perhaps fast riders were used. South from Habitancum however, after a march of 2½ miles near Four Laws, the Roman Wall is sighted at a distance of seven miles in a direct line to the Limestone Bank Milecastle (MC 30). Here, under the lee of the hill, and so invisible from the north, several circular platforms are found. It was long thought these platforms were the basis of a Roman signalling system, although no-one could explain their intelligent use. We now know they are of recent construction. They are foundations for storing bracken which was used for bedding cattle. It is fairly certain that where signalling was needed on Dere Street, signalling stations like the one shown here were constructed.

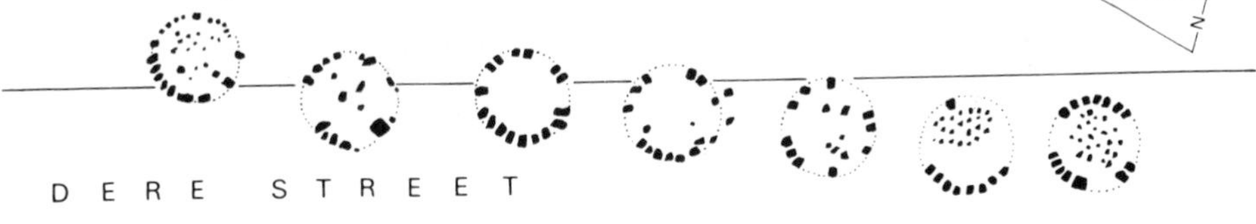


*Seven Platforms*

## HIGH ROCHESTER (Bremenium)

Bremenium is one of the finest forts in Britain and is on a site of great strategic interest. The earliest Roman occupation of the site was represented by the turf rampart of an Agricolan fort. After a few years it was replaced by timber but was not occupied during the Hadrianic period, for not long after 105 A.D. it was destroyed by fire. While Lollius Urbicus was Governor of Britain it was succeeded by a stone fort. A building inscription dated 142 A.D. shows he stayed here when on his way north to build the Antonine Wall in Scotland. It was reconstructed under Severus at the beginning of the 3rd century, when the Scottish Wall had been abandoned, and became a place of great importance. Its occupation came to an end about 340 A.D. The fort was destroyed by fire and not restored, although Habitancum was.

IMP · CAES · T · AELIO
HD ANTONIO · AVG · PIO · P · P
SVB · Q · LOL · VRBICO
LEG · AVG · PRO · PRAE
COH · I · LING
E Q F

Imperatori Caesari Tito AElio
Hadriano Antonino Augusto Pio
patri patriae
sub Quinto Lollio Urbico
legato Augusti pro-praetore
cohors prima Lingonum
equitata fecit

To the Emperor Caesar Titus AElius
Hadrianus Antoninus Augustus Pius,
father of his country
under Quintus Lollius Urbicus

imperial legate, and propraetor,
the first cohort of Lingones,
having a due proportion of cavalry,
erected (this building)

The garrison was in the 2nd century *coh. I Lingonum,* then the *Coh. I Delmatarum.* In the 3rd century it was *coh. I fida Vardullorum milliaria.* Two of these units appear on the illustrations illustrated.

The fort we see today is basically Severan with later alterations. It is almost square measuring 485 by 445 feet, and covers almost five acres.

G · D · N · ET
SIGNORVM
COH · I · VARDVLL
ET N EXPLORA
TOR · BREM · GOR
EGNAT · LVCILI
ANVS · LEG AVG PR PR
CVRANTE CASSIO
SABINIANO TRIB

Genio Domini nostri et
signorum
cohortis primae Vardullorum
et numeri explora-
torum Bremeniensium Gordianorum
Egnatius Lucili-
anus legatus Augusti propraetor
curante Cassio
Sabiniano tribuno.

To the genius of our lord (the
Emperor) and
of the Standards
of the first cohort of the Vardulli
and the exploratory Bremenian
troop styled the Gordian,
Egnatius Lucilianus,
imperial legate and propraetor,
(under the inspection of Cassius
Sabinianus, the tribune)
(erects this altar)

IMP CAE . . . . . .
. . . . . .P · F. . . . . .
. . . .COH · I · F VARD
. . . .BALLIS · A SOLO R. . . .
SVB · C · CL · APELLINI LE(G) AVGG
INSTANTE · AVR QVINTO TR

Imperatori Caesari . . . . . .
. . . . . .pio felici . . . . . .
. . . .cohors prima fida Vardullorum
. . . .ballistarium a solo refecit
sub cura Claudii Apellini legati Augustorum
instante Aurelio Quinto tribuno

To the Emperor Caesar (Marcus Aurelius
Antoninus) Pius, happy . . . . . .
. . . . . .the first cohort of Vardulli styled the faithful
. . . . . .this ballistarium from the ground restored
by direction of Claudius Apellinius the legate of the emperors
Aurelius Quintus the tribune superintending the work.

The fort at Bremenium is famous for its 3rd century artillery defences. On the ramparts large platforms were constructed for machines like the *onager* (a small version of the *ballista),* whose power was derived from hair rope in torsion. From the north and west ramparts these machines could be used against anyone advancing down Dere Street.

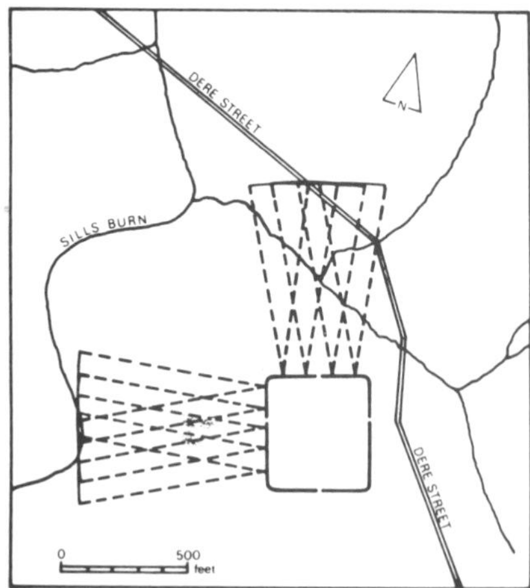

*High Rochester during excavation*

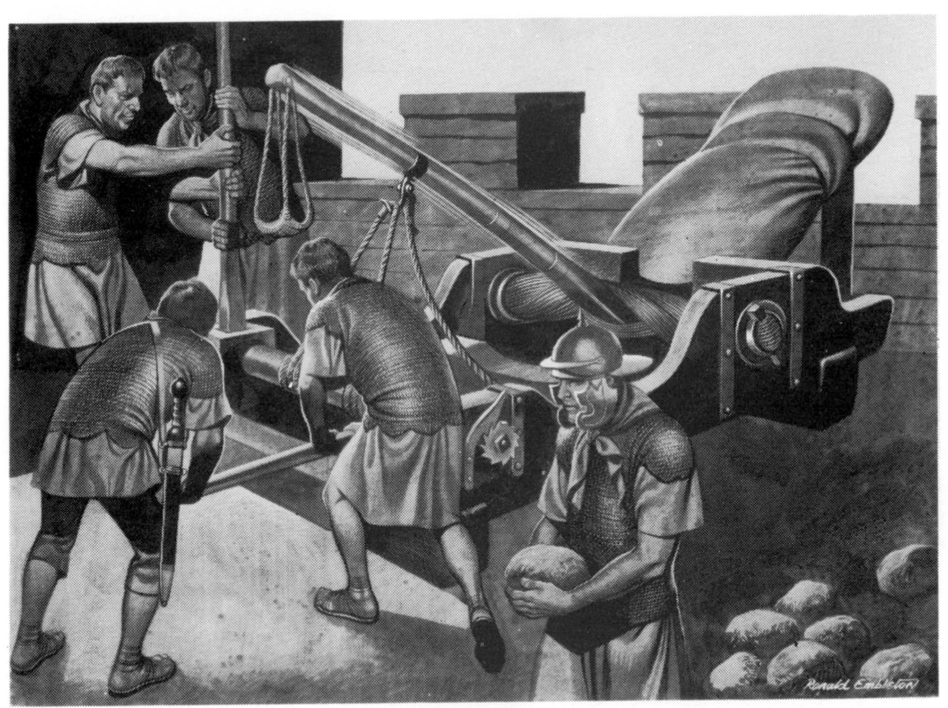


*A Catapult*

*Barrier for gateway to temporary camp*

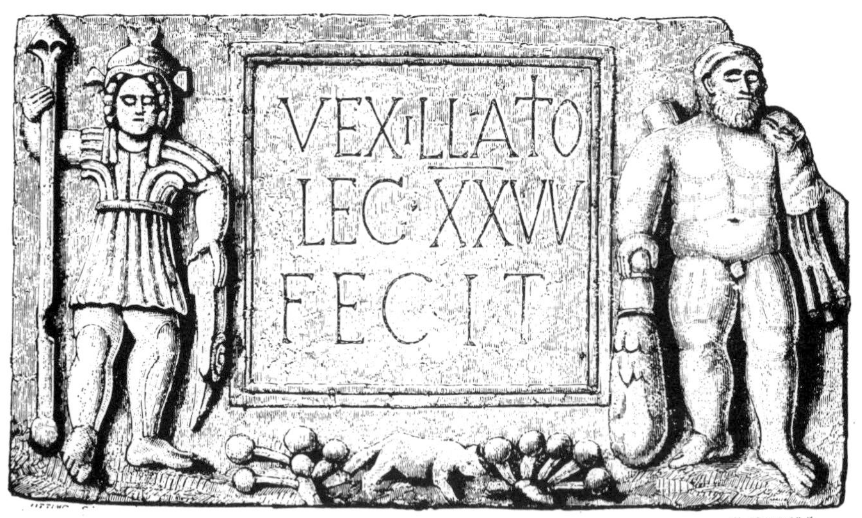


Size, 4 feet 6 inches by 2 feet 6 inches.

**ONAGER**

The Onager (wild ass) was the largest weapon used in the Roman Army. The word *scorpio* is also used. It worked on the torsion principle. A skein of rope was tightened and a wooden arm drawn back on to a loose hair spring. When released the arm is flung upwards throwing a huge stone from a sling at its end. Five soldiers worked this machine, one to fire and four to twist the rope.

Stones about a hundredweight each were used, double usual size, perhaps showing improvements in artillery.

There were smaller machines called catapults *(catapultae)* and *ballistae.* They were like a large cross-bow and threw large metal-headed bolts.

The fort of Bremenium was excavated in 1852 and 1855. The work was not very scientific and was poorly recorded. Fortunately part of the area was left unexplored and a modern excavation would probably yield valuable results. A small dig was carried out in 1935.

The plan of the first excavation shows that the interior of Bremenium was very crowded and the plan of the forts found on Hadrian's Wall was not strictly adhered to. A very large number of buildings had hypocausts — necessary in the very inclement weather encountered here. An extraordinary number (four) of large underground tanks were found. Their use is not known.

To provide for *ballistae* the walls of Bremenium were very thick. On the west wall (L. in the plan), a section is twenty-eight feet thick. The sketch shows how the artillery covered the approaches from the north. The excavation of 1935 revealed one of these large gun platforms extending several feet behind the thick walls. Two of the missiles used can be seen on the gable of the former school at Rochester and two inscriptions recording *ballistae* have been found. One is shown here.

Two religious altars have been found at Bremenium giving the name of the fort. One is shown on page 289. It is now at Alnwick Castle. The Vardulli came from the north of Spain, and since the first cohort of Vardulli is named on several of the inscriptions found at Bremenium, we can assume it was the garrison here. Gordian reigned from A.D. 238 to 244.

Although the fort is now part of the village green of High Rochester there is a fair amount still to see. The west wall is the best preserved with a steep bank nine feet high and facing stones in places. The south gate is entered by a modern road and a guard chamber with walls ten feet high can still be seen, and the west gateway is complete to the springing of the arch. However, the remains are now suffering from neglect and unless consolidated and cleared of undergrowth there will soon be little to see.

The fort has provided many interesting inscriptions, almost fifty in all, of which we reproduce two outstanding examples:—

1. *Venus with nymphs.* The relief is based on a classical scene, showing the goddess of beauty emerging from a pool formed by a woodland spring and preparing to dress her hair. Two nymphs with ewer and basin attend her. The Celtic artist was however unable to produce such a classical scene and the carving is crude. The stone is now at Alnwick Castle.

Size, 3 feet 6½ inches by 2 feet 4 inches.

2. *Building inscription of the 20th Legion.* The inscription reads: *A detachment of the Twentieth Legion, styled Valeria and Victorious, made this.* Mars, the God of War, is on the left, and Hercules on the right. The boar between them is the symbol of the legion. Mars is dressed in full armour, bearing a spear and shield. Hercules is represented as fully grown and bearded with a massive muscular frame. He carries a club and a quiver full of arrows with a lion skin on his shoulders. Both figures are crudely carved but show great vigour. They are soldiers, not 'artists' sculptures.

*Roman Tombs in Watling Street near High Rochester*
*(Reconstruction by Gill Embleton)*

*Altar to*
*Rufinus*

Size, 3 feet 1 inch by 2 feet 6 inches

Size, 2 feet by 1 foot 7 inches

IMP · CAES · M · AVR . .
. .PIO · F..
TRIB · POT (II)I COS III P(RO) . .
P · P · BALLIST · A SOL COH . .
VARDVL . . . .
TIB · CL · PAVL . . . . . .
PR · PR · FE . . . .
P · AEL . . . .

Imperatori Caesari Marco Aurelio
Antonino pio felici
tribunitiae potestatis tertium consuli tertium proconsuli
patri patriae ballistarium a solo cohors (prima fida)
Vardullorum (Antoniniana sub)
Tiberio Claudio Paulino (legato Augusti)
propraetore fecit (instante)
Publio Aelio . .

Travellers in the third century when approaching Bremenium from the south would have seen a large cemetery flanking the road. Among the funeral monuments our traveller would have seen four important tombs here reconstructed. Built tombs of the Roman period are rare in Britain, so the circular tomb whose remains can still be seen is important. The base consists of two course millstone grit. One stone in the lower course has been decorated with an animal's head. Cremated remains were found, an urn with bones (probably those of a Roman officer), and a coin of Severus (222-235). The tomb was discovered and excavated in 1850 by William Coulson, an Inland Revenue officer who was stationed at Bremenium to prevent whisky smuggling from Scotland. He found three other rectangular tombs whose stones have since been used to build a sheep-fold nearby.

The circular tomb was probably conical, the upper portion being composed of earth. There was probably a panel bearing the name of the deceased on the side of the tomb nearest to the road, and, perhaps, the whole was surmounted by a pine-cone ornament as a finial. (Ian Richmond).

A tombstone, now in Elsdon church, briefly records the official career of one Rufinus and his wife, stating that she herself was a woman of high social standing, being a senator's daughter.

Although the lettering is badly damaged it can be read from the 5th line:—

(praef(ecto)) coh(ortis) I Aug(ustae) (pr(aetoriae)) Lusitanor(um)
item coh(ortis) II Breucor(um), subcur(atori) viae Flaminiae et
aliment(orum), subcur(atori) operum pub(licorum), Iulia Lucilla
c(larissima) f(emina) marito b(ene) m(erenti); vix(it) an(nis)
XLVIII m(ensibus) VI d(ie)b(us) XXV.

This is an interesting stone because it is the only one in Britain describing the career of a Roman officer. Of his five appointments the first two were as military prefect in charge of cohorts in Egypt and Mauretania. Then he held two posts in the civil service in Italy as sub-curator of the Flaminian Way and Corn Doles, then sub-contractor of public works at Rome. He died while tribune of Coh. I Vardullorum at Bremenium fort at the age of 48½ years. His career shows that Roman officers were often transferred from one country to another and sometimes served to, what was in this case, an advanced age.

DEAE SANCTAE
MINERVAE
FLAVIVS SE
VERINVS
TRIB ARAM
DEDIT

Deae sanctae
Minervae
Falvius Se-
verinus
tribunus aram
dedit.

To the holy goddess
Minerva,
Flavius Se-
verinus,
the tribune, this altar
dedicated.

*An Altar from Bremenium*

*This altar has carved upon its capital two palm branches and two crescent moons. The palm branch is a token of victory. The crescent on a tombstone usually indicates hope for the future.*

*Decorated Harness Mountings from Newstead*
*(from J. Curle. A Roman Frontier Post and its People. 1911)*

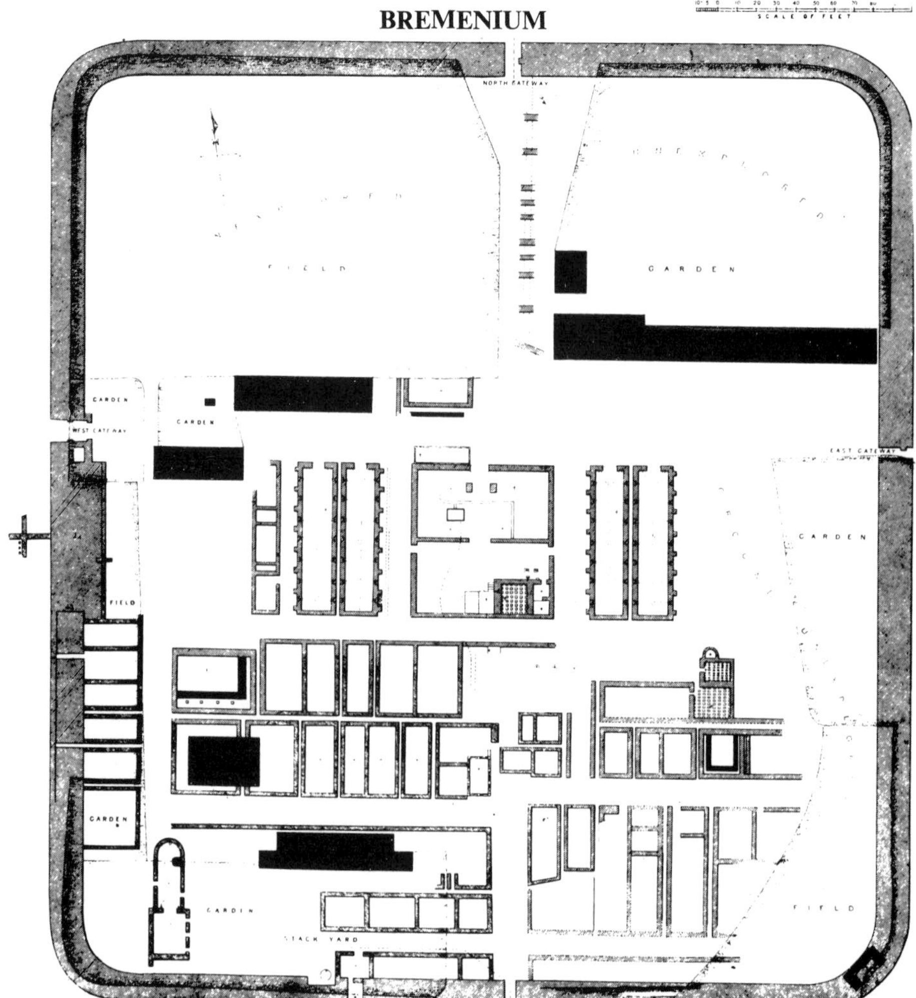


Across the Sills Burn from Bremenium is **Birdhope Camp.** It consists of two camps, one inside the other. The large camp was a temporary one and could hold a legion, the smaller camp, which is the better preserved, was probably occupied for a period when its occupants were probably engaged on engineering works in the neighbourhood. North of Birdhope along Dere Street are four more temporary camps which were revealed by air photography. Sills Burn South and North camps have both been affected by agricultural work and are difficult to trace. Further on is the large camp of Silloans. Dere Street passes through it. Since Dere Street was the work of Agricola, Silloans is one of the earliest dated camps in North Britain.

The next camp discovered from the air is Featherwood East, four miles north of Silloans, a large camp over 400 yards square with prominent ramparts. Nearby is Featherwood West built in the shape of a diamond. These two camps are in the most exposed site in Britain for Roman occupation. Nearby is the summit of Foulplay Head (1,500 feet). From here to the border the only suitable place for a camp is Chew Green, and here there are three temporary camps and two fortlets, all crowded together.

Between Featherwood and Chew Green however is an interesting part of Dere Street. Here can be seen the sockets of two crosses which were probably Roman guide posts. They are called the Outer Golden Pot and the Inner Golden Pot. Roy, in his *Military Antiquities,* speaks of five or more of these stones remaining between Redesdale and Chew Green.

*Outer Golden Pot, Chew Green*

**CHEW GREEN**

The collection of camps and forts at Chew Green is of great interest. Amid the chaos of forts overlapping each other and the crowded and complicated site there is definite order which explains the various purposes for which these fortifications were built.

The camps at Chew Green provided a defence and a refuge at a lonely and exposed part of Dere Street. Extra horses stationed here would provide replacements for convoys and travellers including the Imperial Post.

First to be built was the temporary or marching-camp (A). It was part of the Agricolan defences. It was abandoned after a short period when a small permanent road post was built on its eastern rampart. We have marked it (B) on the main plan.

In the second century it was decided to strengthen the post at Chew Green. The groups of fortifications now seen on the site is unique. On arrival to carry out the developments the troops built within a few hours the north marching camp (C). They left the best part of the site vacant for the forts they intended to build. The temporary camp was 982 by 625 feet with six gates defended by traverses and a ditch. Probably half a legion came here at first, but within a few weeks half of them would leave and those left built the Labour Camp (D), within the earlier marching camp. This was a strong and semi-permanent fortification and during the occupation of Chew Green would only occasionally be occupied when a large force was passing along Dere Street.

The Labour Camp had four gates defended by both traverses and clavicles. The rampart was 12 feet in width, and the ditch ten feet wide and four-and-a-half feet deep. Metalled streets were laid down showing it was occupied for a fair period and a *ballisterium* was erected inside the south wall.

The troops in the Labour Camp erected the fortlet (E) on top of the original fortlet (B). The turf rampart was eighteen feet wide and on three sides was defended by a triple ditch. Since this ditch was dug with difficulty out of slate, which here comes to the surface, it illustrates the importance of this fortlet. On the south there was a single ditch, for here the rampart was covered by two annexes which were entered separately from Dere Street. Here waggon trains could take shelter, especially during the blizzards which swept the area during winter. Dere Street was the main road into Scotland and military and commercial traffic would be considerable. A special unit was probably stationed here for the repair and maintenance of Dere Street.

*A cobbler at work, attached to most Roman forts would be a cobblers' shop, either in the* vicus *or in the fort workshops*

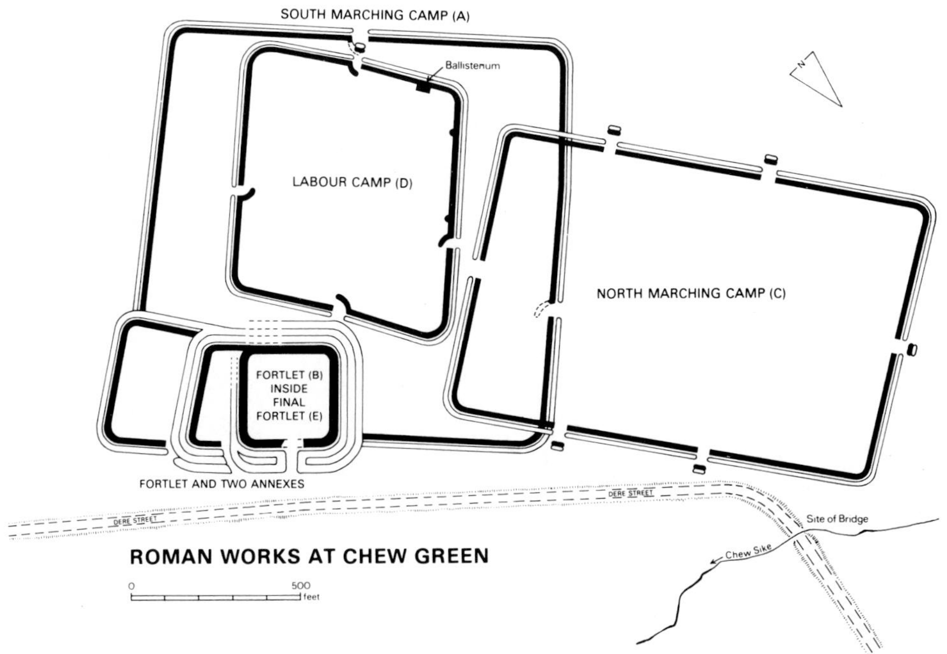


**ROMAN WORKS AT CHEW GREEN**

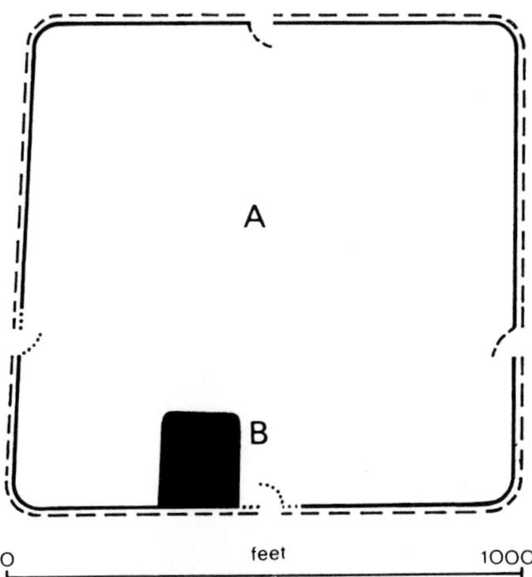


**DIAGRAM OF FIRST-CENTURY TEMPORARY CAMP AND SMALL PERMANENT ROAD POST AT CHEW GREEN**

## CAPPUCK (Eburocaslum?)

It may be disputed whether Cappuck was part of the Roman Wall system, but two altars, surviving in part, suggest it was garrisoned from High Rochester and Risingham. The name *Eburocaslum* is given in the *Ravenna List* as lying between High Rochester and Newstead. It could refer to Chew Green but more likely is Cappuck. Today the site is dfficult to find.

Excavations have revealed four periods of building in each of which changes were made. The Agricolan fort has a clay rampart, a northern gateway and a single ditch. In the second Flavian period (c. 90 - c. 105), the rampart was strengthened and the ditch enlarged, but the plan of the timber buildings is unknown as a result of destruction by fire.

The next fortlet was probably built by the Twentieth Legion during the Antonine re-occupation of the Scottish Lowlands. The new fort was larger, 303 by 260 feet across the ramparts, with a double ditch and stone buildings. Later the fort was reduced in length from 303 to 252 feet. The date of its abandonment is unknown.

Two inscriptions built into Jedburgh Abbey (3 miles to the west) probably came from Cappuck. (RIB 2117, 2118).

Julius Severinus was almost certainly the same man who rebuilt the third century bath-house and dedicated an altar to Fortuna at Risingham, where the Raetian Spearmen were stationed.

The Vardullians on the second altar were stationed at High Rochester.

*I(oui) O(ptimo) ue(x) / il(l)atio Reto/ rum Gaesat(orum) / q(uorum) c(uram) a(git) Iul(ius) / Seuer(inus) trib(unus).*

*'To Jupiter, Best and Greatest, the detachment of Raetian Spearmen, under the acting command of Julius Severinus, their tribune, (set this up)'.*

*. . .) / coh(ors) I Fid(a) Vardul(lorum) / c(iuium) R(omanorum) m(illiari) eq(uitata) et G(aius) / Quintius Seurus / trib(unus) coh(ortis) eiusdem / dom(o) Camil(ia tribu) Ra- uenna u(otum) s(oluerunt) l(aeti) l(ibentes) m(erito).*

'. . .the First Loyal Cohort of Vardullians, Roman citizens, a thousand strong, part-mounted, and Gaius Quintus Severus, tribune of the same cohort, of the Camilian voting-tribe, from Ravenna, gladly, willingly, and deservedly fulfilled their vow'.

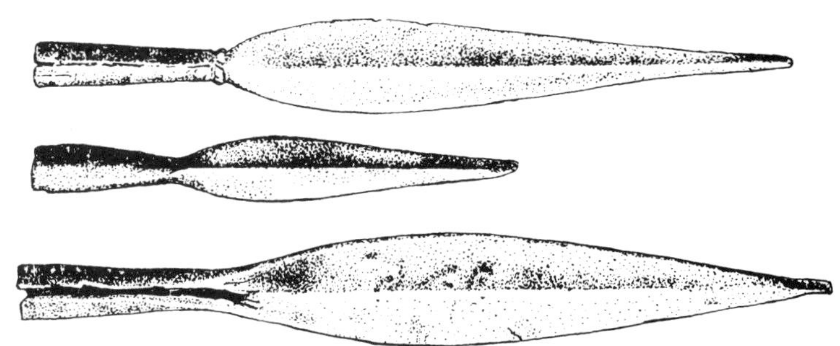

*Lance and javelin heads from Newstead, late 1st — early 2nd centuries. Museum of Antiquities, Edinburgh*

## NEWSTEAD (Trimontium)

The fort at Newstead, situated on the southern bank, commands the valley of the Tweed. Although it cannot be traced the Romans almost certainly built a bridge here. The fort was a key defensive site throughout the Roman period. The *Ravenna List* gives the name as TRIMONTIUM, the "place of the three peaks"; referring to the Eildon Hills nearby. Nothing can be seen on the site today although the excavations from 1905 to 1910 produced a remarkable collection of finds illustrating many aspects of Roman life. The excavations were recorded in a fine illustrated book written by James Curle on behalf of the Society of Antiquaries of Scotland.

The earliest remains on the site are a series of large marching camps, two of which were 40 and 50 acres in extent. There are four large superimposed forts at Newstead. The first, of 10½ acres, was built in 80 A.D. during Agricola's northern campaign. The Agricolan fort departs from the standard layout. The lines of the rampart in each quarter are staggered, compelling those who approached the gates to do so obliquely where they were exposed to side fire. Other Agricolan forts in Scotland displayed similar characteristics but the idea was exceptional and samples are rare. The defences were completed with two ditches.

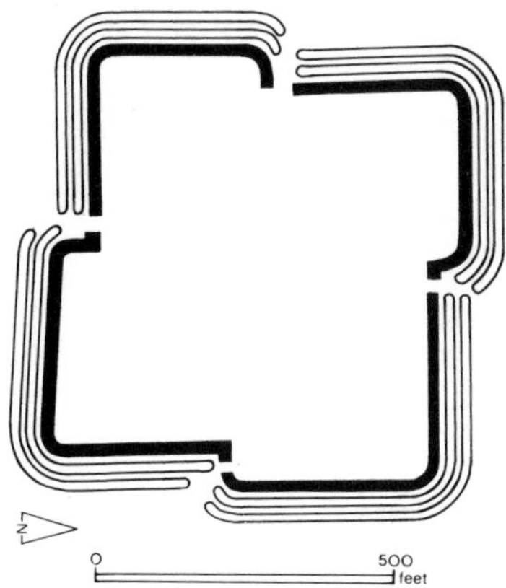


OUTLINE OF AGRICOLAN FORT
AT NEWSTEAD

The second fort replaced it in 86 A.D., and was increased in size to 14½ acres. The rampart was strengthened and at 43 feet wide and 28 feet high was a massive defence. Both forts were defended by turf ramparts with internal wooden buildings, but in the second fort stone foundations were used with timber structures above. The internal arrangements of both forts are unknown.

An interesting feature of Newstead were the three annexes, the western (7 acres) and the eastern (20 acres) probably Agricolan, and the southern annexe of 14 acres from the second fort.

The western annexe during this earlier period received a bath-house and a *mansio* or inn. The second fort was destroyed by fire in 105 A.D.

Newstead was rebuilt in the 140's. It was now provided with a stone wall backed by a 36 foot rampart, two ditches completing the defences. The garrison at this time was probably two cohorts of the Twentieth Legion, occupying half of the fort. The other half, separated by a cross-wall, probably housed the *Ala Vocontiorum,* a 500 strong cavalry unit.

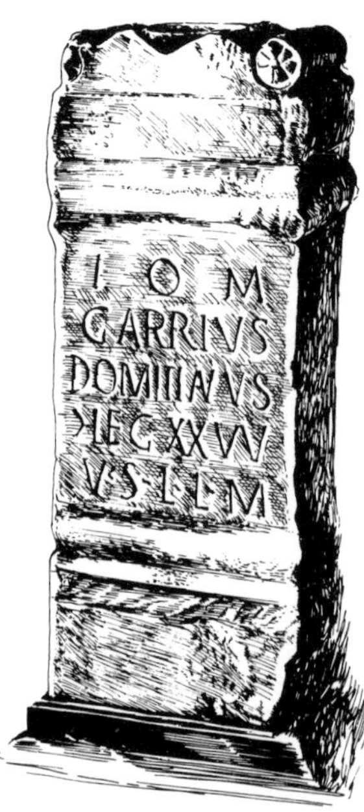


*I(oui) O(ptimo) M(aximo) / G(aius) / Arrius / Domitianus / c(enturio) leg(ionis) XX V(aleriae) V(ictricis) / u(otum) s(oluit) l(aetus) l(ibens) m(erito).*

'To Jupiter, Best and Greatest, Gaius Arrius Domitianus, centurion of the Twentieth Legion Valeria Victrix, gladly, willingly, and deservedly fulfilled his vow'.

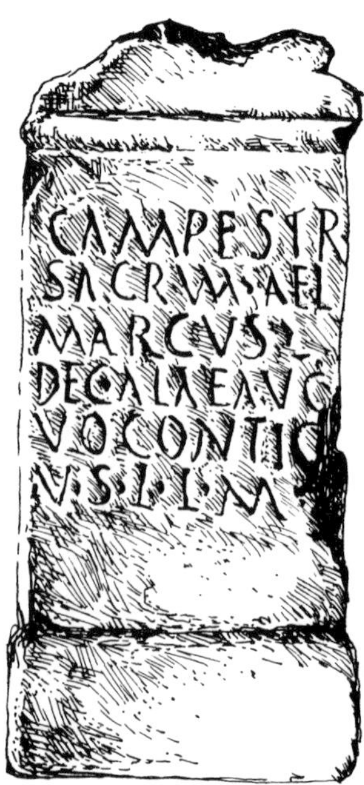


*Campestr(ibus) / sacrum Ael(ius) / Marcus / dec(urio) alae Aug(ustae) / Vocontio (rum) / u(otum) s(oluit) l(aetus) l(ibens) m(erito).*

'Sacred to the Goddesses of the Parade-ground: Aelius Marcus, decurion of the Augustan Cavalry Regiment of Vocontians, gladly, willingly, and deservedly fulfilled his vow'.

*Altars set up by the Twentieth Legion and the Vocontians*

The defences were remodelled in 158 or 163 and the internal buildings repaired. The rampart was extended across the Intervallum to the extraordinary width of 54 feet. The internal dividing wall was demolished. Our plan (page 308) shows the fourth and final fort. Only one building (almost certainly a stable) was found in the northern part of the *retentura.* We have suggested more stables in this area.

Although the garrison of the last fort at Newstead is unknown it was almost certainly a cavalry unit because a huge cross-hall was built in front of the headquarters building to be used for drilling and training cavalrymen.

The fort was abandoned towards the end of the second century.

All the objects discovered at Newstead are in the Museum of Antiquities, Edinburgh.

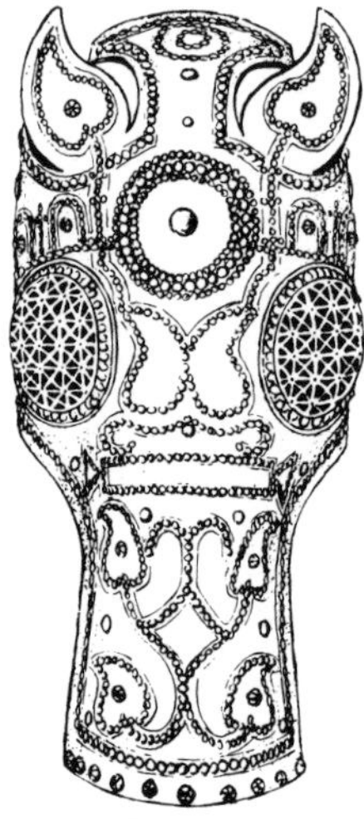

*Reconstruction of the chamfron from Newstead with eye-guards restored*

Water pipe

## THE MANSIO AND BATH HOUSE

Although the two early forts at Newstead were of timber and earth, these two buildings in the western annexe were of stone. A bath-house of wood would have been a danger because of the heating arrangements. The *mansio* shows that Newstead was an important road-post. The plan suggests that as at Vindolanda the building was grouped around a central courtyard but specific details can only be guessed at. The original bath-house outlined in black was of a remakably simple plan but as the fort was altered during the four periods of its building the bath-house also changed and the additions (shaded) means its original outline was entirely lost in the extensions. At some stage a ditch was dug between the *mansio* and the bath. This ditch was part of the defences of the annexe. At about the same time a defensive rampart was built around the bath-house, a unique arrangement. One of the larger water pipes is here reproduced. It is fifteen inches long with a faucet joint of 1¾ inches in diameter. The latrine next to the *mansio* was probably built after the rampart. It is similar to the famous one at Housesteads, but was open to the air or had a lean-to light wooden roof.

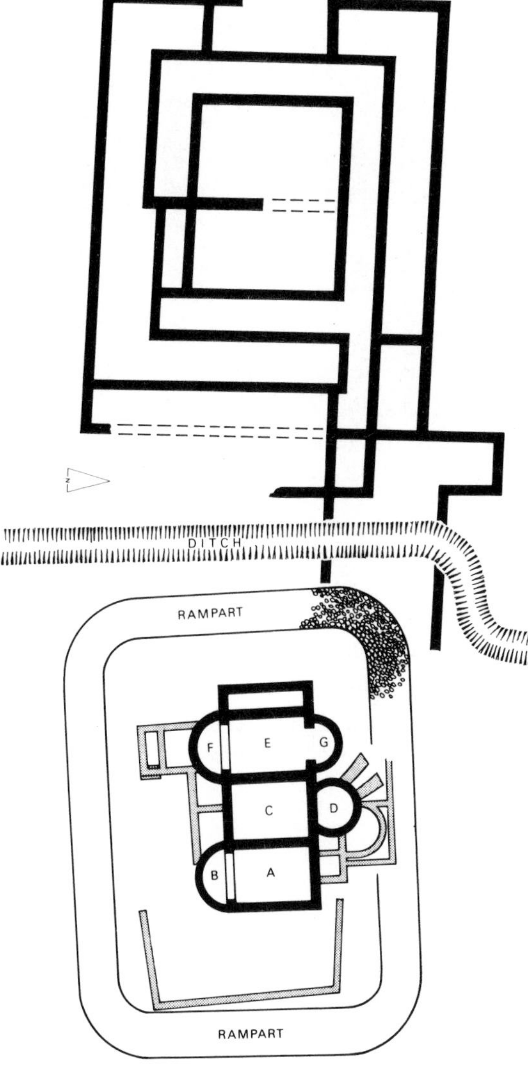


**MANSIO AND BATH HOUSE AT NEWSTEAD**

A. Apodyterium and Frigidarium
B. Cold Bath
C. Tepidarium
D. Laconicum or Sudatorium
E. Caldrium
F. Warm Bath
G. Labrum

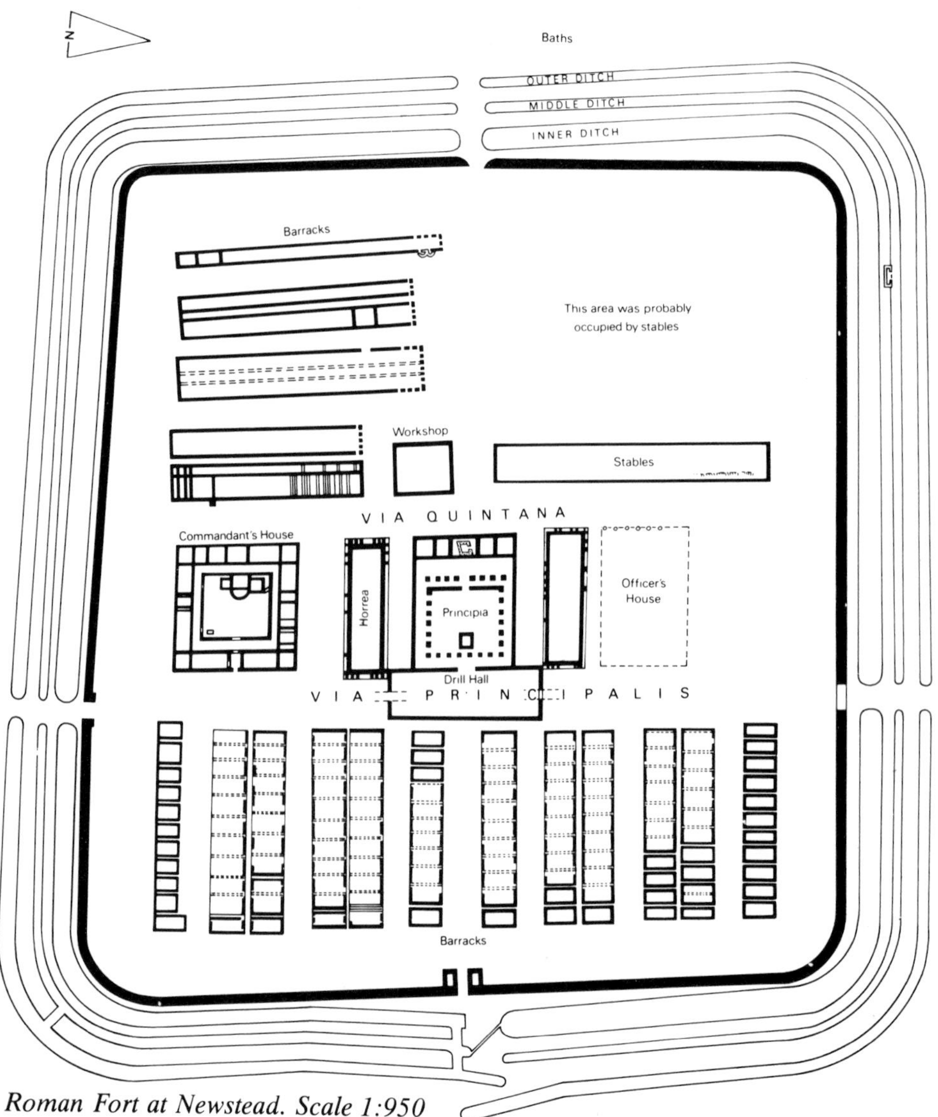


*Roman Fort at Newstead. Scale 1:950*

## THE DEVIL'S CAUSEWAY

To the north of Hadrian's Wall a network of roads led into Scotland. They were originally built before Hadrian's Wall or the Antonine Wall and were intended as a road system to control northern Britain. There were two main routes. On the west was a road from Carlisle which passed through Netherby and Birrens, eventually reaching Edinburgh. On the east was the famous Dere Street which ran from Corbridge through High Rochester and Newstead to Dalkeith. Dere Street was duplicated by another road, the Devil's Causeway.

The Devil's Causeway was clearly a minor route since no important Roman fort was stationed on it. It is difficult to trace today but fortunately a detailed survey of the road was made by H. MacLaughlan and published in 1864. It branched off

*Carlisle Gateway Interior*

from Dere Street at the farm of Bewclay which lay 1½ miles north of Portgate on the Roman Wall. Midway between Bewclay and Learchild aerial photographs have revealed a fortlet at Hartburn which was clearly placed there to control the road.

At Learchild (ALAUNA), near the bridge of Aln, two successive forts have been revealed showing it was a key point on the Devil's Causeway, and was probably garrisoned by a cavalry regiment. It seems not to have been occupied after the building of Hadrian's Wall.

From Learchild a branch road ran west to High Rochester. The main road, however, continued north through Powburn and Lowick to Springhill (one mile south of Tweedmouth) where it seems to have ended. Aerial photography revealed a fortlet here which is covered by a reservoir so only limited excavation has been possible and the fort here has provided material of the third century only.

Aerial photography has revealed a fortlet at Mitford (near Morpeth). It has been suggested (without any evidence as yet) that it guarded a road from Newcastle to Learchild, which would have joined the Devil's Causeway at the Coquet crossing.

A number of Roman objects have been found east of the Devil's Causeway, but they cannot be linked into any definite pattern of Roman settlement.

The most interesting find was part of an altar found at Gloster Hill near the mouth of the Coquet. The surviving inscription reads M PESTRI/OHI which may be expanded to *Matribus campestribus cohors prima.* (To the Godesses of the Parade-ground . . . the First Cohort . . .). (RIB 1206). The only other altar to the Campestral Mothers has been found at Benwell.

Size, 1 foot 5 inches by 1 foot 5 inches

Whether the Romans used the mouth of the Coquet or Aln as ports we do not know.

## STANWIX FORT (Petriana)

From Castlesteads to Stanwix the Wall runs for eight miles. When approached in Roman times the station at Stanwix could be seen in an advantageous position on an elevated platform above the river Eden. It was a grand sight, the greatest fort on the Wall, the seat of the commander of the northern frontier, with a crack regiment the *ala Petriana* which had probably been stationed here since its foundation in Hadrian's time.

Its full name is *ala Augusta Gallorum Petriana bis torquata milliaria civium Romanorum,* meaning the Royal Gallic ala Petriana of 1,000 cavalry twice decorated with torques for valour and made Roman citizens. The fort was named after its garrison.

Today little can be seen since the site is covered with buildings and roads and little excavation has taken place.

In 1939 excavations were carried out which traced the Wall line finding an angle and interval tower. A granary and barracks were also uncovered. The size of the fort was found to be 700 feet from east to west and 580 north to south.

Only a few inscriptions have been found. The tombstone to a cavalry man was found in the wall of the Parish Church. There is a fine relief of Victory here illustrated, and another tombstone set up by Aelia Ammillusima for her husband.

## CARLISLE (LUGUVALLIUM)

The Roman town of Luguvallium was on the south bank of the Eden opposite Stanwix, at a distance of 400 yards. It was a thriving commercial and manufacturing town, the walls of which were one of the wonders of the North in St. Cuthbert's day. It is sometimes stated, without any evidence, that the medieval walls ran on the foundations of their Roman predecessor. Because the site is heavily built on, excavation and discoveries have of necessity been piecemeal. Moreover, a large number of Roman stones were extensively used to build the medieval fortifications. It has been stated (probably correctly) that the fort here was founded by Petilius Cerialis, circa 71 A.D.

It was built of turf and timber and guarded the western end of the Stanegate, as well as the Roman road south, and lay south of the medieval castle. It was replaced at an unknown date by a similar turf and timber fort which remained in occupation until Stanwix was built.

LEGIO IX

The early garrison is uncertain. Two stones were found under the *Carlisle Journal* building in 1860. One records the *Ala Augusta, ob virtutem appelata,* and the other, here reproduced, is a fragment only of a monument set up by its commander recording the *Ala Petriana.* Could these two stones be recording the same regiment? In any case the *Ala Petriana* was transferred to Stanwix when Carlisle ceased to be a fort.

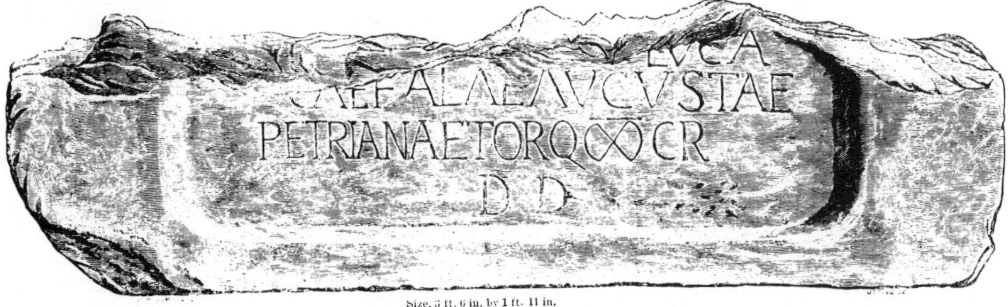


Size, 3 ft. 6 in. by 1 ft. 11 in.

Carlisle is estimated to have covered about 74 acres, so it was an important settlement, and by the middle of the third century had become a *civitas,* the capital of the local tribe, the *Carvetti.*

*Roman soldiers playing dice*



*Opposite. Roman legionaries in battle formation.*

*Carlisle Gateway Exterior*

## GATEWAY TO CARLISLE FORT

Recent excavations in areas of Carlisle scheduled for development have contributed greatly to our knowledge of the Roman occupation. In 1978 Miss Dorothy Charlesworth in excavations in Annetwell Street uncovered the gateway of the Flavian fort, whose massive oak timbers were preserved in the waterlogged ground. The main timber supports were sunk six feet into the soil. The gateway had two portals and was similar to others known to us built in wood or stone.

From the photographs of the remains and the plans of the excavations Ronald Embleton has been able to do the two drawings showing the inside and exterior of the gateway.

The upper portion is mainly conjectural, and is based on reconstructions of other wooden gates found elsewhere.

The boundaries of the Roman fort are now known. It was situated in the centre of medieval Carlisle, extending from and including the Castle site almost to Botchergate, where outside the Walls a Roman cemetery was placed.

(See *Carlisle, A Frontier City* by Mike McCarthy. 1980).

Numerous buildings have been traced at various times and a variety of inscribed stones discovered. One of the best (found in 1829 at Gallow Hill) is dedicated to Aurelia Aureliana. The lady is carrying a bunch of flowers and the pine cones surmounting the pilaster are symbols of eternal life.

Size, 5 feet 4 inches by 2 feet 9 inches

D M AVR AVRELIA VIXSIT
ANNOS XXXXI VLPIVS
APOLINARIS CONIVGI CARISSIME
POSVIT

Diis manibus Aurelia Aureliana vixit
annos quadraginta unum Ulpius
Apolinaris conjugi carissimae
posuit

Another fine uninscribed tombstone shows a lady with a child carrying a fan. The child is playing with a dove in her lap. The sphinx and two lions above are symbols of death. The main cemetery at Carlisle lined the Roman road south.

The following two stones are religious. One shows a man offering sacrifice to the *Parcae* or weird sisters, the other probably represents the god Silvanus. In his right hand he holds a goat for sacrifice, in his left a globe resting on his knee.

*Roman Bronze Horse Bridle*

*Roman Officer's costume with muscle cuirasse*

# INDEX


*Page*

AESICA, ........ *see* Greatchesters
AESICA BROOCH, ........ 173, 174
AMIENS SKILLET, ........ 26
ANCHOR, ........ 37
ANTENOCITICUS, ........ 55
ANTONINE ITINERARY, ........ 25
ANTONINE WALL, ........ 10
AQUEDUCT, ........ 179
AQUEDUCT STONE, ........ 33
ARBEIA, ........ *see* South Shields
AURELIA AURELIANA, ........ 315
AUXILIARIES, ........ 22

BALLISTA, ........ 292
BARCOMBE, ........ 196, 198
BATH HOUSES, ........ 82, 90, 107, 108, 177, 217, 241, 269, 307
BEGGARS, ........ 262
BENWELL, ........ 51-57, 61
BEWCASTLE, ........ 244, 245
BIRDHOPE CAMP, ........ 298
BIRDOSWALD, ........ 234-242, 252, 257, 258
BIRRENS, ........ 272, 273
BLACKSMITH'S SHOP, ........ 104, 105
BLAKEHOPE CAMP, ........ 285-286
BLATOBULGIUM, ........ *see* Birrens
BREMENIUM, ........ *see* High Rochester
BRIDGES, ........ 19, 48, 49, 50, 62, 111, 206
BROCOLITIA, ........ *see* Carrawburgh
BRUNTON TURRET, ........ 94
BURNING VILLAGE, ........ 271
BURYING MONEY AT RUDCHESTER, ........ 67, 80
BUTCHER'S SHOP, ........ 137

CAMBOGLANNA, ........ *see* Birdoswald
CAPPUCK, ........ 301
CARANTINUS, FLAVIUS, ........ 92, 93
CARELGATE, ........ 195
CARLISLE, ........ 311-316
CARLISLE GATEWAY, ........ 309, 314
CARRAWBURGH, ........ 117-121
CARRIER'S INN, ........ 156, 160, 161
CARVETTI, ........ 313
CARVORAN, ........ 187-192
CASTLE NICK MILECASTLE, ........ 159, 162
CASTLESTEADS, ........ 251, 254, 255, 259-261
CATAPULTS, ........ 270, 291, 292
CAVALRY DRILL HALL, ........ 86, 89
CAWFIELDS MILECASTLE, ........ 165
CENTURIAL STONE FROM VALLUM, ........ 65, 66
CHARCOAL, ........ 110
CHESTERS, ........ 98, 113
CHEW GREEN, ........ 299
COBBLER, ........ 300
COCIDIUS, ........ 244, 283
COLLECTING TRIBUTE, ........ 194
CONDERCUM, ........ *see* Benwell
CORBRIDGE, ........ *see* Corstopitum
CORSTOPITUM, ........ 203-210, 212
COUNT THEODOSIUS, ........ 14
COVENTINA'S WELL, ........ 117, 118
CRINDLEDYKES, ........ 196
CUCULATTI, ........ 268
CULVERT AT DENTON BURN, ........ 65
CUTLER, ........ 41

DACIANS, FIRST COHORT, ........ 65
DENTON BURN, ........ 64
DERE STREET, ........ 90, 195
DEVIL'S CAUSEWAY, ........ 308
DICE, ........ 313
DIPLOMA, ........ 23, 84, 85
DODECAHEDRON, ........ 212
DOWN HILL, VALLUM, ........ 78,79
DRAUGHT BOARD, ........ 110
DREAM ALTAR, ........ 284

FAIR AT STAGSHAW BANK, ....91
FIBULA, ....44
FLAVINUS, ....16
FOOTWEAR, ....160, 218
FUNERAL, ....36, 38, 87

GAMING BOARDS, ....207
GATEWAY, ....277
GATEWAY BARRIER, ....291
GIANT'S GRAVE, ....71
GILLALEES BEACON, ....242, 243
GLENWHELT LEAZES CAMP, ....199
GLOSTER HILL, ....310
GOLDEN POTS, ....299
GRANARIES, ....144
GREATCHESTERS, ....172-179

HABITANCUM, .... *see* Risingham
HADRIAN, ....10
HADRIAN'S MONUMENT, ....43, 59
HADRIAN SURVEYS SITE FOR WALL, ....81
HAIRSTYLES, ....222, 223
HALTWHISTLE BURN FORT, ....169-171
HALTONCHESTERS FORT, ....78-87
HARNESS MOUNTINGS, ....297
HARROWS SCAR MILECASTLE, ....233
HEDDON-ON-THE-WALL, ....66
HIGH ROCHESTER, ....288, 290-298
HOSPITALS, ....56, 63, 136
HORSLEY, John, ....68
HOUSESTEADS, ....130-151
HUNTING THE BOAR, ....168
HUTTON, William ....69, 76, 91, 96, 97, 248

IRON SIGN INN, ....72

JOINERY SHOP, ....147, 148

KING ARTHUR, ....121
KITCHENS, ....140, 229

LAMP, ....162
LATRINE, ....143, 225
LEARCHILD, ....309
LEGION, ....19
LEGION, SECOND, ....83
LEGION, SIXTH, ....82
LIGHTNING OF THE GODS, ....91
LIMESTONE BANK VALLUM, ....115, 122
LONGSTONE, ....196
LUGUVALIUM, .... *see* Carlisle

MAINS RIGG SIGNAL STATION, ....201
MANSIO, ....211, 307
MARE AND FOAL, ....199
MAUSOLEUM AT CORBRIDGE, ....204
MEDICAL INSTRUMENTS, ....258
MERCHANT'S WIFE, ....36, 39
MAIDEN WAY, ....242
MILECASTLE, ....18
MILECASTLE 37; ....155
MILECASTLE 50; ....246, 247
MILESTONE, ....74
MILITARY ROAD OF GENERAL WADE, ....67, 73
MILKING GAP, ....158
MILITARY STANDARD, ....226
MILITARY UNITS, ....27-32
MITHRAS, ....71, 121, 141
MODIUS FROM CARVORAN, ....193
MOGONS, ....280, 281

NAVY, ....23
NINE NICKS OF THIRLWALL, ....181
NEWSTEAD, ....303-308
NEWCASTLE UPON TYNE, ....47-51
NETHERBY, ....264, 265, 268, 269
NOTITIA DIGNITATUM, ....25

ONAGER, 290, 292
ONNO, *see* Haltonchesters
OUTPOST FORTS, 263-308

PAENULA, 152
PARCAE, 316
PASSWORD, 95
PATERA (skillet), 34, 246
PETRIANA, *see* Stanwix
PHALLIC SYMBOLS, 230
PIKE HILL SIGNAL TOWER, 248, 256
PONS AELIUS, *see* Newcastle upon Tyne
PORTGATE, 88, 90
POTTER, 60
PURSE, 224, 232

QUARRYING, 230, 231

RAVENNA COSMOGRAPHY, 25
RING, GOLD, 86
RISINGHAM, 276-284
RISINGHAM BROOCH, 283
ROAD BUILDING, 202
ROBIN OF RISINGHAM, 281-283
ROMANO-BRITISH VILLAGE, 267
RUDCHESTER, 67-72
RUDGE CUP, 26
RUFINUS, ALTAR, 294, 295

SACRIFICE, 151
SEATSIDE MARCHING CAMPS, 199
SEGEDUNUM, *see* Wallsend
SEVERUS, 11
SEWINGSHIELDS, 183, 184
SHIP, 37
SIGNAL STATIONS, 196, 287
SLAVE, 86
SLINGERS, 270
SOUTH SHIELDS, 33-42
STAGSHAW BANK, 91
STANDARD BEARER, 125
STANEGATE, 186, 195-204
STANWIX FORT, 310-311
STONE MASON, 35
STRIGIL, 255
STUKELEY, William, 72
SURVEYOR, 182

TANNERY, 215
TESTUDO (TORTOISE), 278
TOMBS ON WATLING STREET, 294, 295
TOMBSTONES, 79
TRIMONTIUM, *see* Newstead
TURF WALL, 239
TURRET, 18
TURRET RECONSTRUCTION, 74, 75, 77

UNQUENTARIEM, 212
UXELLODUNUM, *see* Castlesteads

VALLUM, 18, 19
VARDULLI, FIRST COHORT, 78
VINDOBALA, *see* Rudchester
VINDOLANDA, 210-232
VIRGIN OF THE ZODIAC, 193

WALLSEND, 45
WALLTOWN CRAGS, 184, 185
WATER MILL, 171
WEAVING FRAME, 42
WELTON TOWER, 74
WILLOWFORD BRIDGE, 233, 249
WINSHIELDS, 163
WRITING TABLETS, 227, 228
WRITTEN ROCK, 92, 93
WRITTEN ROCK OF GELT, 250, 251